Matías Saidel
Neoliberalism Reloaded

De Gruyter Contemporary Social Sciences

Volume 13

Matías Saidel

Neoliberalism Reloaded

—

Authoritarian Governmentality
and the Rise of the Radical Right

DE GRUYTER

ISBN 978-3-11-161988-0
e-ISBN (PDF) 978-3-11-072393-9
e-ISBN (EPUB) 978-3-11-072401-1
ISSN 2747-5689
e-ISSN 2747-5697

Library of Congress Control Number: 2022946482

Bibliographic information published by the Deutsche Nationalbibliothek
The Deutsche Nationalbibliothek lists this publication in the Deutsche Nationalbibliografie;
detailed bibliographic data are available on the internet at http://dnb.dnb.de.

© 2024 Walter de Gruyter GmbH, Berlin/Boston
This volume is text- and page-identical with the hardback published in 2023.
Cover image: tilo / iStock / Getty Images Plus

www.degruyter.com

To Bruno and Felipe

Acknowledgements

This book was made possible by my work as a researcher at the National Research Council of Argentina-Institute of Social Studies (CONICET-INES) which includes my participation in the PIP "Neoliberal governmentality and processes of subjectivation: towards a critical ontology of the present" (2017–2019) and as a Professor-Researcher at the National University of Entre Ríos, where I supervise the Research and Development Project 5132 "Politics and subjectivity in neoliberal capitalism: governmentality, dispossession and construction of the common". It was also possible by the kind invitation of De Gruyter to further develop the ideas presented in chapter 3 of this book, part of which appeared in "¿Se puede hablar de un momento fascista del neoliberalismo? Crisis de la democracia liberal y guerra contra las poblaciones precarizadas como síntomas de época", *Revista Argentina de Ciencia Política*, 2020, 1(24), 70–100. This invitation allowed me to revisit earlier work and to conduct new research that has been sent to various academic reviews over the past two years. Chapter 1 draws in part on arguments first presented in "La fábrica de la subjetividad neoliberal: del empresario de sí al hombre endeudado", *Pléyade* 17, July 2016, 131–154. Part of chapter 2 develops reflections first presented at the XI National Congress on Democracy (Rosario National University, 2014) and another part has been published in "Consideraciones sobre las críticas neoliberales a la democracia", *Perspectivas. Revista de Ciencias Sociales* 7(13) Enero–Junio 2022, 449–473. Most of chapter 4 has been published in "El neoliberalismo autoritario y el auge de las nuevas derechas", *História Unisinos* 25(2), May/August 2021, 263–275. Parts of chapter 5 were published in "Hacia una genealogía del populismo de derechas actual. Una aproximación a la corriente nacional-(neo)liberal en Europa y Estados Unidos", *El banquete de los Dioses* 9, Jul–Dec 2021, 339–373. A longer version of chapter 6 was published as "¿Anticomunismo sin comunismo? La construcción del feminismo como enemigo estratégico de las nuevas derechas y el dilema de la reproducción social", *Razón Crítica* 11, 2021, 255–288, https://doi.org/10.21789/25007807.1746 (with Julia Expósito). Chapter 7 draws on a lecture presented at Lund University in May 2018.

I would like to thank Andrea Fagioli, Iván Dalmau, Fiorella Guaglianone, Betania Parodi, Pablo Manfredi, and Dana D. Nelson who have read and commented parts of this book during the process of writing; Alejo Stark and Gastón Souroujon, for commenting on the book proposal; Julia Expósito, Emilio Lo Valvo, Emiliano Sacchi, for years of discussions and shared work that have nurtured my academic formation and with whom I have written the book *Ensamblajes neoliberales: mutaciones del capitalismo contemporáneo,* (Vicente López: Red Edi-

https://doi.org/10.1515/9783110723939-001

torial, 2022) which draws on different aspects of—and theoretical approaches to —neoliberal capitalism; the colleagues of the PIP and Debates Actuales with whom I discussed many ideas during the last decade (Silvana Vignale, Luciana Álvarez, Pablo Méndez, Osvaldo López-Ruiz, Ric Esteves, Adrián Velázquez). I also want to thank my family, and especially the love I received from Yanina and our sons Bruno and Felipe, to whom I would like to dedicate this book.

Contents

Introduction

Can we speak of a fascist moment of neoliberalism? This question, which initially motivated the writing of this book, refers to two interrelated issues. On the one hand, to the increasingly violent, cruel, and unfair means that neoliberal practices and discourses have acquired in recent decades, especially after the global financial crisis and the austerity and punitive response that followed. On the other hand, to the rise of a neoliberal far-right that has not only managed to set the agenda of the ruling political parties in liberal democracies, but also to produce common sense through a relentless battle in social networks, the media, the streets, think tanks and even academia. In this way, discourses and policies marked by hatred of immigrants, women, sex-gender dissidents, the poor, those who receive social aid, etc., are being normalized.

Of course, this question was hardly original. The denunciation of "fascism" by the left and even the proud use of this label by part of the radical right, such as Vox in Spain, has become increasingly frequent. Moreover, the question has been raised repeatedly in academia, especially after the electoral victory of Trump, Modi, Johnson, the Brexit, and Bolsonaro. It also emerged with the arrival of the Lega to the Italian government and the possible victory of Fratelli d'Italia in the 2022 elections, with the consolidation of Fidesz in Hungary and PiS in Poland, with the permanent possibility of a *Rassemblement National* government in France, with the rise of Vox in Spain, and with the growing influence of the far-right in Latin America, not to mention undemocratic regimes elsewhere that have adopted free-market policies combined with political and social authoritarianism.

In this sense, this question implies a specific geo-political framework, since neoliberalism and fascism arose in a particular historical and geographical context: specifically, Europe and then the rest of the West in the first postwar period. Therefore, given that this past haunts and besieges our political experience, and that *the weight of the dead continues to oppress the brains of the living*, we are interested in analyzing the rise of authoritarian neoliberalism, fundamentally in Europe and America. These societies were marked by the history of both processes, but also by the rise of liberal democracy which, as it did a century ago, is once again facing a severe crisis.

In order to address this issue, I take into account different studies on the peculiarities and genealogy of the present. Some of them have focused on the features of the "new neoliberalism", following the global financial crisis and the way in which it has favored the rise of the far right. Others focus on the disruptive aspects of these currents, even pointing to a distancing, in some cases, from

https://doi.org/10.1515/9783110723939-002

neoliberal coordinates. Taking up part of these debates, this book seeks *to pon-der the reasons, characteristics, and antecedents of the becoming authoritarian of neoliberalism, its link with the crisis of liberal democracies and with the rise of the new radical right.* In this context, I will analyze which traits distinguish the present from previous historical periods, how to think about current neoliberalism as a strategic project, how its field of adversity is configured and what the alternative projects to it are. In particular, I seek to explore the relationship between neoliberalism as a *governmental rationality* and the authoritarian practices and ideas that have historically characterized it, taking into account its antagonistic dimension towards egalitarian or collectivist political currents and, in that framework, to mass, class, gender, decolonizing movements and racialized subjects. To this end, the book draws on different theoretical and disciplinary sources. In the first place, from the grid of governmentality, elaborated by Foucault, complementing it with contributions from some of the excellent existing intellectual histories of neoliberal thought. This allows us to understand what they conceived as the desirable social order and the governmental practices necessary to achieve it. In this sense, I take up elements of some of the most influential currents and authors of Euro-American neoliberalism of the twentieth century, understanding that the term "neoliberal" refers to a heterogeneous and in some points contradictory set of economic, social and political proposals. However, I will discuss this governmental dimension in the light of recent mutations of capitalism and a consideration of the way in which human populations are effectively being governed through often violent and coercive processes of neoliberalization. This will imply complementing that analytical framework with other traditions, especially from the critique of (neo)Marxist political economy and its analysis of neoliberalism as a current stage of capitalism. (Duménil & Lévy, 2004; Duménil & Lévy, 2013).

At the same time, to approach the different dimensions of this radicalization of neoliberalism, I will draw on contributions from political philosophy around the links between the anti-democratism of the most influential neoliberal currents and the reactionary thought that today is openly expressed in the rise of the new radical right-wing; of the historical transformations of really existing neoliberalism and its authoritarian becoming; of contemporary political sociology on the characteristics of these currents; of the discourse of these new radical rights in their antagonism to egalitarianism and "gender ideology"; of certain critical feminisms and their foregrounding of the problem of social reproduction; and of diverse knowledge and practices of the commons that would allow us to imagine new political horizons and modes of (self-) government.

Thus, the book proposes to use a series of theoretical and methodological tools that are combined according to the problems to be addressed in each case, to consider different dimensions of the problems studied. In many parts of the book, an archaeo-genealogical approach will predominate, taking into account the historical contexts of enunciation of neoliberal discursivity and the institutional devices through which these ideas were able to develop and become hegemonic. In this framework, emphasis is placed on the reactionary and anti-democratic aspects that link some prominent members of the *neoliberal thought collective* (Mirowski & Plehwe, 2009) with the authoritarian evolution of neoliberalism and the rise of the radical right. At other times, emphasis is placed on an interpretation and commentary of reflections that different contemporary theorists make on these processes and discursivities from different disciplines of the humanities and social sciences. Far from attempting a synthesis between the different theoretical-methodological proposals, I will seek to strategically articulate elements of each hermeneutic grid in their heterogeneity to ponder different aspects of the issues at stake. In Foucault's terms, I will not make use of a dialectical logic, which seeks to homogenize the contradictory, but a logic of strategy, which establishes connections between disparate elements that remain disparate, without seeking to reduce them to unity (Foucault, 2008, p. 42). On the other hand, I will seek to avoid a characterization of these processes and concepts to think of them as universal, starting with that of neoliberalism, although grammar—as Nietzsche already warned us—often leads us down that path.[1]

Towards a minimal definition of neoliberalism

The concept of neoliberalism presents problems for the social sciences due to its breadth, vagueness, and indeterminacy. For this reason, some scholars consider that, since it designates so many things at the same time, it would be better to abandon it. However, these features are constitutive of any concept that is part of the political-hegemonic disputes of a society. In this sense, neoliberalism could be defined as an empty and, at the same time, floating signifier.[2] Like "popu-

---

1 In a famous passage of *Twilight of the idols* that reflects on Being and Language in the realm of Reason, Nietzsche states: "I'm afraid we're not rid of God because we still believe in grammar". (Nietzsche, 1997, p. 21)

2 An empty signifier is a signifier without a signified. According to Ernesto Laclau, empty signifiers allow us to understand the logic with which hegemony is constructed, when a particular identity manages to contingently represent that place of the universal through the articulation of a chain of equivalences between different social demands within the same discursive field. On the other hand, the floating signifier is subject to the pressure of different equivalential chains, even between antagonistic fields. (Laclau, 2005; Laclau, 2007).

lism", "fascism", "socialism", "capitalism", "authoritarianism", "totalitarianism" or "democracy", the concept of neoliberalism presents the impossibility of a univocal definition, while at the same time it is indispensable for the exercise and study of contemporary politics. Indeed, this concept makes it possible to identify the configuration of a chain of equivalences between different social demands that trace an antagonism and a hegemonic dispute of the extreme defenders of market freedom against what they consider collectivist, egalitarian and/or protectionist positions which, for thinkers such as Friedrich von Hayek or Wilhelm Röpke, are the prelude to totalitarianism. This allows us to visualize two things at the outset: on the one hand, there is no such thing as "neoliberalism", as a kind of essence or substance that manifests itself through different accidents.[3] On the other hand, if there is a heterogeneous series of theoretical and political currents that can be identified as neoliberal, this unity in dispersion takes place not only in theoretical but, above all, in *political-strategic* terms. In this sense, neoliberalism is a political rationality that adapts itself to the different contexts in which it intervenes. (Dardot, Sauvêtre, Guéguen & Laval, 2021).

It is important to note this from the beginning, because in the use of the concept, even in the field of studies inspired by Foucault's pioneering work on this subject, we tend to underestimate the theoretical and political differences within this universe. In this reading, at least from the Walter Lippmann colloquium onwards, the neoliberal project would be reduced to transforming—through a strong state that establishes and safeguards the rules of the market—*omnes et singulatim* into *homines economici*, entrepreneurs of themselves subjected to the rule of competition and alien to any logic of collective solidarity, producing an economization of all spheres of existence (Brown, 2015).[4] However, in addition to considerable theoretical and political differences between the various neoliberal currents, there are also differences in what is understood by concepts such as *enterprise, competition, social justice, market,* etc. not only between authors but also at different moments in history.

---

3 As Serge Audier points out, terms change their meaning according to the historical-political context and neoliberalism is no exception. However, most studies of neoliberalism adopt essentialist or teleological points of view, where there would be a linear development between its intellectual origins and its subsequent applications, whether they place the starting point in 1930 or 1970. On the contrary, Audier shows that there is not one but many neoliberalisms, which enable very different policies. (Audier, 2012)

4 This totalizing character of neoliberal rationality, which seeks to govern not only from the outside but also by transforming the internal forum and thus avoiding the possibility of a critical distance, leads Villacañas (2020) to consider neoliberalism as a political theology.

In any case, although a theoretical-political study such as mine, which is far from being a conceptual history of neoliberalism, cannot avoid establishing generalizations such as those mentioned above and looking for common elements among the leading figures of neoliberalism, I will try to specify in each case the meanings, authors and currents that I analyze in this journey through the authoritarian and reactionary aspects of neoliberalism. In fact, any genealogy, as well as histories of ideas and conceptual history, requires a permanent effort of contextualization.

Hence, there are multiple conceptions and dimensions of neoliberalism. First, it refers to a thought collective and a set of ideas that are present in different schools, whose minimum common denominator is the need for a strong state that guarantees a free economy and promotes competition in society, to the point that each economic-social unit and each institution—including the state itself—is regulated as an enterprise guided by efficiency criteria. This entails policies such as the elimination of customs tariffs and taxes on property and income, supply-side monetarist approaches, the elimination of subsidies and social policies, and so on. Second, neoliberalism is a class project that sought to re-establish the conditions for capital accumulation after the crisis of the 1970s. Third, neo-liberalism names a phase of global capitalism characterized by "a structural re-orientation of the state towards export-oriented, financialized capital, open-ended commitments to market-like governance systems, privatization and corporate expansion and deep aversion to social collectives and the progressive redistribution of wealth on the part of ruling classes" (Fabry, 2019, p. 3).

In order to take these different definitions into account, a genealogy of authoritarian neoliberalism should take elements from at least four approaches: (a) an archaeo-genealogical approach that conceives neoliberalism as a governmental rationality that was elaborated and promoted by a specific thought collective and its organizations; (b) a structural approach that understands neoliberalism as a new phase of capitalism characterized by financialization, automation and intellectualization of labor, fiscal orthodoxy, just-in-time production, labor flexibilization, exctractivism and accumulation by dispossession; (c) a historical-political approach to the different political and cultural forms through which neoliberal policies were implemented; d) readings of neoliberalism from its margins, such as those proposed by feminism, postcolonial thought, queer theory or from the peripheries of capitalism, which mark the continuity of neoliberalism with patriarchy, colonialism, racism and imperialism (Callison & Manfredi, 2019).

The historical-structural approach has been developed by neo-Marxist scholars and allows us to understand to some extent how capitalism has been transformed and how populations have been governed within this framework. For example, David Harvey analyzes the economic, legal, and political measures taken during the processes of neoliberalization, emphasizing the measures of liberalization, privatization, deregulation, and financialization that unbridled capitalism from its Keynesian, Welfarist and Fordist shackles.

The history of neoliberalism proposed by Harvey analyzes fundamental milestones of this transition, such as the dollar-gold inconvertibility decreed in 1971, the oil crises and the Volcker shock, which were fundamental in the transition to monetarism, in the production of the Third World debt crisis and the financialization of the world economy under the aegis of the United States. This view focuses on the processes that took place in different geographies, starting with the "Chilean experiment" and followed by the neoliberal reforms of Thatcher and Reagan, Latin America, Asia, and the capitalist-neoliberal transformation of China. These supply-side policies, the monetarist fight against inflation, tax cuts for the richest and corporations, the privatization of industries and public goods, the domination of shareholders, creditors, and financial markets, led to a rise in unemployment, a fall in wages, and were part of a war against unions and the working class in general. Fundamentally, according to different neo-Marxist authors, neoliberal globalization entailed a re-actualization of primitive accumulation, involving the plunder of natural resources, the exploitation of cheap labor in conditions of semi-slavery, the "debt trap", and the privatization of public goods and services. Particularly in the West, neoliberalism entailed the undermining of social gains and rights obtained after generations of class struggle, leading to levels of inequality that are similar to those which existed before the First World War (Piketty, 2014), and to working conditions in some parts of the planet that resemble more those of nineteenth-century capitalism described by Marx than the images of the Fordist worker fully satisfied and integrated into mass consumption.[5]

These measures were not taken in isolation. There were a series of global institutions created with the Bretton Woods treaties, which, although erected in a stage dominated by Keynesianism, Welfarism and developmentalism, would gradually transform their own doctrines in an increasingly neoliberal direction. Since the post-war model of Keynesian capitalism went into crisis, organizations such as the IMF, the World Bank and the GATT (later the WTO) were fundamental not only in the ideological dissemination but also in the political implementa-

---

[5] This image can be traced from the passive revolution that Americanism and Fordism meant for Gramsci (1971)—which tended to produce a new type of worker and man, a new conformism that standardizes ways of being and thinking—to the Marcusian critique of one-dimensional man (Marcuse, 1991), which have been taken up by alt-right ideologues, such as Samuel Francis and Paul Gottfried.

tion of neoliberal measures.[6] The advantage of these institutions for neoliberals —especially the "globalists" in Geneva—was that they are not subject to the whims of the democratic majorities of each state, and thus allow a kind of global governance that promotes economic freedom and the rights of capital, even when they challenge human rights (Slobodian, 2018). In particular, the IMF, which had emerged to maintain monetary stability, played a major role with the external debt crises suffered by different countries in Latin America, Africa and then Asia, since the late 1970s, promoting measures that were later embodied in what is known as the Washington Consensus.[7] These ideas and institutions were central to the project of the global capitalist class, whose greatest success was to consolidate its power and put an end to inflation in most countries, at the price of a slowdown in economic growth, an increase in unemployment and informality, and a deterioration in the living conditions of most of the population worldwide. Proof of this is that, when countries followed the measures imposed by the IMF and the WB to the letter, growth was slower, while the opposite happened in countries that followed their own growth paths, especially in the new industrial powers that emerged in Asia in the 1980s (Harvey, 2005).

According to this view, neoliberal capitalism represented a second wave of enclosures of the commons and a re-edition of primitive accumulation (Midnight notes, 1990). In this sense, Harvey points out that neoliberalism has been characterized by a type of accumulation, which is not extended reproduction but accumulation by dispossession, a reenactment of the methods of primitive accumulation in societies already traversed by capitalism (Harvey, 2005).

---

6 As Slobodian points out, several of the neoliberal theorists—especially Michael Heilperin, Philip Cortney and Ludwig Erhard—played a key role in defeating the International Trade Organization, which, together with the IMF and the World Bank, was to complete the Bretton Woods agreements. The reason for fighting it had to do with preventing economic democracy from being transferred to the realm of international trade, at a time when Keynesian doctrines dominated economic policy and the countries of the global South wanted to maintain a space to protect their own industries from foreign competition and promote full employment in their countries. In such a framework, to the human rights of individuals, neoliberals responded with the rights of capital. (Slobodian, 2018, ch. 4)

7 Dieter Plehwe recalls that the Washington Consensus "combined a set of macroeconomic policies intended to restore economic stability and a set of liberalization policies aimed at structural reform. The WC's rallying cries were "structural adjustment" and "getting the prices right." Williamson's ten policy instruments included reduction of federal deficits, privatization of state-run enterprises, deregulation of key industries, and trade and financial sector liberalization". Even though these measures could be subscribed by neoliberals, Williamson takes distance from that label, since he reduces neoliberalism to the Chicago school doctrine and Thatcher and Reagan policies of supply side economics, monetarism and minimum government. (Mirowski & Plehwe, 2009, p.8)

Although Harvey maintains that exploitation and dispossession obey to different logics, his theory could be linked to others that focused on the multiple forms of extractivism and dispossession that have characterized neoliberalism in the peripheries of global capitalism (Federici, 2014; 2020; 2021; Gago & Mezzadra, 2017; Svampa, 2019; Shiva, 2002). At the same time, this perspective can be linked to readings of neoliberalism as the last phase of racial capitalism (Mbembe, 2017; Bhattacharyya, 2018), imperialism, and colonialism.

Within the neo-Marxist approaches, it is also worth mentioning Italian post-operaism, which has contributed to understanding the productive mutations of contemporary capitalism, which implies both transformations in the way of working and the way in which value is produced, with respect to the predominant logics of the Fordist and Keynesian stage. In fact, these approaches often combine the critique of Marxist political economy with post-structuralism and, especially, with the philosophy of Deleuze, Guattari and Foucault. In this framework, the transformations in the exercise of power during the neoliberal stage are read from what Deleuze called the *society of control* and the transformations of capitalism towards a primacy of the immaterial and the digital. Hence the centrality of cognitive, affective, relational, and communicative labor as realities of the new subject of production and politics that operates from the *singular* and the *common* and that the authors call *multitude* (Hardt & Negri, 2004). Indeed, the multitude cannot be reduced to a unitary or homogeneous logic such as the people, the mass, or the class. It is the effect of the end of Fordism and the transition to an increasingly heterogeneous capitalism, where the forms of work are ever more precarious, fragmentary, individualized, singular, and where social cooperation is progressively decentralized. In contrast to the reading of neoliberalism in terms of dispossession, Hardt and Negri consider that neoliberalism cannot be reduced to the plunder of already-existing wealth, since capitalism is fundamentally a system of production and therefore it organizes the creation of new wealth. For this very reason, in the new forms of expropriation of socially produced value they see not so much a pillage as an expropriation of the commons. If the notion of *dispossession* is better suited to the extraction of natural resources that should be collectively owned or accessed or to the processes of privatization of public enterprises, the notion of *biopolitical exploitation* refers to the expropriation of the artificial commons, which is produced by social cooperation, and which, for Hardt and Negri, is increasingly autonomous with respect to capital (Hardt & Negri, 2009). However, as we will see in chapter 7, for Dardot and Laval capital continues to configure the common and to organize social cooperation according to its own needs, which is why it is imperative to elaborate a new instituent theory and praxis of the common as an alternative to neoliberal capitalism. (Dardot & Laval, 2019a)

As I have anticipated, if Marxist approaches understand neoliberalism as a phase of the capitalist mode of production, the archaeo-genealogical approach inaugurated by Foucault focuses on neoliberalism as a political-governmental rationality that seeks to produce a type of entrepreneurial subjectivity and govern society through competition. In that framework, subjects are induced to behave as entrepreneurs of the self who must maximize their own interests, hence becoming calculable and easy to rule. Instead of imposing an external norm to the governed, this type of power takes people's desires and motivations into account. Precisely the different focus provided by Marxists and Foucauldians offers the possibility to have a wider view of neoliberalism and to link the transformations in capitalist mode of production and accumulation with the transformations in the modes of subjectification enabled by neoliberalism.

In this framework, I will seek to trace the elements that allow us to grasp the authoritarian evolution of neoliberalism, which I will refer to at the end of the book as *neoliberalism reloaded*. In this sense, although my approach focuses on governmental rationality and is tributary to the line of inquiry initiated by Foucault in his seminars, it cannot be dissociated from the structural transformations of capitalism which we cannot address in depth in this work. Indeed, this book will concentrate more on the political-cultural aspects of a project of government of human behavior through the market, which requires coercive mechanisms that have often been minimized by critics. It is against this authoritarian and violent background of neoliberalism that the new radical right finds fertile ground to impose its reactionary and exclusionary visions.

Outline of this book

The book begins by taking up the governmentality grid initially proposed by Michel Foucault, during his courses on this subject at the Collège de France (Foucault, 2007; 2008). This approach allowed to complexify and complement certain readings—predominant in the 1990s—that reduced neoliberalism to a mere ideology or to a series of macroeconomic measures, such as those summarized in the Washington Consensus. According to Foucault, neoliberalism can be understood as a governmental rationality that seeks to establish the norm of competition and the enterprise-form as decisive instruments for governing populations and producing subjectivities (Dardot & Laval, 2017). This conception on the conduction of subjects' behaviors through an intervention on the frameworks of social action is the one that predominates when conceiving the governance of populations today. However, this would not imply the end of disciplinary power or sovereign power, as some readings of governmentality studies suggest (Han, 2015),[8] but its transformation in view of the constitution of a *homo economicus* that is governed in all spheres of its existence by a new set of rules, linked to entrepreneurship, competition, maximization, performance, etc. (Dardot and Laval, 2017). In this framework, theories of human capital and the new forms of management of institutions and the workforce that arise from them take center stage. As an example, in chapter 1 I will make a brief commentary on the techniques of management as prevailing governance apparatuses today in business (Nicoli & Paltrinieri, 2014; Paltrinieri, 2013; Pézet, 2004) and of its paradigmatic function for neoliberal governance in the social and institutional fields in general. Such developments resonate with characterizations of neoliberal society as a society of control (Deleuze, 1992) and performance (Friedrich, 2016; Han, 2015) in which power would be exercised through performance-enjoyment apparatuses (Dardot & Laval, 2017), the promotion of *co-opetition* (Dardot & Laval, 2019a) and where the excess of positivity (Han, 2015) and the felicist ideology (Berardi, 2009) would result in a constant search for self-optimization (Friedrich et al., 2016), to the point of self-exploitation (Han, 2015). However, I will argue that self-exploitation and violence against oneself are not the product of a power operating from vaporous performance imperatives, but the effect of concrete and material practices of coercion, incitement, and disciplining. The performance imperative operates under the constant pressure of debt, and of the possible loss of employment, income, rights, and self-esteem. In this sense, performance is the other side of the material, labor, and spiritual precariousness to which neoliberal subjects are constantly subjected.

---

8 In some cases, such as that of Byung-Chul Han, the distinction between sovereign, disciplinary and biopolitical techniques is taken as a kind of succession of historical stages. This has led to debates on how to locate biopolitics historically, either by emphasizing its common origin with sovereign power in the production of bare life (Agamben, 1998) or by pointing out the specificity of modern biopolitics in its articulation with the paradigm of immunization (Esposito, 2008). In fact, Foucault makes it clear that there is no replacement of one type of power by another, but that what changes in certain historical moments is the dominant technique. Disciplinary and sovereign techniques can function perfectly well within security devices, fulfilling different functions: "There is not the legal age, the disciplinary age, and then the age of security. Mechanisms of security do not replace disciplinary mechanisms, which would have replaced juridico-legal mechanisms. In reality you have a series of complex edifices in which, of course, the techniques themselves change and are perfected, or anyway become more complicated, but in which what above all changes is the dominant characteristic, or more exactly, the system of correlation between juridico-legal mechanisms, disciplinary mechanisms, and mechanisms of security" (Foucault, 2007, p. 8)

As I have anticipated, this has led me to rethink the grid of governmentality from different contributions that attempt to link Foucault's analyses with contemporary transformations of capitalism, which are not part of the Frenchman's inquiry. Already a decade ago, Maurizio Lazzarato stressed the limits of the figure of the entrepreneur of the self to think neoliberal capitalism, emphasizing the social and machinic subjection apparatuses characterized by violence and cruelty exerted on subjected bodies (Lazzarato, 2012). In this sense, I will dedicate a section of chapter 1 to the role of debt as a key power *dispositif* for the functioning of neoliberal capitalism, in terms of economic extraction and the moralization of subjectivities. (Lazzarato, 2012; Graeber, 2012; Lazzarato, 2015). Debt thus possesses an extractive aspect and another clearly productive one, insofar as it manufactures, shapes and modulates—through cruel mnemotechnics —the forms of contemporary subjectivity (Lazzarato, 2012). However, far from thinking of the indebted subject—or human capital—as universal, I consider it necessary to recognize the differential modalities of subordination, exploitation and extraction according to which debt operates in terms of sex-gender, race, geography and class. (Cavallero & Gago, 2021; Sacchi, 2020). In that sense, it becomes necessary to understand neoliberalism as an economic and political technology that operates by exploiting, producing, and governing racial, colonial and sex-gender differences. In this framework, the question of reproductive labor (feminized, racialized and permanently exposed to violence) and, in a broader sense, the question of reproduction and its relation to production, labor, value and subjectivity, will be central to my critical analysis of neoliberalism and to understand antagonisms in force today (Expósito, 2021).

Within this framework, the grid of governmentality is not opposed to that of war. In fact, war against populations has been a central element of neoliberal capitalism (Alliez & Lazzarato, 2016). For Lazzarato, such violence would take on a "fascist" tinge, connecting the violent origins of neoliberalism in Chile with the figures of Trump and Bolsonaro today (Lazzarato, 2021). In a similar vein, after an exhaustive archaeological work on liberalism and neoliberalism, Dardot et al (2021) will recover the Foucauldian paradigm of civil war as a grid of intelligibility of neoliberal politics, in its declared antagonism to any political or social current that seeks to counteract the inequalities produced by capitalism (Dardot, Sauvêtre, Guéguen & Laval, 2021).

In this framework, from chapter 2 onwards, the problem of violence will lead me to problematize neoliberalism as a political-strategic project, as a discourse of social division that defines and redefines the frontier between the market economy and its antagonists, and thus to put at stake the relationship between neoliberalism(s) and authoritarianism(s). In part, the chapter will attempt to explore neoliberal polarization strategies by focusing on the proposed antagonism

between "free market" and "totalitarian dirigisme". To understand this antagonism, it is possible to recover the idea of politics as a continuation of war (Foucault, 2003b), showing the antidemocratic and authoritarian features of the neoliberal thought collective itself and of its project of society, for which it does not
hesitate to appeal to civil war against egalitarian currents in the name of freedom
(Dardot et al., 2021).

In this framework, after identifying tensions between liberalism and democracy, and between sovereignty and government, chapter 2 explores some of the
main conservative features of the thought of authors such as Röpke and Hayek
and makes a brief commentary on the criticisms of democracy by institutions
such as the Trilateral Commission. As we shall see, the neoliberal defense of economic freedom as the only relevant one, to the detriment of political participation and the extension of civil, political, and social rights of the majorities,
plays a decisive role in the crisis of liberal democracy itself. At the same time,
this conception of freedom—which is the word that inherently defines liberalism
and neoliberalism—implies a phobia of the poor, the racialized, the feminized,
the sexual dissidents, and of any politics that attempts to correct inequalities.
In that sense, it is a freedom that only concerns white and male owners, and
that legitimizes and encourages the current far-right (Brown, 2019).

These exclusions allow us to understand the deep link between the most influential streams of neoliberalism—from the Austrian and ordoliberal school to
the contemporary paleolibertarians—and reactionary thought (Perrin, 2014),
which does not consider racialized, colonized, feminized, and impoverished
subjects as equal to white and male owners, and for that very reason does not
believe them fit for democratic self-government (Cornelissen, 2020; Slobodian,
2014; 2018). In this violent, hierarchical and exclusionary logic is situated the punitive moment that has characterized the neoliberal stage (Fassin, 2018), where
the notion of "social enemy" is redefined and also erects a fertile ground for the
emergence of authoritarian neoliberalism, which we will analyze in chapters 3
and 4, and of national-neoliberal currents, whose unrestricted defense of property goes hand in hand with ethno-nationalist supremacism, as I will analyze in
chapter 5.

In this framework, chapter 3 focuses on the context of the emergence of "actually existing neoliberalism" by briefly reviewing its evolution from the 1970s to
the present, in a transition from "combative neoliberalism" to "punitive neoliberalism". Therefore, it is asked whether the present radicalization of neoliberalism leads us to a form of "neoliberal fascism" or whether in fact—considering
the substantial differences between the present moment and the rise of fascism
in the twentieth century—there are better conceptual tools to think about the present. To this end, different theoretical contributions that characterize the present

moment in terms of neo-fascism, neoliberal fascism, or post-fascism are traced. Then, the scope of such views is questioned, since they seem to think of authoritarianism as something exclusively given by the political and cultural forms of the new radical right, which entails the risk of ignoring the violence intrinsic to the specifically neoliberal apparatuses of power.

In continuity with these reflections, chapter 4 explores the notion of *authoritarian neoliberalism* and its relationship with the rise of the new right. I return to the contemporary debate, where the concept of authoritarian neoliberalism seeks to mark a new stage within neoliberal governance following the global financial crisis of 2008, which is transversal to different types of political regimes and party configurations, while it also refers to the violent and authoritarian origins of neoliberalism itself. In turn, it allows us to nuance the sharp opposition between democratic, consensual, and progressive neoliberalism in the global North and a neoliberalism imposed by force in the South. Within this framework, I analyze the new national-liberal and social-identitarian radical rights, which have emerged strongly in recent years, as an effect of neoliberal globalization itself. Both currents criticize different aspects of globalization and the undermining of state sovereignty without putting capitalism or neoliberalism as a system of power into question. Although I draw on contributions made by the notion of authoritarian neoliberalism, I also point out its limits, because it exaggerates its novelty and because it is possible to think of an authoritarianism that is inherent to neoliberal rationality that such a conceptualization seems to blur.

This genealogy of authoritarian neoliberalism and its link with the radical right continues in chapter 5. There I propose a brief historicization of some national-neoliberal political currents within the framework of a strategy known as right-wing populism, which consists of appealing to the people against the establishment in an (ethno)nationalist key. In this framework, I will comment on some of the criticisms of this current to transnational institutions and its defense of the nation as a platform from which to promote free trade and competition in the global market. In this framework, I first recover the role played by Thatcher and Eurosceptic think tanks in the rise of European national-liberalism and then comment on some key political and intellectual figures of the paleoconservative and dextro-libertarian currents, such as Murray Rothbard, Patrick Buchanan, and Llewellyn Rockwell, which inspired contemporary right-wing populisms in the United States. Finally, I address the link between these currents and the alternative right, in a drift from libertarianism and paleoconservatism to neo-fascist positions. This exploration allows us not only to better understand the link between neoliberalism and the new radical right, but also to grasp some ideological characteristics of the reactionary wave that is sweeping over different parts of the world.

In this framework, in chapter 6 I analyze the construction of "feminism" and "gender ideology" as strategic enemies of the new radical right, which designates them as the spearhead of a communist advance-guard that would have conquered the political-cultural hegemony in the West and in Latin America, and which they call "cultural Marxism". In my reading, this hatred is due to the fact that anti-capitalist feminism, with its struggle against exploitation and dispossession of reproductive labor, is currently the most powerful mass movement in its ability to question both patriarchy and neoliberal capitalism, and thus counteract the advance of the far-right, which seeks to defend class, race and gender privileges. In this framework, drawing on Julia Expósito's reading of intersectional and social reproduction feminism, I will comment on some elements of social reproduction, which critically recovers the materialist and dialectical method of Marx. Within that framework, the modes of exploitation, oppression, alienation, and extraction are fused in the contradiction that operates in social reproduction between the production of capital and the sustainability of life, which materializes in neoliberalism as a crisis of civilization and care (Expósito, 2021). Reproductive work guarantees the fundamental sustenance through which the very capacity to work and, therefore, life itself is (re)produced. However, being feminized and racialized, it is subjected to multiple forms of social violence that our patriarchal society legitimizes. Therefore, anticapitalist feminisms not only question the very foundations of our socioeconomic system, but also open new potentialities for social coexistence, production, and reproduction.

In the face of the dispossessive, extractive and configuring logics of neoliberal capitalism, the question of *the common* emerges as an alternative to capitalism and neoliberal governmental rationality, but also to the old state-centered socialism. Thus, chapter 7 makes a political approach to the common, where at stake is not an ontological duty towards any other, but a political project that aims to subvert the neoliberal logics that govern us, appealing to self-determination and self-management. However, this appeal should not lead us to state-phobia nor to individualism, but to be able to situate the state as a field of struggles that the commoners cannot renounce.

In sum, this book the hypothesizes that in order to carry out a critical ontology of the present we must take into account the strategic character of the neoliberal project and the modalities of violence that are inherent to it. Within this framework, I situate entrepreneurial and competitive rationality as the central axis of neoliberal governmentality, which implies specific forms of coercion that differ according to race, gender, sexuality, and class, and which must be thought of in the light of the contemporary transformations of capitalism in the forms of accumulation, production, and reproduction. Although I recognize its internal differences and its plurality of theoretical and political currents, I will understand neoliberalism as a social, theoretical, political, and cultural project whose mission is to defend property and the freedom to undertake and compete in the face of any collective search for equality or social justice. Hence the proliferation of inequalities, exclusions, and social protests, which have led to an increasingly authoritarian, anti-democratic and punitive neoliberalism, and its confluence with authoritarian currents of the far-right in its rejection of mass democracy, feminism, and racialized subjects. In the face of this authoritarian governmentality, it is imperative to think about how we can govern ourselves differently.

1 Neoliberal reason

1.1 The emergence of neoliberalism

Although the Austrian School of neoliberal thought finds its roots in the subjective theory of value developed at the end of the nineteenth century by Carl Menger,[1] neoliberalism emerges as such in the interwar period, in opposition to the rise of political and economic nationalism and "collectivist ideas" (Dardot & Laval, 2017; Slobodian, 2018; Hoppe, 2000) which followed the fall of the Empires and monarchies of Central and Eastern Europe (Austro-Hungarian, Ottoman, Russian, Prussian). According to Dieter Plehwe, this explicit redefinition of liberalism and the role of the state in securing a free market first appears in the book *Old and New Economic Liberalism* by the Swedish economist and later member of the Mont-Pèlerin Society Eli F. Heckscher (1921), and then in *Trends of Economic Ideas*, by the Swiss economist Hans Honegger (1925). Later, the term "neoliberalism" appears in a paper by Ludwig von Mises in 1927 and in a speech by Alexander Rüstow in 1932. However, the Walter Lippmann Colloquium[2] is usually considered as a founding moment of the "neoliberal thought collective", which is institutionally embodied in the Mont- Pèlerin Society[3], created in 1947 under the aegis of Hayek and Röpke, and which will

---

1 In contrast to classical economics, according to which the value of things is determined by the labor socially necessary to produce them or by the costs of the various factors of production, the subjective theory of value maintains that value is decided by the subjective preferences of consumers. For a development of how this theory is reinterpreted by the leading members of the Austrian school of economics, see De Büren (2020) and Audier (2012).

2 The Walter Lippmann Colloquium was a conference of intellectuals organized in Paris in August 1938 by the French philosopher Louis Rougier to discuss the publication of Lippmann's 1937 book *An Enquiry into the Principles of the Good Society* which was translated to French as *La cité libre*. Some of the most prominent liberal thinkers and some big entrepreneurs of that time took part of the conference. During the latter, they created an organization to promote liberalism which was called the *Comité international d'étude pour le renouveau du libéralisme* (CIERL). This organization has inspired the creation of the Mont-Pèlerin Society in 1947. The conference is considered by many scholars (Foucault, 2008; Reinhoudt & Audier, 2018) as the keystone of the *neoliberal thought collective* (Mirowski & Plehwe, 2009). In that meeting, different schools coincided in the need to renew liberalism, analyzing the causes of the decline of *laissez faire*, and to oppose collectivism and socialist planning. However, while in the conference there was a big influence of representatives of "social liberalism", they will be absent from the MPS (Audier, 2012)

3 The MPS is an international organization that promotes a free market society. It's first meeting was held in 1947, with the participation of leading intellectuals of different branches of neolib-

https://doi.org/10.1515/9783110723939-003

have a decisive influence on the spread of neoliberal ideas and policies through-out the world.

As early as the 1938 colloquium, divergent positions were put forward on the causes of the crisis of liberalism and, therefore, on the proposals for founding a new liberalism. Austrians such as Hayek and Mises argued that the crisis of cap-italism and liberalism was not due to an intrinsic dynamic or to the failure of the liberal project of a self-regulated market, but precisely to the interventions of the state in the economy in the preceding phase.[4] On the other hand, the diagnosis made by the theorists who were fundamentally part of the Freiburg School in Germany, together with French theorists such as Rougier, and Walter Lipp-mann—an American journalist who advised several presidents from Wilson to Johnson—is quite different. In fact, in *The good society* (1937), Lippmann states that it was liberalism itself that produced its own crisis. One of the problems with classical liberalism for these theorists was its naive naturalism (Foucault, 2008). That is, classical liberalism presupposes that the market is a natural realm of ex-change. However, for most neoliberals the market is a historical and institutional construction and, therefore, this market must be produced through legal rules and other social and environmental conditionings. Therefore, the state is a deci-sive actor in the promotion of competition through certain legal rules and struc-tural interventions that make it possible to regulate and promote this market game without intervening directly in it.[5]

---

eralism such as the philosopher Karl Popper and the economists Friedrich Hayek and Ludwig von Mises (Austrian school), Ludwig Ehrhard (ordoliberalism), and Milton Friedman (Chicago School). Its original statement of aims maintains that their core mission is to defend freedom, which can only be preserved through private property and competitive markets that diffuse power in opposition to collectivism in which power is concentrated in few hands. It has had a great influence in the promotion of neoliberal thought throughout the world. It started its ac-tivities when neoliberal thought was marginal and had a great success in transforming it into a hegemonic and commonsensical *Weltanschauung*. According to Hayek, the intention of the SMP was to facilitate the "personal contact between the defenders of neoliberalism", develop a struc-ture of neoliberal thought, and "its practical application to the problems of different countries". (Slobodian, 2018, p. 127)

4 It should be noted that in 1938 this position was minoritarian. It was in the second post-war period that the ideas and the figure of Hayek came to dominate the neoliberal collective.

5 Sébastien Caré proposes a typology of the main variants of neoliberal thought in the 1930s, taking into account two criteria: a political one, ranging from those in favor of state intervention-ism to thinkers who remained more anchored in *laissez faire*; an epistemological one, distin-guishing positivist tendencies from those more reluctant to use the methods of the natural sci-ences within the social sciences. Crossing the two variables, we obtain four broadly defined positions: the ordoliberal Freiburg school (Wilhelm Röpke, Alexander Rüstow, Franz Böhm, etc.), interventionist and anti-positivist; the Chicago school (Milton Friedman, Gary Becker,

Despite these divergences, the different schools that took part of the Collo-quium coincided in their progressive identification of socialism, Keynesianism, economic dirigisme, economic planning and state interventionism as enemies[6], which would form a system that, for authors such as Hayek and Röpke, inevita-bly leads to totalitarianism.[7] While since the 1920s Mises denounced the irration-ality of socialism as it could not give an adequate response to consumer prefer-ences through the spontaneous operation of the price system (Mises, 1951),

---

etc.), non-interventionist and positivist; the Vienna school (Ludwig von Mises, Friedrich Hayek, Murray Rothbard, etc.), anti-interventionist and anti-positivist; the Paris school (Louis Rougier, Jacques Rueff, Maurice Allais, etc.) interventionist and positivist (Caré, 2016; Caré & Châton, 2016). For an extraordinary survey of these divergent positions that calls into question rigid clas-sifications and shows how variegated the neoliberal universe is see Audier (2012; 2018).

6 In his course, Foucault comments mainly on the ideas of the Freiburg and Chicago schools, with some references to Hayek and Giscard d'Estaing's neoliberalism. However, the neoliberal thought collective (Mirowski and Plehwe, 2009) is multiple and varied according to geography and generations. In this sense, Callison and Manfredi point out that: "Animated by a shared hos-tility to democratic dynamics and state planning, neoliberalism is best understood as a family tree with different branches consisting of their own idiosyncratic philosophies and commit-ments. These included the Austrian School's "catallactic" model of market dynamics in which exchange is superior to value-laden "social engineering"; the Freiburg School's conviction that only an independent "strong state" can prevent democratic and corporate powers from de-stabilizing the competitive market order; the Chicago School's belief that almost all forms of state intervention and public ownership produce worse outcomes, disrupt market rule, and in-fringe upon individual liberty; the Virginia School's claim that all government officials use power to self-interested, inefficient, and wasteful ends, and thus require strict constitutional lim-itations like "debt brakes"; and the Geneva School's strategy of international institutional de-sign to lock in market-friendly policies and legally delimit state sovereignty over capital flows" (Callison & Manfredi, 2019, p. 7). In this mapping, one of the most influential and least known branches is the Geneva school, where Austrians and Germans met in the 1930s and where a neoliberal globalism emerged that sought to rebuild the international economy after the fall of empires and against economic nationalism (Slobodian, 2018). Slobodian uses such a label: "to describe a genus of neoliberal thought that stretches from the seminar rooms of fin-de-siècle Vienna to the halls of the WTO in fin-de-millennium Geneva [...] the Gen-eva School includes thinkers who held academic positions in Geneva, Switzerland, among them Wilhelm Röpke, Ludwig von Mises, and Michael Heilperin; those who pursued or presented key research there, including Hayek, Lionel Robbins, and Gottfried Haberler; and those who worked at the General Agreement on Tariffs and Trade (GATT), such as Jan Tumlir, Frieder Roessler, and Petersmann himself. Although they shared affinities with the Freiburg School, Geneva School neoliberals transposed the ordoliberal idea of "the economic constitution"—or the totality of rules governing economic life—to the scale beyond the nation". (Slobodian, 2018, p. 8)

7 Isabella Weber points out that "The importance of socialism and Marxism specifically for the formation of neoliberal thought is reflected in the great number of writings by some of the core neoliberal thinkers on socialism. The figureheads of neoliberalism articulated their ideology in explicit opposition to planning and collectivism". (Weber, 2018, p. 220)

Hayek argued in his 1944 book *The road to Serfdom* against the Beveridge plan that Nazism was a necessary outcome of planning and state interventionism. In opposition to the latter, neoliberalism would aim to build a free market society, governed by competition, which made necessary a legal framework, and, more fundamentally, the production of a corresponding *ethos*, a new form of subjectivity.

To this end, as I anticipated, neoliberalism seeks to overcome the naturalistic assumptions of classical liberalism and *laissez faire* politics. Indeed, for ordoliberals, the market is an institutional construction that must be conceived in terms of competition and inequality and no longer in terms of exchanges and equivalence. Competition must be promoted and monitored by means of an active policy that includes legal interventions, regulatory and ordering actions.[8] "One must govern for the market, rather than because of the market" (Foucault, 2008, p. 121). Specific to neoliberal politics will be not the degree of interventionism but the "governmental style" (Foucault, 2008, p. 123) and aims. Within this framework, full employment—a central goal of Keynesian public policies developed by most Western states after the Great Depression and the Second World War—should no longer be sought by economic policies since it would inevitably lead to distortion of spontaneous price equilibria. At the same time, Ordoliberalism will argue that social policy must not compensate for the effects of economic processes and cannot set equality as its goal but must let inequality do its job. According to Foucault, the only social policy they conceive is economic growth (2008, p. 144). Therefore, the state should promote the creation of a society of self-sufficient individuals and enterprises regulated through competition to avoid massification (*Vermassung*) and proletarianization. "It is a matter of making the market, competition, and so the enterprise, into what could be called the formative power of society" (Foucault, 2008, p. 148) and "obtaining a society that is not orientated towards the commodity and the uniformity of the commodity, but towards the multiplicity and differentiation of enterprises" (Foucault, 2008, p. 149).

Ordoliberals will coincide with the Chicago neoliberals in the affirmation of the entrepreneurial model as the interpretative framework of society and the nodal point of the technology of the neoliberal self. In both cases, neoliberal governmentality will seek to configure a *homo economicus* that is not that of exchange but that of the enterprise (Nicoli & Paltrinieri, 2014). However, if for ordoliberals the notion of enterprise had a moral component, the Chicago school

---

8 In Eucken's theory, regulatory actions seek to control inflation through credit policy while organizing actions intervene on structural market conditions (Foucault, 2008, pp. 137–143).

considers this *homo economicus*—and not the subject of exchange of classical economy or an anthropological subject of normalization—beyond any moral or communitarian implications, as the interface between subjects and government, allowing efficiency and cost-benefit rationality to be established as the main criteria to analyze human action.

In this framework, following a line that had been prepared by the Austrian school with the subjective theory of value and praxeology (Mises, 1998; Murillo, 2011; De Büren, 2020), the Chicago school will argue that economics must assume the point of view of the agent and his choices, dealing with behaviors that involve "a strategic choice of means, ways and instruments" (Foucault, 2008, p. 269), allocating scarce resources to antagonistic ends. Thus, first Jacob Mincer, then Theodore Schultz and finally Gary Becker developed the theory of *human capital*, which can be defined as the set of physical, cultural, and psychological elements invested to value one's own life (Foucault, 2008). From this perspective, all behaviors and decisions, even the most intimate and non-utilitarian, can be analyzed in economic terms of costs and benefits, supply and demand, since "the object of economic analysis" is defined as "the set of systematic responses to the variables of the environment" (Foucault, 2008, p. 270).[9]

I would like to suggest that, despite the original intentions of their proponents, these theories became not only heuristic but also normative and strategic for the neoliberal technologies of government and their regime of veridiction, by hegemonizing the discourse and practice of all kinds of institutions. They do not only make up for the inadequacies of a classical economics that would not have thought of work and value beyond the time factor, or that would not have been able to think of it from the worker's point of view. Rather, they were used to force us to think and function as entrepreneurs of ourselves, seeking to maximize profits through an optimal use of available resources in all spheres of existence. Moreover, by making us all magically possessors of capital, the capital-labor conflict itself seems to be overcome, since the capacity to produce appears as a cap-

---

9 In 1992, Gary Becker was awarded the Nobel Prize in economics for having extended the domain of microeconomics to the analysis of hitherto non-market behavior. In the same vein, David Friedman proposes an explanation of the economic rationality of crime and marriage in terms of costs and benefits. For example, marriage would not only reduce transaction costs, but also allow for functional specialization. It would be a long-term bilateral monopoly contract in which, although we choose our partner in a highly competitive market, once the choice is made, the costs of switching are too high to try (Friedman, 1997, p. 317). It would be interesting to ask how the high divorce rates in Western societies are explained under this paradigm.

ital of the worker, a resource that he must use efficiently and responsibly to achieve a satisfaction that depends only on himself. In such a situation, if the subject makes responsible use of his own life, he will be rewarded with an increase in his own capital and his own satisfaction, while if he does not, he must assume the corresponding costs, such as poverty, unemployment, precariousness, etc. Thus, with the theory of human capital there is a total fusion between capital and the subject who holds it. The worker is now someone who invests his capital, his skills, and competences, in order to obtain an income, entering into a relationship of equal exchange with the employer (Leghissa, 2008). To do so, he must sell and manage his work properly, positioning himself in a market, getting a customer, negotiating the contract price (Nicoli & Paltrinieri, 2014). In short, he must become an enterprise.

1.2 The neoliberal subject as entrepreneur of the self

As we can see, neoliberal reason seeks to introduce competition as a social organizer and the entrepreneurial logic in every decisional sphere. It is a technology of government that intervenes in the environment, trying to configure ways of behaving, thinking, and desiring, with the aim of creating the conditions for self-management and self-surveillance that allow subjects to compete in the market through an entrepreneurial ethics. Within this framework, exploitation and inequity are no longer perceived and explained as social outcomes of an economic system in which few people own the means of production and the majority only their capacity to work. To the extent that the body itself and its aptitudes come to be considered as a capital with the capacity to generate an income, inequalities will no longer be explained by a socio-economic context but as the consequence of a misuse of one's own investments and choices. The failure of the individual derives from a "mismanaged life" (Hamman, 2009), from a moral failure. Based on these assumptions, neoliberals separate economic policy from social policy and propose an "individual social policy". The aim is no longer to free subjects from the risks of existence by means of the welfare state but to make everyone assume his own risks as an entrepreneur of himself, "being for himself his own capital, [...] his own producer, [...] the source of [his] earnings" (Foucault, 2008, p. 226) and thus responsible for his success or failure.

Within this framework, according to Nikolas Rose, neoliberal governmentality prescribes "adopt[ing] a calculative prudent personal relation to fate now conceived in terms of calculable dangers and avertable risks" (Barry, Osborne & Rose, 1996). Indeed, risk is not only central to explaining the functioning of late modern society (Beck, 1992), but also plays a strategic role for neoliberals.

As Marzocca (2011, p. 106) points out, the notion of risk enables to think of the uncertainty associated with individual and societal life as both inevitable and valuable.[10]

This insecurity is taken for granted by the new forms of workforce management that appeal to horizontality and network organization through commitment, management by results, continuous evaluation, and the search for personal fulfillment and self-esteem in and through work.[11] In a context of growing labor precariousness and the existence of a large proportion of workers who globally live in uncertainty regarding their material livelihood, these techniques, combined with the constant threat of unemployment, personal failure, indebtedness and poverty, make the neoliberal subject "eminently governable" (Foucault, 2008, p. 270) and make it possible to diversify and intensify the modalities of exploitation. The (neo)liberal subject must learn to "live dangerously" (Foucault, 2008, p. 66) and must know the fear of the risk-taker, even if the most likely outcome is depression. The need for constant adaptation and improvement and the subjection to continuous evaluation processes mean that, far from being self-confident, as advertised by management schools, the neoliberal subject must strive to make his life goals coincide with the demands of the company, to find a glimpse of security and self-esteem:

> [...] the entrepreneur of the self is subjected to a process of continuous transformation/adaptation that coincides with the infinite search for a truth of the self that should be the key to both his fulfillment and his happiness, in any case to his insertion "in the world", that is, in the "reality" of the market. For this reason, the indefinite reinforcement of the will in the search for oneself and one's own truth is functional to the governability of the entrepreneurial subject and becomes the central hinge of neoliberal management. (Nicoli & Paltrinieri, 2014, p. 73).[12]

---

10 This was explicitly stated by the former Minister of Education of Argentina during one of his speeches within the framework of strongly exclusionary and precarious economic, labor, and educational policies: "we must create Argentines who are able to live in uncertainty and enjoy it" (Bullrich, 2016a). Another famous phrase of the then minister, which allows visualizing the colonial character of the human capital project, referred to education as a new "Campaign of the Desert"—which in Argentinian history refers to the process of colonization of Patagonia through the extermination of the native peoples. (Bullrich, 2016b)

11 As Pézet (2004) points out, managerial governance seeks to create devices that make it possible to mobilize the subjectivation objectives of individuals themselves in favor of the company they work for. Concomitantly, Paltrinieri (2013) speaks of "instrumentalization of the care of the self" to improve the company's performance hidden behind the promotion of new forms of subjectivation and emancipatory empowerment that the company proposes at all levels.

12 When sources are cited in the bibliography in a foreign language, the translation is the author's own.

In this way, fear is combined with another, more affirmative mechanism of control of subjectivity that Dardot and Laval call the performance-enjoyment apparatus. For them, the strength of neoliberal rationality lies in producing situations where subjects are forced to function according to rules imposed on them that are presented as if they had been chosen by themselves, as we pointed out in relation to management. This is part of the performance culture, which implies the need for constant self-improvement, and which is accompanied by an imperative to enjoy one's own performance. According to the Frenchmen, in the past, performance and enjoyment were separate. One gave the best of oneself at work to then enjoy the remuneration and free time. Today, instead, the "new subject is requested to produce 'ever more' and enjoy 'ever more', and thus to be directly connected to a 'surplus-enjoyment' that has become systemic. Life itself, in all its aspects, becomes the object of apparatuses of performance and pleasure" (Dardot & Laval, 2017, p. 313).

In this sense, marketing seductions are fundamental to exploit expectations of enjoyment. They complement the new forms of coaching as a fundamental tool for each "collaborator" of the company to give the best of himself at work. In this sense, Nicoli and Paltrinieri point out that contemporary forms of management seek that the working subject, far from renouncing his self, pursues an infinite self-improvement that must coincide with what suits the company (Nicoli & Paltrinieri, 2014, p. 66). In fact, along with the labor contract, the worker assumes a psychological contract that involves adhering to the "mission" of the company, fully identifying with it (Gallino, 2008, p. 16). Therefore, the enterprise becomes the main rule-dispensing institution, and it is as an enterprise that any other institution acquires legitimacy to set rules and social identities, according to a logic of efficiency and competitiveness. This entrepreneurial subjectivity places its truth in the verdict of success, in which it puts its value and its being to the test. Truth becomes identified with performance, as defined by managerial power, which generates various pathological effects (Dardot & Laval, 2017). In this sense, Byung-Chul Han points out that we live in a performance society, in which everything seems possible and in which "[p]rohibitions, commandments, and the law are replaced by projects, initiatives, and motivation" (Han, 2015, p. 9). This society, characterized by an excess of positivity,[13] would

---

13 According to Han, this has to do with the absence of an outside and of an Other against which to immunize oneself. For example, the foreigner would not be perceived as a threat but as a burden. "The violence of positivity does not presume or require hostility" (2015, p. 6). Neuronal violence derives from an overload of the identical. Han's assertions account for part of the violence with which neoliberal capitalism functions. As we will see, the violence

no longer produce madmen and criminals but depressives and losers (Han, 2015, p. 9). It is not by chance that non-infectious pathologies such as depression, attention deficit, occupational burnout syndrome, or panic attacks—not to mention cancer (McMurtry, 1999)—have become epidemic (Berardi, 2009; Han, 2015). According to Han, "it is not the excess of responsibility and initiative that makes one sick, but the imperative to achieve: the new commandment of late-modern labor society" (Han, 2015, p. 10). In that framework, the "depressive human being is an animal laborans that exploits itself—and it does so voluntarily, without external constraints" or following the "free constraint of maximizing achievement" (Han, 2015, p. 11).

Although, as I will try to show, I disagree with the assumption that the obligation to maximize one's own performance or self-exploitation is achieved through non-coercive means, Han contributes to problematize an important aspect of neoliberal governmentality, for which—as Foucault pointed out with respect to liberalism—the increase in freedom implies the intensification and sophistication of control mechanisms. In this sense, as Berardi points out, the imperative of multiplying freedom actually means multiplying productivity (Berardi, 2010). This dialectic, added to the interests of pharmaceutical companies allied to a neuropsychiatry that reduces mood problems to chemical imbalances, has favored the proliferation of psychological disorders—and their diagnoses—in recent decades.[14] In this sense, for Berardi, the connection between the expectations set in motion by the ideology of happiness of the euphoric neoliberal stage, especially in the sectors linked to the "cognitariat", and the catastrophic result for the subjects is evident: the promise of happiness and success led millions of young *cognitarians* to accept to work under highly stressful and hyper-exploitative conditions in a context of exaltation of competition and self-entrepreneurship (Berardi, 2009).

This exploitation of affections and expectations is achieved, at least ideally, by appealing to genuine motivations of the exploited. According to Paltrinieri, if

---

that has been registered with the rise of the extreme right is not only based on a supposed otherness, but also constructs enmity from the perspective of an ethnocultural differentialism.

14 This can be seen in the proliferation of mental pathologies in the various versions of the *Diagnostic and Statistical Manual of Mental Disorders* (DSM) of the *American Psychiatric Association*. On the other hand, there is an increasing amount of sociological literature that marks depression as the morbid condition typical of the neoliberal era and, at the same time, the dialectic of valorization that the new mental pathologies and the neurochemical interpretation of the self and its discomfort, set in motion, especially in reference to the pharmaceutical industry (Berardi, 2009; Barry, Osborne & Rose, 1996). In this framework, Rose (2003) characterizes advanced liberal societies as *psychopharmacological societies*.

management organizes existence in the company, marketing appears as a subjectivizing force, a key device of noopolitics (Lazzarato, 2006). This corresponds to what Deleuze called the society of control, in which the disciplinary molding exercised in closed institutional spaces would be less relevant than the modulation of subjectivities that takes place in open spaces, in a transition from school to permanent training, from prison to electronic anklets, and from the factory to the company. It is within this framework that generalized competition, the empowerment of subjects and the incitement to proactively seek self-realization are imposed. In other words, "the deployment of the logic of the market as a generalized normative logic, from the state to innermost subjectivity" (Dardot & Laval, 2017).

That said, I would like to ask under what conditions our societies produce subjects who are incited to believe that there are no limits to reach self-realization and if the "excess of positivity" can be universalized. Should we not analyze structural aspects of neoliberal capitalism that allow us to understand why "we fight for our servitude as if it were our liberation"? In this sense, an example I would like to highlight has to do with the role of debt in the production of new forms of social and machinic subjection to the neoliberal norm.

1.2.1 Debt, between social subjection and machinic servitude

In the previous section, I tried to show that neoliberal governmentality puts at stake a form of existence, ways of relating to others and to ourselves through generalized competition in every realm of social life, which implies an a priori acceptance of inequalities, both in the design of public policies and in the framework of interpersonal relationships: "After all, inequality is the same for all" (Foucault, 2008, p. 143).[15] In this framework, in which social policy cannot set as its goal the leveling of living conditions in order to achieve equality of opportunities and economic policy relies on inequality as a mode of regulation, there arises an obligation to conduct oneself as an enterprise, which is achieved through a variety of apparatuses immanent to society. One of them has been indebtedness, to which the process of financialization of recent decades has made a notable contribution. This not only refers to the preponderance of finance over other sectors of the economy, but also to the extension of the logic of capitalist rent to all activities capable of producing value (Hardt & Negri, 2009). If for some neoliberal theorists human capital was already configured by a kind of fixed cap-

---

15 Foucault (2008) attributes this phrase to Röpke, but we have not found it in his texts.

ital, including the body itself and its genetic equipment, and a variable capital (culture, education, aptitudes, relationships, etc.), capable of obtaining an income, it is not surprising that in the neoliberal context, in which we are witnessing a cut in wages and social spending, labor precariousness and reduction of social services, the *entrepreneur of the self* is progressively transformed into *indebted man*. To put it very schematically: this entrepreneur is a capitalist who possesses no capital other than his own aptitudes, modulated by ever-increasing possibilities and imperatives of consumption, and with fewer and fewer means of his own to satisfy them. The gap between these expectations and these means, in a context of wage deflation and commodification of access to previously public goods and services, is filled by indebtedness, which, in turn, forces the acceptance of new working and living conditions to make repayment possible.

Although debt is key to impose neoliberal policies and to produce a corresponding subjectivity, its functioning as an apparatus of control is far from new. In this sense, reading together the theory of currency in Marx and then in Deleuze and Guattari and Nietzsche's *The Genealogy of Morals*, Lazzarato puts forward the following hypotheses: first, that the social sphere is not constituted by exchange (economic and/or symbolic), but by asymmetrical credit/debt that historically and theoretically precedes the dynamics of production and wage labor. Secondly, that debt is an economic relation inseparable from the production of the debtor and his morality. In this sense, the economy of debt duplicates labor in the classical sense of the term, imposing a work on oneself, in such a way that unifies economy and ethics, production of value and of subjectivity (Lazzarato, 2012). Thirdly, debt works hand in hand with the objectively machinic character of capitalism, shaping not only the intra- and intersubjective sphere (social subjection) but also traversing the infrapersonal, the preindividual and the asubjective realms (machinic servitude) (Lazzarato, 2012).

Now, to bring up indebtedness as a power apparatus implies introducing into the analysis the financialization of the economy and society. The most obvious side of this process would be the hegemony of financial capital, an element without which neoliberalism as it has been imposed on a global scale cannot be understood, in a dialectical relationship with the indebtedness of families and nations. In many cases, as in Latin America and Africa, public indebtedness served to promote neoliberal reforms supported by the great world powers and multilateral lending agencies. These structural reforms dismantled welfare policies in a coercive manner within the framework of a globalization that implied trade liberalization, privatization and financialization of economies, producing a dramatic increase in inequalities in a context of ultra-exploitation of common goods. As John McMurtry (1999) points out, once the borders are open to its influence, financial capital tends to reproduce itself in an uncontrolled manner, without any consideration for the lives of people or the effects on the environment. And although—as Bifo Berardi (2009) anticipated two decades ago—the euphoric stage of neoliberalism seems to have ended, especially with its successive crises, financial capital continues to drive modes of accumulation and decisively influences the entrepreneurial modes of subjectivation and the functioning of various institutions that are part of the neoliberal governance. In this framework, in which every income is transformed into rent and in which existential precariousness must be assumed as a resource, debt, as a deterritorialized power relation of an economic, political, and moral nature, plays a dual role. On the one hand, it is a source of profit for large international creditors. On the other hand, it produces a specific form of subjectivity.

In fact, when Deleuze announced the passage from the enclosed man to the indebted man, he was making the caveat that three quarters of humanity had always been too many for enclosure and too poor for debt (Deleuze, 1992). However, the financialization of the last decades achieved the "inclusion" of these subjects in the debt economy, through mortgages, consumer credit, micro-credits, etc. and sovereign debt whose interests are paid by taxpayers, helping to impose the entrepreneurial subjective norm. As Lazzarato points out, "in the current economy, the production of subjectivity reveals itself to be the primary and most important form of production, the 'commodity' that goes into the production of all other commodities" (Lazzarato, 2012, p. 34).

As I was saying, this strategic role of debt as a driver of economic relations is nothing new. It even precedes historically the creation of currency and the mythical barter.[16] Currency was not invented to overcome the inadequacies of a primitive mode of exchange, since it is the expression of an exchange that originates in debt. In fact, since currency is always the product of a political institution, it is itself configured not only as a means of exchange and a store of value, but first and foremost as debt. While not all debt is monetized, currency has been (at least until the invention of blockchains and cryptocurrencies)[17] always-already

---

16 Contrary to what mainstream economics has maintained since Adam Smith, David Graeber shows that barter occurs either between men who do not have permanent social relations and are potentially enemies or in societies that habitually exchange using currency and are facing an economic collapse, as happened in Russia in the 90s and Argentina in 2001–2002. (Graeber, 2011, p. 37).

17 Without entering the discussion of whether cryptocurrencies can be equated with traditional currencies or whether they maintain the same functions as fiat money, the fact is that they are no longer based on state-controlled issuance but on a series of decentralized technical protocols and user participation. This decentralized character of cryptographic money makes both anarcho-capitalist libertarians and communists see in it an emancipatory potential (in one case from the state and in the other from the state-capital binomial). In this sense, Mark Alizart

debt because from its very invention it is issued or guaranteed by an authority with coercive power to which the money must be repaid.[18]

In this context, Lazzarato affirms that the debt-currency expresses "an asymmetry of forces, a power to prescribe and impose modes of future exploitation, domination, and subjection" (2012, pp. 34–35). This is true for both individual and public debt, making the "creditor-debtor relationship" constitute "the subjective paradigm of modern-day capitalism [...] in which economic activity and the ethico-political activity of producing the subject go hand in hand. Debt breeds, subdues, manufactures, adapts, and shapes subjectivity" (Lazzarato, 2012, pp. 38–39). According to Lazzarato, debt and money constitute, since the late 1970s, the strategic apparatuses of neoliberal government. (2012, p. 90) As Nietzsche already warned, debt gives birth to this always-already guilty subject (*Schuld* means both debt and guilt in German), capable of making promises and developing consciousness and interiority. The guilty/debtor subject is forced to develop a memory not of the past but of the future. In that sense, the morality of debt allows capitalism to dispose of the future in advance (Lazzarato, 2012, p. 46).

In fact, money functions as one of the *asignifying semiotics* that are indispensable for the functioning of capitalism. If as a medium of exchange money refers to the intersubjective sphere, its decisive role as debt-currency implies an anticipated capture of the possible. Thus, currency not only makes it possible to produce a social subjection that mobilizes the consciousness and memory of the subject, but at the same time, debt-currency produces a machinic subjugation, which possesses "a molecular, infrapersonal, and pre-individual hold on subjectivity that does not pass through reflexive consciousness and its representations, nor through the 'self'" (2012, p. 146).

In this sense, the transversality of finance is made possible by that of machines and signs, which insert themselves into our minds and bodies, producing interfaces between the organic and the inorganic (chips, data banks, etc.) that constantly transmit information and produce new forms of subjection and servitude that do not have to do with the intersubjective but with the pre-subjective or pre-individual realm. For this very reason, capitalism does not refer only to language and meaning but fundamentally to asignifying semiotics. The power appa-

---

(2020) argues that bitcoin is revolutionary because it eliminates the intermediary role of banks, because it creates a trust that does not depend on subjectivity and because it can alleviate the dysfunctions of the market. This is what communism would have lacked for the organized destruction of the state.

18 As Graeber (2011) points out, while money can be issued by a private entity, such as a bank, it is the state that guarantees the agreements and legal terms.

ratuses of contemporary capitalism not only produce a subject-entrepreneur of the self that administers its own human capital but also configure and modulate a dividual, whose operations can be expressed in samples, data banks, etc. and which does not act but functions as a human element of a mechanism that he does not control: "he functions according to the programs that use him as one of its component parts" (Lazzarato, 2012, p. 149). In this modulation, the governance of behavior through algorithms plays an important role, not only in terms of indebtedness but also in various forms of control (marketing, electoral campaigns, surveillance, data mining, etc.).

This cybernetic aspect is fundamental to complement the Foucauldian diagnosis of neoliberalism, because although in today's capitalism the processes of social subjection are centrally carried out around human capital, which turns us into economic subjects responsible and guilty of our own actions, this goes hand in hand with a machinic servitude, which exploits the *dividual*[19], where the human being functions as a component, or interface, of machines that directly exploit his pre-subjective impulses and affections. Bio-informational and pharmaco-pornographic capitalism seeks to give impulse to the somatic device that regulates the excitation-frustration-excitation cycle and produce mental and psychosomatic states that allow the control of subjectivity (Preciado, 2013). To do so, it acts by decomposing and recomposing modules of subjectivity and information, intervening on chemical, genetic and neuronal elements of the body. (Lazzarato, 2015).

In this context, Lazzarato argues that in financial and neoliberal capitalism the main capture apparatuses are income and taxes, relegating the role that profit had in the preceding phase.[20] With the passage from the welfare to the debt-

---

19 The dividual appears in Simondon in relation to the concept of individuation and is taken up by Deleuze in *The Image-Movement* and *A Thousand Plateaus*, where it corresponds to the affects, a deterritorialized image beyond the individual and the collective. However, in the *Postscript on societies of control*, Deleuze uses the notion of dividual to characterize the mode of operation of modulation devices, which reconfigure individual preferences in a series of samples expressed in anonymous algorithms, which is propagated by digital technologies and allows new forms of surveillance. (Rodriguez, 2015).

20 Although the wealthiest sectors are the ones who tend to protest high taxes, the tax structure of most countries is frankly regressive, with a greater relative impact on the lower and middle sectors. One need only think of the systematic reduction in the tax burden on large capital and higher incomes that has taken place since the 1980s throughout the world. For example, in the United States, the marginal tax rate on top earners fell from 70% in 1980 to 28% in 1988, while inheritance taxes fell from 70% to 35% for the same group of taxpayers. The same evolution is observed in all North-Western countries (Piketty, 2014) and in the rest of the world as well. Thus, the states went from being financed primarily by progressive taxes

fare state, it is now the rich who are permanently assisted by the states at the expense of the wage earners, since taxes are no longer used to provide services to society but to pay to big creditors who send their money to tax havens. In any case, debtfare is not only an anonymous mechanism of plunder, but it is also productive of subjectivity. From the subjective point of view, taxation would make it possible to expiate collective guilt in the face of debt. On this point, the neoliberal strategy has been very clear: to replace social rights with the right to go into debt.

In this sense, it is worth insisting that the constant appeal of neoliberal governmental rationality to the desires and motivations of the subjects in order to be able to deploy itself was accompanied from the beginning of its implementation by extremely violent interventions, which is aggravated in the face of crisis contexts. This repressive governmentality is articulated with centuries-old non-state biopolitical apparatuses centered on consumption, which have been enriched by marketing, surveys, television, internet and social networks. These biopolitical devices—today articulated by finance—produce at the same time economic value, subjectivity and police control (Lazzarato, 2015).

In this context, Lazzarato states that since the 1980s a large-scale mortgage on the future of humanity has begun, in which individuals and countries are increasingly subjected to the owners of capital, while the goals of companies are increasingly subordinated to the pressure of shareholders. The financial market has become a disciplining agent for all corporate actors, leading to a high concentration of profits and wealth. At the same time, wage deflation has put the workforce in competition on a global scale and driven many wage earners into debt. In this context, companies and states are subject to the same rules of governance, the new watchword of neoliberal reason, which presupposes a series of decentralized and more horizontal consultative and decision-making bodies which, in theory, would give greater legitimacy to the solutions offered by technocrats than government, with its top-down representative and administrative logic. These governance techniques are as valid for companies as they are for states, which "have been placed under the control of the international financial community, bodies of experts, and ratings agencies" (Dardot & Laval, 2017, p. 219).

In this sense, the seemingly neutral notion of governance implies a break with the pillars of modern politics, representative democracy and legislative in-

---

on income and wealth, especially from the late 1930s to the 1980s, to being financed by debt, whose services now take a large part of the resources previously devoted to welfare and socio-economic promotion.

stitutions, which are based on the centrality of a people and a territory (Ferrarese, 2014). Instead, it is now the creditors and investors who must judge the quality of public action, that is, its conformity with respect to their own financial interests (Dardot & Laval, 2017). But, as we know, these debts fall on society and have become unpayable, mortgaging the collective, if not individual, future.

In this context of neoliberal governance and generalized indebtedness, we must conceive ourselves as bearers of a capital to be valorized, eroding the logics of solidarity, and behave as managers of our own risks. This entrepreneurial and accounting management of one's own life becomes a norm not only for those who work but also for people who have not even entered the labor market (Lazzarato, 2015). Thus, what was presented by the neoliberal narrative as an expansion of autonomy, of the possibilities of consumption and enjoyment, has lost all its attractiveness. According to Lazzarato, neoliberalism promised that we would all be shareholders, owners, entrepreneurs, but the only thing it achieved was to precipitate us into the condition of indebted man, responsible for his own fate. Within this framework, the population must take care of everything that companies and the welfare state externalize to society, starting with debt. It is debt that forces us to become *homines oeconomici*. And it is debt, and not immaterial or cognitive labor, that marks the pace of neoliberal societies:

> In the debt economy, to become human capital or an entrepreneur of the self means assuming the costs as well as the risks of a flexible and financialized economy, [...] especially those of precariousness, poverty, unemployment, a failing health system, housing shortages, etc. [...] taking responsibility for poverty, unemployment, precariousness, welfare benefits, low wages, reduced pensions, etc., as if these were the individual's "resources" and "investments" to manage as capital, as "his" capital. As we can very clearly see, the concepts of entrepreneur of the self and human capital must be interpreted by way of the creditor-debtor relationship. We must start from the most general and most deterritorialized power relation trough which neoliberal power governs the class struggle (Lazzarato, 2012, p. 51).

As we can see, although some readers of Foucault see governmentality as a type of oblative and consensual power, the economy of debt studied by Lazzarato takes us back to class struggle. In fact, it is Warren Buffett himself, one of the richest men on the planet, who points out that we are facing a class war and that it is being won by the 1% of which he is part (Lazzarato, 2012). In this context, debt is, at the same time, a key device for transforming the incitement to behave as entrepreneurs in all decisions into an almost obligatory norm of conduct and an impersonal and deterritorialized mechanism of domination, increasingly difficult for individuals and states to confront. However, this mechanism of subjection and domination cannot be fully grasped without taking into account the differential modes of exploitation that debt produces in terms of sex, gender, race and location. In this sense, Argentine feminist theorists and activists Verónica Gago and Luci Cavallero explain that debt must be made visible, transforming it into a collective problem, but also showing that it produces differential modes of exploitation and extraction according to sex, gender and geography. Therefore, the "indebted man" cannot be conceived as a universal subjective figure of current capitalism, or "a sole debtor-creditor relation that can be separated from concrete situations and especially from sexual, gender, racial, and locational difference, precisely because debt does not homogenize those differences, but rather exploits them" (Cavallero & Gago, 2021, p. 4). Within this framework, the authors mark not only a difference in terms of the way in which feminized subjectivities are exploited but also in terms of their potential for disobedience. With respect to the former, they emphasize the existence of

> (1) a particular form of moralization directed toward women and feminized bodies; (2) a differential of exploitation due to the corresponding relations of subordination; (3) a specific relation between debt and reproductive tasks; (4) the concrete impact of sexist violence, to which debt is connected; and (5) fundamental variations in possibilities "for the future" involving financial obligation in the case of feminized bodies (Cavallero & Gago, 2021, p. 4).

But if debt exploits these subjectivities in a broader and deeper way, it is also within the feminist movement that new forms of disobedience to the power of debt are being articulated. If the debt economy is part of a new form of war on populations, not only is this war not the same for everyone, but today resistance is fundamentally based on an anti-capitalist feminism which, as we shall see in chapter 6, questions not only patriarchy but also neoliberal capitalism.

1.3 Neoliberal governmentality: not such a soft power

As I have anticipated, the characterization of governmental power as conduction of behaviors (Foucault, 2007) gave rise to sweetened interpretations of governmentality as a soft power, which differs from the struggle between forces and war in the filigree of peace, that characterized the Foucauldian interpretation of power in *Surveiller et punir*, *La volonté de savoir* or courses such as *La société punitive* and *Il faut Défendre la Société*.

On one hand, these interpretations derive from the disruptive inflection that Foucault himself gave to the notion of governmentality as different from the juridico-political tradition of sovereignty and from the knowledge-power apparatuses that had been crucial in his previous work. On the other hand, they stem from the context of reception of his seminars. Indeed, the notion of governmentality circulated first in the Anglo-Saxon world since the publication in 1991 of the compilation *The Foucault Effect*, where the reader can find not only Foucault's class of February 8, 1978, but also inquiries from academics that followed his seminars at the *Collège de France* and even an approach to his vision of neoliberalism in Colin Gordon's introductory chapter. However, Foucault's seminar on neoliberalism *Naissance de la biopolitique* was not published until 2004, precisely when the hegemonic stage of neoliberalism was ending (Davies, 2016). At that moment, while neoliberal policies were producing evident inequalities at the socioeconomic level and they had not been able to recover the levels of growth of the "glorious thirty", they could nonetheless legitimize themselves in a normative, efficient, agile, meritocratic, individualistic, and hedonistic logic that resonated with the genealogy proposed by Foucault in 1979. However, over the years, the image of neoliberalism as a current that undermined traditional hierarchies and morals, expanding the spaces of freedom of choice proved wrong, especially in periods of crisis. That image does not reflect the centrality of traditional morality and family values for the ethos of the entrepreneur of the self, as a subjective figure of neoliberalism (Cooper, 2017; Whyte, 2019) nor the conservative and reactionary aspects of neoliberal thought that will be analyzed in the next chapters.

Moreover, at the time when Foucault was studying neoliberal thought, very material wars were being waged that would aim to radically transform society in that direction. Such wars were no longer primarily interstate, but had, and continue to have, as their target, an internal enemy. In the 1970s, this would be verified in the Southern Cone with the arrival of the Chicago Boys to give assistance to the bloody dictatorship of Pinochet, and in Argentina with adjustment plans that initiated a cycle of recession, indebtedness, unemployment and poverty that weighed like a death sentence on a country that half a century ago had the best socioeconomic indicators in the region.

Without resorting to state terrorism or military dictatorship, this combative neoliberalism was also that of Thatcher and Reagan, who destroyed the power of the organized working class, reduced taxes for the rich and wages for workers, and commodified public goods so that there was no alternative to neoliberalism. This process was consolidated with the fall of the USSR and the rise of neoliberal globalization accompanied by a multiculturalist opening promoted by governments that, like those of Mitterrand, Blair, Clinton, Schroeder and others, had come to power with a center-left discourse and took the policy of privatization, mercantilization and the culture of narcissistic and meritocratic individualism to its ultimate consequences, to the point that Thatcher would recognize New Labor as her greatest achievement.

However, in recent years, especially after the crisis of 2008, we have witnessed at a global level an accelerated growth of political forces that contain unabashedly authoritarian, reactionary, and xenophobic features. In this sense, if the commodification of everything seemed to give place to a society in which everything solid and substantial vanished in the icy waters of competition and the wet dreams of mass consumerism, today we are witnessing the rebirth of strongly exclusionary identities and a consolidation of different forms of war both by its means (military, psychological, financial, commercial, legal, political, economic, social and cultural) as well as by their declared or implicit targets (wars against immigrants, women, sexual dissidents, the poor, the precarious, drug traffickers, peasants, terrorism, Muslims, Indians).

In this sense, where Foucault saw an epistemological novelty in the figure of *homo oeconomicus* proposed by the theorists of human capital, such as Gary Becker, who questioned both the subject of exchange of classical economics and the anthropological subject of the disciplinary society, the sociopolitical reality of neoliberalism indicated that beneath the formalism of these theories was hidden a white, salaried man, provider of his family. When he feels his patriarchal privileges and the privileges of the salary of whiteness are threatened, this subject will not blame the social system that generates his discomfort but the subjects that come after him in the "cascade of contempt" of neoliberal society.

This situation should provoke a certain perplexity in those visions of neoliberalism for which the new governmentality was characterized by the reflexivity of the subjects and the absence of negativity. Indeed, as I have pointed out, in order to interpret contemporary power relations, it is not enough to characterize neoliberal capitalism as a performance society, marked by an excess of positivity, in which people exploit themselves and where violence is purely neuronal (Han, 2015). In addition to asking about the power apparatuses that give rise to this type of subjectivities, such as the already mentioned indebtedness, it is necessary to consider the strategic rationalities that organize and produce this society of competition and self-entrepreneurship. In sum, it seems too reductive to think at this point that neoliberal governmentality opposes war when innumerable wars are taking place today within the neoliberal world itself. Such visions seem to take at face value the way in which neoliberal discourse presents itself and in turn seem to focus on the tendentially hegemonic subjectivities and geographies of global capitalism, without considering that violent modes of accumulation have been permanent in the peripheries of capitalism from its birth to the present.

In this sense, far from thinking of current power exclusively as soft, flexible, reflexive and characterized by an excess of positivity, I try to consider the violent ways in which entrepreneurial subjectivities are produced and wealth is extracted. In this sense, Alliez and Lazzarato (2016) argue that governmentality cannot be separated from the conflictual logic of biopower, that there is an increasingly marked continuity between war, politics, and economics (with a hegemonic role of finance) and that liberalism has been from its beginnings a philosophy of total war. Far from the irenic visions that have plagued studies on governmentality in the aftermath of the publication of *Birth of Biopolitics*, Alliez and Lazzarato contribute to a genealogy of the transformations towards increasingly authoritarian and coercive forms of the entrepreneurialization of life.

In our reading, there is no sharp opposition between neoliberalism as governmental reason and the strategic rationality in which such governmentality is inscribed. If, on the one hand, different modalities of behavioral conduction and of modulation of subjectivities are deployed, based on incentives and incitements to the subjects produced by and for that society, at the same time this production of neoliberal, entrepreneurial, competitive subjectivities imply a whole series of disciplinary, biopolitical and sovereign apparatuses that shape them in an often-violent manner.

Indeed, if neoliberal rationality is separated from its strategic component in the reconfiguration of a class, sexual and racial power, it would be impossible to understand the history of actually existing neoliberalism, which is marked by genocidal dictatorships, authoritarian regimes and extremely violent repressions. As Lazzarato (2021) points out, to produce this neoliberal entrepreneurial subject, it was necessary to defeat the revolutionary, libertarian, anti-capitalist, and anti-imperialist subjectivities that populated the universities, factories, neighborhoods, jungles, and metropolis in the 1960s. But this defeat does not happen once and for all. It is permanently reenacted. War continues to operate in the filigree of peace (Foucault, 2003b).

For this very reason, neoliberal governmental rationality, which produces entrepreneurial subjectivities, must be read in the light of the transformations of capitalism itself and of the struggles of classes, sexes, genders, and races. Neoliberalism is a project that from its beginnings opposes socialism, Keynesianism, and social justice and, in this framework, proposes to violently transform the pattern of accumulation, redistributive and social policies, and the very subjectivity of human beings who must compete in the market. To this end, it will not hesitate to undermine democracy and appeal to social and political authoritarianism.

This is precisely what some contemporary scholars show, reading Marx together with Foucault. For example, Wendy Brown stresses that the genealogy of Foucauldian governmentality is incomplete if it is not read in the light of the world-shaping power of capital, studied by Marx:

Capital, and not only the articulation of it in economic reason and governance, dominates the human beings and human worlds it organizes. If this aspect is omitted in the theorization of neoliberalism [...] we will not grasp the intricate dynamics between the political rationality and the economic constraints, and we will also not grasp the extent and depth of neoliberalism's power in making this world and unfreedom within it. (Brown, 2015, p. 76)

Maurizio Lazzarato, who does not cease in his attempts to show the decisive role of capital in our societies, not only has rethought neoliberal governmentality in the light of the economy of debt (2012; 2015) but also reinserts the genealogy of governmentality in a historicization of the relationship between wars and capital (Alliez & Lazzarato, 2016). In such a framework, governmentality cannot be naively thought of as a soft power that definitively leaves behind the din of war, but as a form of regulation of behaviors that makes use of extremely violent and coercive practices as a condition of its exercise. Alliez and Lazzarato point out that "war, money, and the state are constitutive or constituent forces, in other words the ontological forces of capitalism" (Alliez & Lazzarato, 2016, p. 15). The genealogy of capitalism shows that without the exercise of external war and internal civil war, capital could not have been constituted and, reciprocally, without the capture and valorization of wealth operated by capital, the state could never have exercised its administrative, juridical, governmental, and military functions. The expropriation of the means of production and the appropriation of the means of exercising force are the conditions for the formation of capital and the constitution of the state that develop together (Alliez & Lazzarato, 2016).

In this sense, primitive accumulation does not represent the prehistory or the original sin of capitalism but is constantly re-actualized in what Harvey called *accumulation by dispossession* (Harvey, 2005). In such genealogy, the wars against the poor and women in the internal colonization of Europe, and the wars against native peoples in the colonization of the Americas, Africa, Asia and Oceania, not only made possible the emergence of modern capitalism, but were the prelude to the class struggles of the nineteenth and twentieth centuries (Alliez & Lazzarato, 2016). For that reason, the wars of class, race, sex, gender, and subjectivity, with which capitalism was born, are reactivated in the neoliberal stage, configuring a new wave of enclosure of the commons (Bollier, 2014; Caffentzis & Federici, 2014; De Angelis, 2001; Midnight Notes, 1990 & 2009; Mezzadra, 2008; Mattei, 2010).

In this sense, the Foucauldian genealogy of power in the West lacks a more exhaustive development of its relationship with external and internal colonization, and, within this framework, with primitive accumulation as a condition of possibility of disciplinary society and biopolitics. A decisive chapter of this genealogy is represented by the expropriation of women's bodies as the axis of the biological and social reproduction of the labor force, a condition of possibility for the emergence of capitalism and biopolitics (Federici, 2014). On the other hand, Alliez and Lazzarato (2016) point out that although Foucault glimpses a relationship between the deployment of disciplinary power with its model of truth in the West and its refinement in the colonies, taking as one of his cases the application of disciplinary schemes to the Guarani by the Jesuits (Ruidrejo, 2015), he does not develop this point in his later works on the disciplinary society (Foucault, 2003a). Moreover, let us not forget that American silver and gold were decisive for mercantilist policies, on which Foucault dwells in his genealogy of governmentality (Foucault, 2007; Alliez & Lazzarato, 2016). As we have pointed out, Foucault acknowledges the colonial genocide in his genealogy of racism, but then concentrates on the European case (Foucault, 2003b). However, state racism finds its antecedents in the colonies, where it develops as a way to justify the enslavement and extermination of "barbarian" peoples, which were the condition of possibility for the development of capitalism and, at the same time, the laboratory of the war against the nineteenth-century working class and of the total war in Europe in the twentieth century (Alliez & Lazzarato, 2016). As Mbembe (2019) points out, the genealogy of biopolitics and racism must be sought in the enslavement of colonized peoples, where one witnesses, long before than in Europe, the selection of races, the prohibition of mixed marriages, forced sterilization and even the extermination of the vanquished.

Considering primitive accumulation, with intra- and extra-European colonization, there is a deeper genealogy of disciplines, biopolitics and racism that allows us to understand more fully our present (Alliez & Lazzarato, 2016). From this perspective, there is not a properly capitalist accumulation that leaves behind the violence of primitive accumulation. At the same time, war and biopower are not opposed to the government of behaviors but become their inherent condition of possibility. Following Carl Schmitt, Alliez and Lazzarato argue that the economy is the continuation of war by other means, where, as Chinese Army officers Qiao Liang and Wang Xiangsui argue, "financial offensives" constitute a form of non-bloody warfare that can be even more devastating than bloody ones (Alliez & Lazzarato, 2016, p. 306). In this framework, Lazzarato and Alliez maintain that already since the nineteenth century capitalism is eminently financial and that only total war, the revolutionary threat and then the cold war made it possible to put a momentary stop to class conflict: welfare as a result of warfare. However, the planetary civil war and the debt economy have been unfolding again since the dollar-gold inconvertibility, declared by Nixon in 1971, and accelerated with the 2008 crisis, in the absence of any real threat to the unchallenged dominance of capital (Alliez & Lazzarato, 2016).

In this sense, far from naively opposing governmentality and the production of an entrepreneurial *ethos* to violence, Lazzarato and Alliez argue that what is governed and what makes it possible to govern are the divisions that project the wars within the population to the rank of real content of biopolitics: "a biopolitical governmentality of war as differential distribution of instability and norm of "daily life"" (2016, p. 26), that far from "the Great Narrative of the liberal birth of biopolitics" (2016, p. 27) elaborated by Foucault, takes the colonial war—which is a war against populations in which the distinction between peace and war, combatants and civilians, the economic, the political and the military is erased—as a model for all other wars. According to Alliez and Lazzarato, this model of war against populations is the one that has been adopted by finance capital since the '70s on a global scale, thus wiping out the brief history of capital reformism and the relation of forces that had made it possible. (2016, p. 43) In this sense, "the flows of credit and the flows of war are, with the states that integrate them, the condition of existence, production, and reproduction of contemporary capitalism" (2016, p. 14).

1.4 By way of conclusion

Throughout this chapter I have attempted to characterize neoliberal governmentality stressing the production of subjectivity as the central and most successful aspect of its implementation, since the entrepreneurial logic has conquered our most intimate self and our everyday practices. Going beyond *The Birth of Biopolitics*, I have recovered different contributions that attempt to update this diagnosis, connecting it with the passage from the enclosed man to the indebted man identified by Deleuze in his commentary on the *societies of control*, without forgetting that this control of subjectivity implies a series of cruel mnemotechnics applied on human bodies and souls. In this framework, I have highlighted the role of debt as a key apparatus to produce the neoliberal subject who must assume his existential precariousness as a resource of which he must make adequate use or be condemned to deprivation and misery. In this sense, debt connects the systemic dimension of contemporary capitalism with everyday social practices, functioning as an apparatus of control and capture.

In this way, I have tried to show that, far from opposing governmentality and war as a historical and interpretative framework of power relations and as a condition of its exercise, in both liberalism and neoliberalism there is a permanent articulation between coercion and production of subjectivity and a new version of class struggle in which increasingly exorbitant debts, and wars, both bloody and aseptic, multiply.

To implement their *Vitalpolitik*, neoliberal forces have constitutionalized the dependence of monetary policy on the financial markets and promoted an entrepreneurial *ethos* in the various institutional spheres in which we interact within the framework of a growing subjection to indebtedness. To this end, they have resorted not only to noopolitical apparatuses (such as marketing, the cultural industry, mass media, social networks, digital platforms, etc.) and to the production of new laws, but also to bloody dictatorships, police wars against unarmed populations, violent repression of social protests, hard and soft coups against democratic governments, etc.; in short, repudiating the rule of law and combining the deterritorialization of financial flows with an increasingly intense racist, classist and sexist reterritorialization. Moreover, every crisis, war or catastrophe has been an opportunity to create new markets (Klein, 2007) and get rid of superfluous populations. Like the welfare of the "glorious thirty", debtfare is also an effect of warfare. As Warren Buffett (2011a) pointed out, the richest 1% of the planet, of which he is a part, is categorically winning the class warfare in the last decades. Therefore, states should stop coddling them (Buffett, 2011b).

In this sense, an update of the Foucauldian diagnosis on neoliberalism and its modes of subjectivation requires, among other things, a deeper inquiry into its articulations with the hegemony of financial capitalism, on which our own capitalization, the production and exploitation of the commons and of our minds and bodies largely depend. Moreover, as we have argued, capitalism produces not only forms of social subjection but also of machinic servitude, it does not target only the subject but also the dividual, it does not extract value only from individuals and their labor power but also from the pre-individual, which makes the possibilities of resistance much more complex. In this framework, debt plays a decisive role, since the obligation to repay it implies the need to adopt certain behaviors that neutralize and capture potentialities.

Far from any irenic version of (neo)liberal governmentality, and even going beyond the formidable Foucauldian characterization of that political rationality, it becomes clear that indebtedness, dispossession and the increasingly widespread precarization of diverse populations, the rise of inequality, violence and environmental degradation, the "becoming black of the world" (Mbembe, 2017), are not mere collateral effects but central elements of the governance of our time and of the production of *homo economicus* as entrepreneur of himself.

This leads me to the question of the authoritarian becoming of neoliberalism —or neoliberalism reloaded—a moment when increasingly insidious and violent apparatuses of control are exercised with ferociousness on colonized, racialized and feminized populations, combined with the rise of a radical right based on hatred and thirst for revenge towards those same people. In this context, there is an increasingly evident contradiction between neoliberal rationality—with its disdain for mass democracy, economic, social, and cultural rights, popular political participation, and egalitarianism—and liberal democracy, which is based on popular sovereignty and the rule of law, whose legal scope has expanded throughout the twentieth century. For this reason, in the next chapter I will focus on some aspects of the crisis of liberal democracy as a process strongly conditioned by the global rise of neoliberal rationality. I will try to show that this rejection of democracy and even of human rights are constitutive of neoliberal thought and that, because of this fear of the masses, neoliberal antidemocratic spirit ends up combining with forms of social, cultural, and political authoritarianism.

2 The neoliberal era and the crisis of liberal democracy

In the previous chapter, I tried to show that the imposition of a neoliberal governmental rationality at the global level entailed the configuration of a series apparatuses of control—such as performance-enjoyment and indebtedness—that came to complement the logics of government and production of dominant subjectivity in a framework of the rise of post-Fordism and global financial capitalism, redefining the functions of the state and its forms of government. Neoliberal governmentality does not address the citizen, with its rights and obligations, but the *homo economicus*, understood as an entrepreneur of the self. These processes put central aspects of liberal democracy in crisis.

Hence, in this chapter I will address some tensions between the predominance of neoliberalism as a governmental rationality and liberal democracy based on popular sovereignty as the source of legitimacy of political power. On the one hand, this tension is constitutive of neoliberal thought, which from its beginnings distrusted popular sovereignty and democracy, which it considered to be the prelude to communism and, in general, to the sacrifice of freedom on the altar of an illusory and pernicious equality. In this fight against "unlimited democracy", whether in its social-democratic, socialist, or liberal-Keynesian form, several currents of neoliberalism exhibit authoritarian traits that are in tune with the reactionary thinking of the nineteenth century (Perrin, 2014). On the other hand, with the triumph of neoliberal reason and the victory over communism consummated in 1991, liberal democracy, which was presented as the triumphant, unsurpassable, and universal political formula, is being questioned by different internal and external processes. Indeed, the application of neoliberal policies, together with the financialization of the global economy, implied an upward redistribution of political power and economic resources to the detriment of the popular and middle classes. On the other hand, given its distrust of the masses, neoliberal governmentality implies a technocratic control of politics that undermines popular participation, reducing citizens to the role of mere clients of the administration who must limit themselves to validating decisions made by an oligarchy of experts. In the democracy of consumers (Mises, 1951) or customers (Karsten and Beckman, 2013), the only meaningful vote is the one that takes place in the market. Therefore, political democracy, which by its own dynamics would lead to distort the functioning of the market, must be neutralized.

As if this were not enough, also political liberalism is severely questioned. Increasingly subtle and insidious apparatuses of control are blurring the invio-

https://doi.org/10.1515/9783110723939-004

lable private sphere and individual autonomy, which were sacred for classical liberalism. In this context, the spread of police forms of surveillance and control of subjectivities, and the suspension of constitutional guarantees to defend the population from their "enemies", undermine the very values and rules—such as basic civil liberties and rights—that liberal democracy claims to defend. Moreover, the "great guardians of liberal democracy" have first advocated the containment of political participation and subsequently placed the world in a state of permanent war and exception, sacrificing liberal democracy itself and the rule of law in the name of "democracy".[1] In this sense, the acclaimed *Rechtstaat* and the Kantian doctrine of perpetual peace is belied by the permanent reality of preventive, deterrent or even punitive war, which dangerously reintroduces the theological-political doctrine of *bellum justum* onto the global scene.[2]

In the face of the threat that neoliberal governmentality represents to popular sovereignty and the rise of the new radical populist right that promises to restore the broken link between politics and people's feelings, identity and desires, it is worth asking whether we are not witnessing a profound crisis of the marriage between democracy and liberalism that took place in the West throughout the twentieth century, and whether it was not a marriage of convenience from the outset. To attempt a preliminary answer to this question, I will begin with a characterization of liberal democracy, analytically separating forms of sovereignty and government. Then, I will briefly comment on power apparatuses that call this democracy into question, the forms of subjectivity that they configure, and certain discourses that legitimize neoliberal policies by encouraging decisions that undermine liberal democracy from within. In this sense, I will try to

---

1 Libertarian positions, such as that of Karsten and Beckman (2012), oppose these practices— military interventionism, imperialism, technocracy, etc. However, they do not attribute them to neoliberalism but to democracy. From these perspectives, the last decades have not been marked by the advance of the free market but by the intervention and regulation of a state whose influence in economic and social life is growing due to the very dynamics of democracy. Even though it is partially true, the key issue is not the size of the state but its functions. Neoliberals have always advocated a strong state that promotes competition, commodification and entrepreneurialization.

2 The revival of political theology as an interpretative matrix of contemporary politics is perhaps a symptom of the decomposition of the agnosticism that characterized the mainstream demo-liberalism. The "war on terrorism" declared by Bush after September 11, 2001, was presented as a crusade against the infidels in the name of "democracy", in which no neutrality is possible. Bush's speeches on the need to combat the "axis of evil" exemplify wars in the name of humanity denounced by Schmitt (1996) which, by placing the enemy outside the law and humanity, seek to authorize with impunity the most merciless massacres. For an analysis of the use of "democracy" to justify the invasion of Afghanistan and Iraq, cf. Castro Santos and Tavares Teixeira (2013).

show some of the tensions between neoliberal governmental rationality and liberal democracy. To this end, I will focus on some of the main criticisms of democracy from a conservative, pluralist, and technocratic point of view, which are made by different neoliberal thinkers. In this framework, I will place special emphasis on the contributions of Röpke and Hayek to better understand the articulation between the neoliberal critique of democracy and certain conservative positions that will be taken up by the radical right that I will analyze in chapters 4 and 5.

2.1 Brief reflections on liberal democracy

The current crisis of liberal democracy, which occurred at a time when its final triumph was being celebrated (Fukuyama, 1989), is perceived by various intellectuals, whether they subscribe to or reject this tradition. To explain this crisis, one does not have to turn to republican or communitarian critique, nor to models of participatory or radical democracy, nor to feminist or postcolonial currents, which question the ontological and anthropological premises of liberalism[3] (abstract universalism, atomism, androcentrism, sexism, ethnocentrism, etc.), but to the material processes that challenge them. One might say that crisis is constitutive of democracy, or that liberalism has always been elitist. However, I would like to emphasize that the foundations on which this liberal democracy was built are today being challenged not so much by external threats as by internal processes in which neoliberal governmental rationality plays a decisive role.

The concept of liberal democracy implies the combination of two different political rationalities. On the one hand, democracy, which in its minimal definition refers to the power (*kratos*) of the people (*demos*) or popular sovereignty. In modern nation-states, this sovereignty gains in scope and loses in depth. It gains extension as citizenship expands and inequalities based on birth are eliminated, so that the exclusion of social sectors from political participation within the national space loses legitimacy. Not coincidentally, the modern mass democratic movement, which took seriously the postulates of bourgeois egalitarianism, constantly fought for the expansion and realization of political rights to gradually include all adults in active citizenship, regardless of their gender, wealth, and level of education. Moreover, the socialist movement sought to transform this

---

3 Here I use liberalism in the European and Latin-American sense of the term, as a tradition that privileges negative freedom and a formal set of civil rights and is frequently conservative in socioeconomic and cultural terms.

formal democracy into a substantive one by eclipsing liberal institutions and fighting for the reintegration of the state into civil society. On the other hand, the loss of depth has to do with the fact that modern democracy is representative, and this idea of representation even precedes the rise of the modern democratic movement. It is precisely with the doctrines of the social contract that the modern idea of political representation is imposed, which has led over time to the spread of an electoral model for the appointment of representatives of the political body who are autonomous with respect to their constituents.

This autonomy of representatives is at the heart of political liberalism, which emerges as a doctrine that, against the background of religious pluralism, modern individualism, and the emergence of the modern rule of law (Rawls, 2006), considers individual freedom of thought and religious practice, expression, association, etc., and legal equality as core values. In this sense, liberalism adopts the doctrine of the rule of law to limit the reason of the state vis-à-vis the natural rights of the citizen. The autonomy of the individual and his political capacities are founded on private property as an inalienable right, based on the ownership of oneself, from which comes the right to the fruits of labor as an extension of one's own body (Locke)[4]. At the institutional level, liberalism advocates the separation of powers to avoid tyranny and recognizes Parliament as the central space for the exercise of power through legislation and political debate. At the same time, economic liberalism was configured under the idea of governing as little as possible (Foucault, 2007; 2010a). It assumes that society, and hence the economy, can regulate itself and therefore it is necessary to limit the intervention of the state, reserving to it the minimal functions of administration of justice, public works, tax collection and everything that society cannot do by itself.[5] In this sense, if political liberalism originally had to deal with a *homo juridicus* and *politicus* who are subjects of law and must renounce their interests in the public sphere, liberalism as a technology of government presupposes an *homo economicus*, who precisely does not have to renounce his interests in order to become predictable and governable.

In this context, the nineteenth century was the scene of a struggle between liberalism, which sought to keep the political participation of the masses in check, and the democratic movement, which fought for the expansion of active citizenship. Within the framework of the liberal rule of law, citizens acquired constitutional guarantees and civil, political, and social rights that later, in the

---

4 This, of course, applies only to white men and landowners, who in turn can appropriate land they consider unoccupied (*res nullius*) and enslave barbarian and racialized peoples.
5 As we shall see, libertarian currents maintain that these functions would be better fulfilled by individuals.

twentieth century and after the Second World War, allowed liberal democracy to assert itself in the West as the legitimate political formula par excellence, in opposition to what was called totalitarianism, to the point that hegemonic political science celebrates with Kantian reminiscences that democracies do not make war between them.[6] However, the opposition between democracy and communism that prevailed during the Cold War meant the end of any emancipatory vocation of democracy (Ross, 2010), at least in the countries that claimed to be its champions. Democracy and freedom became words of order in the face of attempts to undermine the capitalist organization of society.

In this evolution, constitutional law is proving less and less effective in guaranteeing what it promises. To explain this, I distinguish this juridical-institutional dimension from the concrete forms of exercising power that we associate with the Foucauldian concept of governmentality. In my view, liberal democracy is the result of a compromise between liberalism and democracy that has been successful in the northwestern quadrant of the globe, especially after the postwar period. However, neoliberalism has seriously challenged this compromise through new forms of control that have led to a loss of economic, social, and even civil rights that seemed sacrosanct to the tradition of the liberal rule of law, according to which there should be progressivity in acquired rights. At the same time, these practices and mechanisms have made democratic political activity irrelevant by preventing citizens from having a say in important political decisions. In this sense, while liberal democracy remains an increasingly accepted political formula for government legitimacy and constitutional order in the West, the mechanisms of government seem to have adopted other logics that turn them into empty shells.

---

6 Perhaps it would be better to say: no democracy declares war on another. As we know from Latin America, the direct or indirect interference of the United States has been responsible for nipping in the bud any democratic process of social change that affects the interests of transnational corporations. Moreover, as Karsten and Beckman (2012) point out, the fact that Western democracies did not fight wars among themselves after the Second World War, is not due to the nature of the political system, but to their military alliance in the NATO. As for Kantian reminiscences, they refer to the idea that the citizens of a republic would not be inclined to support a war whose consequences they would have to bear, and that peace would be possible when international law is based on a confederation of states whose constitution's guarantee the prohibition of wars of aggression (Kant, 2016).

2.2 Democracy and liberalism, between sovereignty and government

If one understands by democracy the effective exercise of power by a population which is neither divided nor hierarchically ordered in classes, it is quite clear that we are very far from democracy. It is only too clear that we are living under a regime of a dictatorship of class, of a power of class which imposes itself by violence, even when the instruments of this violence are institutional and constitutional; and to that degree, there isn't any question of democracy for us (Foucault, in Chomsky & Foucault, 2006, p. 39)

As with the concept of neoliberalism, that of democracy is not only marked by an inherent polysemy and by the historical transformations that give it new meanings, but also, as with any authentically political concept, by polemical and hegemonic disputes. In this section, I will try to keep this dimension in mind, but, in order to organize the theoretical-conceptual development, I would like to begin with an analytical distinction between democracy as a form of state that is legitimized by popular sovereignty and as a form of government of/about that same people, a role that we believe (neo)liberalism will increasingly play.[7]

As we have pointed out in the previous chapter, in his genealogy of power in the West, Foucault brackets the problem of legitimacy and the theoretical and political privilege of sovereignty to analyze the concrete mechanisms by which it works, producing subjectivities through disciplinary and biopolitical mechanisms. In this framework, Foucault treats liberalism not so much as an economic or political theory but as the most persistent technology of government in Western modernity. At the same time, Foucault offers tools to distinguish democracy understood in the juridical-political terms of popular sovereignty from democracy as a form of government. In this sense, in reference to Athenian democracy, Foucault distinguishes the problems of *politeia*, related to the constitution— which involves questions of political rights such as *isonomia* or *isegoria*—from those of *dynasteia*, which have to do with the effective exercise of power, that is, with a political experience that involves forms of relationship with oneself and with others. In this framework, democratic *parrhesia* has a hinge role between both dimensions, making the problem of governmentality appear (Foucault, 2010).

This distinction between sovereign power and governmentality has been treated in different ways by Agamben (2007; 2010) and is taken up again in a

---

7 Elías Palti (2009) points out that this distinction was present in the nineteenth century in Latin America and that in the end it would seem that popular sovereignty only took place as constituent power, being incompatible with government.

conference on democracy. Agamben points out the ambivalence of this term since it can indicate either a way of constituting the body politic (through constitutional provisions) or a way of governing (administrative practice). In other words, it can designate a form of legitimization or a modality of exercise of political power. This ambiguity between the juridical-political-constitutional and economic-administrative-managerial paradigm would already be present in the term *politeia*, which, in Aristotle, could be translated both as constitution and as government. Translating Aristotle in modern terms, Agamben points out that his passage from *The Politics* (1279a, 25 ff) could be read as affirming that constituent power (*politeia*) and constituted power (*politeuma*) are linked in sovereign power (*kyrion*). Agamben recalls Foucault's (2007) reading of Rousseau's *The Social Contract*, where the Genevan seeks to reconcile a juridical-institutional terminology (contract, general will, sovereignty) with an art of government. For Agamben, this distinction between sovereignty and government is crucial. Rousseau repeatedly stresses the difference between the sovereign power that legislates, the seat of the general will, and the governmental power that executes. However, in order to show the indivisibility of sovereignty, he ends by pointing out, like Aristotle, that sovereignty (*kyrion*) is at the same time one of the terms of the distinction and the one that holds together constitution and government. On the contrary, according to Agamben, the error of having thought of government as simply executive power is evident today, since we are witnessing an uncontested predominance of government and economy, where popular sovereignty has lost any meaning. This would explain why we get lost in abstractions such as law, general will, popular sovereignty, without being able to address the problem of government and its articulation with the *locus* of sovereignty. (Agamben, 2010)

Therefore, there is a fundamental tension between, on the one hand, *popular sovereignty as a source of political legitimacy,* which takes place in a representative context where the people[8] neither deliberate nor govern, and, on the other hand, a *(neo)liberal* (not "democratic", as in Agamben's conceptualization) *governmental rationality,* which is imposing itself without any consideration for

---

8 In any case, this unitary people (*populus*) is a juridical fiction to be distinguished from the *plebs*, which, as we will see, is feared by liberals. As Palti points out, until the nineteenth century it was always thought that one part of society governed another. It was not conceivable that we are all sovereigns and subjects at the same time. For Agamben, every People generates a people that is in a relationship of exclusive inclusion. For his part, Laclau points out that populism consists in the hegemony of a part (the plebs) that claims to be the whole (populus) and Rancière understands that this is the part that has no part in the current political order.

these juridical fictions, and which seems destined to neutralize popular sovereignty, seeking its legitimacy on the epistemic and even moral level.

Indeed, today most democratic states base the legitimacy of their constitutional and political systems on popular sovereignty. However, when we look at the practices of government, we see oligarchic and plutocratic forms of political leadership and a growing elimination of the social rights obtained during the period 1945 – 1975, which had made our societies more democratic in the economic, social, and political spheres. In my view, this expresses a tension between the people as sovereign that founds the constitutional order and must elect its representatives through the popular vote and a governmental rationality whose legitimacy is sustained by specific forms of knowledge-power placed at the service of what is understood as an optimal or desirable state of life for the population. In this sense, the historical novelty of political democracy based on the legitimacy of popular sovereignty has been superimposed on the forms of governmentality that accompany the forms of the state and traverse them. In modern times, liberalism and then neoliberalism appear as the triumphant rationalities of government, capable of establishing acceptable forms of resource administration and of producing subjectivities through disciplinary, biopolitical and noopolitical power. For this reason, in the preceding chapter I have made some considerations on neoliberalism as a governmental rationality and on the emergence of what have been called societies of control, processes that to a large extent characterize our contemporary ways of being and acting. Now, this governmental rationality is constructed in a strategic confrontation with the modern democratic movement, lamenting the end of empires and the demand for equality of subaltern classes and peoples—also defined as "the revolt of the masses" (Ortega y Gasset, 1993).

Following this thread, in the remainder of this chapter, I will focus on the way in which, both as a system of ideas and as a political project, neoliberalism enters into increasingly evident short-circuits with democracy, which it considers an obstacle to the effective government of the population, to the preservation of freedom and to the existence of a rational system of production and consumption. Within this framework, we will see that, for neoliberals, the juridical legitimacy of power—whether it is a democratic or dictatorial government—is secondary to the effective way in which subjects are governed through economic rationality. Popular sovereignty and the parliaments can establish limitations on private property and market rule, thus undermining negative freedom which, in the (neo)liberal view, is the only authentic freedom. Therefore, neoliberals end up declaring democracy as enemy of freedom as such.

2.3 Neoliberalism against democracy

"My personal preference is for a liberal dictatorship rather than a democratic government where liberalism is absent." (F. von Hayek)

There are several elements that allow us to glimpse that the crisis of liberal democracy and the current rise of the neoliberal far-right, with its hierarchical and ethnocentric conception, are not merely byproducts of the processes of neoliberalization, but also find an ideological predecessor in the neoliberal thought collective. Indeed, the attack on mass democracy from technocratic, elitist, conservative, reactionary, and even libertarian positions has been part of the doctrinal cores of many neoliberal theorists and think tanks since its inception and has continued to develop in new forms ever since. From most neoliberal perspectives, democracy is seen as the fruit of the era of the masses, the spoils of pressure groups, the precursor of egalitarianism, the antechamber of totalitarianism or the vector of decadence. (Solchany, 2016, p. 136) This threat is more serious when democracy is exercised by non-Western peoples or races (Slobodian, 2018; Cornelissen, 2020) whose low level of civilization would make them prone to fall prey to demagogues and encourage socializing policies. In this framework, democracy is seen as the matrix of the worst danger threatening societies: *collectivism* (Dardot et al., 2021, p. 57). Hence the need for institutional devices that contain the pernicious effects of the dogma of popular sovereignty (Dardot et al., 2021, p. 58) and for a strong state that prevents politics and democracy from affecting the functioning of the market (Dardot et al., 2021, p. 74).

Although neoliberal governmental rationality cannot be reduced to an ideology, a political theory, or a conception of the social, this strategic rationality is inseparable from the war of ideas waged by a system of thought for which democratic egalitarianism is unacceptable, since it necessarily leads to an invasion of individual liberties and to make Human Rights—in their post-war version—prevail over the rights of capital (Slobodian, 2021).[9] Democracy would be acceptable only if it is reduced to a mode of selection of representatives that allows a non-violent alternation of governing authorities, but it cannot, and should not, pretend to extend to the economic sphere or to the international level.

Neoliberal positions range from a total rejection of democracy (Murray Rothbard, Hans-Hermann Hoppe, Robert Nozick, Louis Baudin, Alexander Rüstow,

---

9 As evidenced by Jessica Whyte (2019), unlike the first generation of neoliberals, who opposed the rights of capital to Human Rights, from the '70s a neoliberal appropriation of the discourse of Human Rights has begun, as rights of the individual owner, to the detriment of social and economic rights.

etc.) to an acceptance under certain conditions (Friedrich Hayek, Wilhelm Röpke, Milton Friedman, etc.), while strong support for it is rare, especially among neoliberal economists (Caré & Châton, 2016). Indeed, those who accept democracy, reject its "unlimited" (Hayek) or "pure" (Röpke) version. In this framework, neoliberalism and democracy can coexist at the price of a limitation (Caré & Châton, 2016, p. 11) or a hollowing out (Cornelissen, 2020) of the latter. The neoliberal fear of democracy is based on the fact that electorates will seek a redistribution of wealth, the intervention of markets, the defense of corporate interests, and thus will destroy the conditions for a free market, such as free exchange, the protection of private property and the discipline of competition (Cornelissen, 2020, p. 349). Therefore, they will seek to establish legal or constitutional measures that limit the influence of the citizenry.

To order the neoliberal criticisms of democracy, I draw on the analytical distinction of Caré and Châton, who point out three attitudes of neoliberal distrust of democracy, which in some cases are manifested in the same authors: a) a technocratic attitude, b) a conservative one, and c) a pluralist one. To this I will add what Cornelissen (2020) calls "a racialized critique of democracy".

2.3.1 The technocratic critique of democracy

As Caré and Châton point out, there is a technocratic critique of democracy that cuts across different schools and seeks to avoid "unlimited democracy" by removing from collective deliberation issues that can be decided only by a competent elite. Democracy is considered ineffective for solving technical problems. Consequently, an expert elite is needed to make the decisions that are necessary for the best functioning of society. Thus, those who decide public policies must possess technical knowledge. The emblematic figure of this technocracy destined to replace democracy are the Chicago boys who advised the Pinochet regime, although this "expertocracy" is also found in key institutions of the European Union and Multilateral Organizations such as the International Monetary Fund and the World Bank (Dardot & Laval, 2016). This critique of democracy predominates in the Chicago School, given its epistemological and theoretical assumptions based on *homo economicus* as someone who acts rationally in the sense that responds in a systematic way to the modifications in the variables of the environment, who "accepts reality" and therefore is eminently governable. (Foucault, 2008, pp. 269–270).

In this framework, Milton and Rose Friedman argue that taxes and spending should be limited, Keynesian policies banned, monetarism constitutionalized, and regulatory measures that challenge international economic flows prohibited.

Milton Friedman's support for authoritarian regimes in which economic freedom reigns is based on such efficiency reasons. In fact, while he declared that Chile was an exception to the rule and that it was necessary to combine economic liberalism with political freedoms, he not only welcomed the measures of the Pinochet regime, but also opposed the US Civil Rights Act of 1964, supported apartheid in South Africa and was fascinated by the economic performance of Hong Kong, a non-democratic state that had an outstanding economic performance due—according to the economist—to the fact that it did not involve redistributive policies as did England, the United States or Israel (Biebricher, 2020). These measures were a product of democracy, which, by allowing the interference of the masses in politics, led to less economic and civil freedom. Thus, Friedman stated: "There is almost no doubt that if you had political freedom in Hong Kong you would have much less economic and civil freedom than you do as a result of an authoritarian government" (Friedman, 1988, p. 64).

Indeed, Milton Friedman's technocratic critique of democracy will argue that the wider the sphere of the market, the fewer issues will be subject to political decision and, therefore, to the need to obtain consensus, making the functioning of society more efficient. In this sense, neoliberal political economy is unthinkable without its goal of dethroning politics (Rodrigues, 2018, p. 133; Brown, 2019).

2.3.2 The conservative critique

The neoliberal-conservative critique of democracy deplores the irruption of the undisciplined masses into the public sphere and proposes entrusting political power to a virtuous elite. This criticism, very frequent in ordoliberalism, denounces democracy, especially parliamentary democracy, for producing a harmful pluralism, fostering a narrow materialism within the masses, and weakening the virtuous dispositions of individuals. (Caré & Châton, 2016, p. 12)

This rejection of democracy, which finds its roots in the conservative and elitist thought of the late nineteenth century, has developed especially in the context of criticism of the Weimar Republic. In 1932, the ordoliberal Walter Eucken denounced "the democratization of the world", i.e., the universal male suffrage which brought politics closer to "the people and their passions, the interest groups and the chaotic powers of the masses" (Slobodian, 2018, p. 124). Eucken denounced state interventionism as an outcome of the age of the masses, where the distinction between the political and the economic sphere has been lost. In the same year, at the congress of the *Verein für Socialpolitik*, Alexander Rüstow presents the republican state as a "total state" that endlessly extends its prerogatives, but which is also a weak state that has become subject to the influence of interest groups. He takes up the Schmittean critique of pluralism and advocates a strong, neutral state, "serving the highest general interest", embodying "authority" and "leadership" (*Führertum*), based on a "correct and organically constructed constitution" (Rüstow, 1932 apud Solchany, 2016, p. 140). Alexander Rüstow thus prolonged the criticism addressed since July 1929 to parliamentary democracy where he advocated for an executive power that did not have to be tied to parliamentary majorities (Solchany, 2016). For Rüstow, the strong state should remain isolated from the erosive dynamics of mass democracy, and this will later lead him to defend a hierarchical and authoritarian state against totalitarian collectivism. (Biebricher, 2020; Davidson, 2018).

Indeed, against the model of the bureaucratized mass society, the ordoliberals propose the ideal of an organic society united by a shared culture and way of life and of a strong state above corporate interests, which sustains a moral tradition that in turn strengthens it, and which serves at the same time for the proper functioning of the economy. Such a state must be led by a civic-minded aristocracy. (Röpke, 1958 apud Caré & Châton, 2016).

In that sense, although most ordoliberals opposed Nazism for being plebeian and for its racial and economic policies, they also criticized the Weimar Republic as characterized by pluralism, interventionism and a politicization of the economy that transformed the state in a realm of dispute between different interest groups. There are even those who, like Fanz Böhm, had an ambiguous attitude towards Nazism. He published in 1937 a text entitled *Die Ordnung der Wirtschaft als geschichtliche Aufgabe* (The economic order as a historical mission), where the rejection of the democratic experience and a certain indulgence towards the new Nazi order are mixed. (Solchany, 2016, p. 141) In fact, in 1936, Böhm criticizes in harsh terms the situation prevailing during the Weimar Republic, while pondering the possibility offered by the new situation to settle the modern economic nation with a "community of people and destiny". Far from criticizing the quadrennial plan commanded by Göring, Böhm stresses that the existence of a state of emergency would open new horizons for a lasting economic constitution.

With this example, we do not seek to inscribe the strong state promoted by ordoliberalism in the same tradition as Nazism.[10] In fact, the vast majority of ordoliberals opposed the regime and, in many cases, had to go into exile. However,

---

10 In his critique of neoliberal statephobia, Foucault has made it clear that the totalitarian state is not the result of the expansive dynamics of the state as if welfare state and totalitarian state would stem from the same source. In fact, totalitarianism would be the paroxysm of party governmentality (Foucault, 2008).

it is important to underline that this opposition was not aimed at a reestablishment of the Democratic Republic. In those years, the Ordoliberals maintained a close relationship with conservative and religious circles, which, even when they opposed Nazism, maintained a profoundly anti-democratic and anti-parliamentary stance.

A similar position was held in those years by Louis Rougier, a central figure of French neoliberalism and organizer of the Walter Lippmann colloquium. In 1938 he published *Les Mystiques économiques. Comment l'on passe des démocraties libérales aux États totalitaires*. (Economic mystics. How we move from liberal democracies to totalitarian states). There he argues that enrichment, rising living standards and access to secular education have produced "the revolt of the masses".[11] He regrets that economic, budgetary, and monetary policy is made under the pressure of the electoral masses, who have a magical mentality, when statecraft is eminently aristocratic and can only be exercised by elites (Dardot et al., 2021, p. 69).

This same criticism is shared by Wilhelm Röpke, who, from his exile in Istanbul and Geneva, promoted a new liberalism and openly criticized Nazism. Röpke's neoliberalism seeks to be a response to collectivism, which he considers a product of massification (*Vermassung*), proletarianization and secularization. As in Hayek and Friedman, his thought becomes increasingly anti-statist and more critical of democracy. In 1942, in *Die Gesellschaftskrisis der Gegenwart* (The social crisis of our time), he reads democracy as a manifestation and even a profound cause of the modern crisis. The German criticizes parliamentary democracy, which has degenerated into "pluralism". Against this, he proposes a model of directorial and even dictatorial democracy that has certain Schmittean reminiscences.

> One cannot render a worse Service to democracy than to identify it with the complicated and corrupt parlor game of a democracy degenerated into pluralism. We know today that not only a parliamentary, but even a "direct," a presidential, a directorial, yes, even a dictatorial democracy is possible, always assuming that the link between the people and the will of the state is not severed and that whoever wields power must render account to the people, is subject to its control and can, consequently, be removed from office. (Röpke, 1950, p. 102)

---

[11] During the 1930s, neoliberal elitism not only draws on the political sociology of Michels, Pareto or Mosca, but also on the critique of mass society elaborated by Ortega y Gasset, and the reactionary thinking of the nineteenth century. It should be noted that fear of the masses and criticism of democracy are not confined to the neoliberal universe.

As we can see, Röpke's obsession is to ensure the unity of the state and to place its leadership above sectoral interests. The democratic president or dictator must be accountable to the people. In this sense, at an earlier point in the development of his book, Röpke takes up the Roman tradition and opposes *dictatorship* to *tyranny*. He argues that it is a mistake to simply associate collectivism with dictatorship, since dictatorship does not necessarily result in total control by an elite that identifies itself with the state, as the examples of Atatürk and Salazar would show. (1950, p. 84) In these pages it is observed that the only viable democracy for Röpke is that of the market and the only free society is one where consumer sovereignty reigns—to say it with Mises—and where producers are rewarded for offering what people want and are punished with bankruptcy when they offer that which does not arouse the interest of the public. (Röpke, 1950, p. 90; p.105) On the contrary, when democracy derives in socialism, there is no possible free society, because socialism seeks to politicize the economy, and to replace the democratic government of the market by the autocratic government of the state, whose control is exercised by means of criminal law. In that sense, for Röpke, socialism goes hand in hand with a completely authoritarian system of government. Economic dictatorship necessarily derives in an autocratic control of political and intellectual life. (Röpke, 1950, p. 90).

On the other hand, in a diagnosis that anticipates the Trilateral Commission by 30 years (see below) Röpke points out that the crisis of democracy has to do with the spiritual collectivization that leads to plebeianism, vested interests and the fanaticism of certain minorities.

> The crisis of democracy consists in the dogmatic failure to understand the limitations inherent in the democratic and liberal principle, the resulting spiritual collectivization, the arrogance of vested interests, the fanaticism of minorities. It consists in the general leveling down which accompanies spiritual collectivization and leads to "plebeianism," the decreasing understanding of the requisites of a well constructed democratic state and of the sacrifices which have to be made for it, the disintegrating effects of the crisis of the economic System as well as of the policies of economic intervention and planning. All these and a few other factors have rendered the functioning of democratic institutions increasingly more difficult, have led to the dissolution of the authority, impartiality and unity of the state and to a weakening of the political will [...] (Röpke, 1950, p. 17)

The German continued this critique in his 1944 book, *Civitas Humana*, dismissing the concept of popular sovereignty as impracticable. For the post-war world, the economist aspires to a legitimate, decentralized, and cooperative state, which encounters numerous obstacles: the state that extends its field of intervention too far, the influence of interest groups, and socialism, which breaks social consensus and instills the spirit of civil war. These "symptoms of decomposition" derive from the decline of the sense of responsibility or perhaps also from universal suffrage, whose dangers can be corrected by a "government of responsible people" for which a series of measures are required: the decentralization of power, the erection of a second legislative chamber, which will counterbalance the first chamber elected by universal suffrage, measures tending to exclude the youngest and to modulate the right to vote by giving more influence to parents and to those who have demonstrated capacity at the professional level (Solchany, 2016, p. 146).

In 1958, Röpke published *Jenseits von Angebot und Nachfrage* (Beyond supply and demand) in which he deepens his critique of the predominance of what he considers Jacobin-centralist mass democracy, which is a consequence of modern massification, to the detriment of the English and Swiss models, and of the disastrous path leading from the Jacobinism of the French Revolution to modern totalitarianism. For Röpke, the pluralist state suffers from the paraconstitutional influence of pressure groups, demagogues, and partisan apparatuses, which direct, stir up and exploit "opinions, feelings and passions of the masses" and lead to its decomposition. To prevent democracy from degenerating into arbitrariness and omnipotence of the state, it is necessary to oppose to the will of the state determined by universal suffrage the barriers "of natural law, of intangible norms and of tradition", which must be inscribed in the Constitution and imprinted on consciences (Solchany, 2016, p. 147).

Faced with the revolt of the masses, Röpke proposes the revolt of the elites. The backbone of a healthy society must be a true *nobilitas naturalis*, a "class of censors". Its members will be clothed with the "natural dignity" conferred by an existence made of "dedication to the community" and "unshakable integrity", of "proven maturity in judgment" and "irreproachable private life". In short: of courageous and unfailing commitment to what is true and just. The survival of our free world would depend on the ability of our time to produce such aristocrats of civic spirit, who were abundant in the feudal era (Solchany, 2016, p. 148). These elites must defend the order of competition against interventionism and that of civilization against nihilism. To achieve this pre-democratic utopia in which the weight of authority is imposed, democracy must necessarily be limited in terms of participation and in terms of the issues it can address: "Democracy and freedom are only compatible in the long run if all those who exercise the right to vote, or at least the majority of them, are aware that there are certain higher principles and norms of state life and economic constitution, which lie outside the democratic decision-making process". (Röpke, 1950 apud Solchany, 2016, p. 148)

2.3.3 The pluralist critique of democracy

There would be a pluralist critique of democracy, which seeks to defend "minorities" against the omnipotence of majorities. In this sense, Hayek argues that the conformism of majorities prevents society from benefiting from the contributions of innovative minorities, who make better use of freedom. This elite would not be more virtuous or more expert, but would express divergent ideas, which oppose the dominant opinion of today, but which could inspire that of the future. However, rather than openness to the future, Hayek's neoliberalism ends up favoring traditional morality and hierarchies (Perrin, 2014; Brown, 2019).

In comparison with Röpke's critique of democracy, Hayek's is developed within the framework of a more comprehensive political philosophy. However, his distrust of democracy is no less intense: when in 1962 he sends his copy of *The Constitution of Freedom* to Salazar, he declares that he hopes that he can help the efforts of a constitution that is protected against the abuses of democracy. Hayek would later point out that in his regime—as in Pinochet's later—there were more personal freedoms than in many democratic regimes. In *Law, Legislation and Liberty* of 1979, Hayek elaborates a model of a constitution that keeps power in the hands of a carefully selected elite, protected from the influence of the masses.

Hayek's argument is based first on his theory of knowledge. The democratic principle would be contrary to the mode of operation of society governed by the norms of just behavior, which are not the product of rationalist constructivism, but the gradual result of a process of trial and error extending over several centuries and embedded in tradition. This epistemology would be compatible with a liberal, limited democracy, which is opposed to a social or unlimited democracy, where popular sovereignty finds no containment and becomes totalitarian.

Later, however, Hayek will make a distinction between democracy, as a method of producing laws, and liberalism, as a doctrine of what the law should be. Liberalism would be opposed to totalitarianism and democracy to authoritarianism. As we have already seen in Röpke, just as democracy can lead to totalitarianism, there can be authoritarian and even dictatorial regimes that are liberal.

Liberalism (in the European nineteenth-century meaning of the word [...]) is concerned mainly with limiting the coercive powers of all government, whether democratic or not, whereas the dogmatic democrat knows only one limit to government—current majority opinion. The difference between the two ideals stands out most clearly if we name their opposites: for democracy it is authoritarian government; for liberalism it is totalitarianism. Neither of the two systems necessarily excludes the opposite of the other: a democracy may well wield totalitarian powers, and it is conceivable that an authoritarian government may act on liberal principles. (Hayek, 2011, p. 166)[12]

Furthermore, Hayek stresses the incompatibility between unlimited democracy and the functioning of the market. That is why the political process must be managed by elites with neoliberal visions with minimal possibility of popular control and democratic election. This should include constitutional measures that avoid social democratic outcomes in taxation and the extension of democracy to the economic sphere (Rodrigues, 2018, p. 132).

Indeed, Hayek rejects a democracy that is the "arbitrary rule of the majority", that attempts to seek social justice or that is subject to pressure from interest groups such as trade unions, professional or employers' organizations. To avoid these influences, democratic government must be limited in its attributions and the majorities of the moment must obey broader general rules. Legislation must be kept as far away as possible from the influence of the masses. In that sense, Hayek's demarchy is very much like an oligarchy whose source of legitimacy is tradition.

Hayek was so concerned that majorities could legislate because he considers economic liberalism to be the only authentic philosophy of freedom, while democracy is always on the verge of leading society into servitude. For the Austrian, if liberalism is a philosophy that limits the exercise of power, democracy multiplies it, since it has a tendency towards the unlimited. Even if the regulations of the rule of law are respected, democratic governments may try to intervene in the economic sphere—for example, by seeking to guarantee real equality of opportunities—and thus insensibly lead to tyranny. An example of this is the income tax, defended by some liberals, but defenestrated by Hayek. In the same vein, Lippmann argued in 1940 that democracy's attempt to develop an egalitarian social policy was incompatible with economic liberalism. In short, as the epigraph to this section points out, the source of legitimacy of political power does not matter. It can be of democratic and constitutional origin, but to the extent that it interferes with economic freedom, it is no longer a free regime. On the

---

12 Of course, the distinction drawn by Hayek is not uncommon in Western political thought. On the one hand, the great studies on totalitarianism—which emerged during the Cold War—find that totalitarian movements were made possible by the advent of the masses into the political arena—that is, by mass democracy—and by the breakdown of traditional ties. They also point out that these movements were illiberal. What many seem to forget is the link, clearly established by Arendt (1973), between the imperialism of the nineteenth-century liberal powers and the racism tested in the colonies as the first antecedents of total domination and the systematic and bureaucratic extermination of human beings.

other hand, as we have already seen with Röpke, a dictatorial government may well exercise a liberal government as far as it does not interfere with economic freedom. If the first case would be that of Allende's democratic socialism, the second would be represented by the liberal dictatorship of Pinochet in Chile or Salazar in Portugal.[13] In this sense, neoliberal demophobia is due to its defense of an absolute conception of property and economic freedom against the search for equality to which democracy would inevitably tend. For Hayek, to intervene for the sake of promoting social justice—a mythical concept that makes no sense from a rational point of view—would be a gregarious atavism that destroys civilization.

As we see, these currents presuppose that the only true freedom is economic freedom and that the only power capable of infringing on freedoms is political power, whose intervention also makes the functioning of society less efficient. Politics would be a mere appendix of economic processes, over which it cannot—and should not—exercise any control (Polo Blanco, 2018). These premises derive from liberal and conservative thinking of the nineteenth century, with its fear of the masses and the tyranny of majorities. (Tocqueville, 2002). For this thinking, the fundamental question is not who holds political power but how it is exercised, with what scope and intensity. From this perspective, a democracy can be more tyrannical than a monarchical government.[14] The goal is to limit political power, regardless of its origin. As Isaiah Berlin (2002) points out in his famous lecture *Two Concepts of Liberty*, following the line traced by Benjamin Constant in the revolutionized nineteenth century, the only authentic liberty is the negative one, the liberty of the moderns, that is, the non-interference or absence of external coercion.

In this sense, neoliberal opposition to mass democracy is heir to liberal-conservative and sometimes even reactionary thinking of the nineteenth century. Thus, as we shall see, it is no coincidence that the ideas of today's far-right, whose central concern is the reestablishment of traditional hierarchies, can be

---

13 The Salazar regime is praised early on by various neoliberal intellectuals. In the late 1930s, the liberal press organ *Neue Zürcher Zeitung* is in favor of Franco and Salazar. In the 1950s, Louis Baudin fully supports the Salazar regime and considers it a successful neoliberal experience, capable of combining liberalism and conservatism (Audier, 2016).

14 According to Hans-Hermann Hoppe (2001), power is always more limited in a monarchy, a government of private property that must preserve its wealth for future generations, than in a democracy, which is based in public property and in which the government must exploit the citizens as much as possible during a short period of time.

easily combined with the defense of the free market.[15] This confluence can also be seen in the racialized critique of democracy.

2.3.4 The racialized critique

Distrust of democracy was also expressed by neoliberals in racial terms, especially after the Second World War, and with the process of decolonization. For neoliberals, empires could end, but only if they guaranteed the rights of capital and did not erect barriers to the circulation of capital and goods (Slobodian, 2018). This was unlikely in a context of decolonization, in which multilateral institutions and U.S. policy promoted a global new deal and the developmentalist idea that industrialization was possible and necessary for the progress of the global south (Slobodian, 2018). In the face of this, neoliberals will argue that industrialization is not the only path to development, which is only possible by maintaining a market economy where production is guided by comparative advantages. But it does not end there: from a racialized position, they will argue that being culturally underdeveloped, the colonial population was not ready for self-determination, since it would fall prey to communist propaganda, thus destroying any prospect of economic and civilizational development (Cornelissen, 2020). In this framework, democratization in the global South was seen by neoliberals as an obstacle to economic development and the establishment of a market economy. Therefore, a choice must be made between economic development and democratic self-government. "The problem, as they imagine it, is that what they call 'underdeveloped' populations lack the cultural or civilizational 'maturity' to be entrusted with self-rule, as they are unlikely themselves to establish the legal and institutional framework necessary for material growth" (Cornelissen, 2020, pp. 348–349).

According to Cornelissen, the neoliberal framing of postcolonial populations moved in two main registers. First, it functioned to discursively trap the colonized in the past, confining them to a premodern regime of temporality. This is most clearly reflected in the ordoliberal position on the complexities of postcolonial governance. Alexander Rüstow in the late 1950s and Röpke a few years later asserted that many postcolonial populations live in a "stone age" environment and therefore do not possess the sociological and spiritual conditions for

---

15 This goes against the assumptions of classical philosophy. For example, Aristotle argued that the market erases traditional hierarchies, putting those who are different by nature on an equal footing. By contrast, in a society where hierarchies are fundamentally economic and political, with strong and extensive property rights, we see that the deregulated market reinforces them.

democracy and the rule of law. Fritz Machlup was still of the opinion in the late 1960s that democracy only works for informed people who can distinguish between deceptive promises and realistic programs, something that populations with little political experience and a high degree of illiteracy cannot do. In this context, the Austrian-American recalled Mill's dictum that "there is no liberty for savages". (Cornelissen, 2020, p. 352). Allowing the unlimited right to vote in such a context could lead to the destruction of many other freedoms and the possibility of economic development. (Machlup, 1969, p. 142 apud Cornelissen, 2020, p. 352). From this point of view, to be pre-modern or underdeveloped is also to be ignorant, inexperienced, immature. (Cornelissen, 2020, p. 352)

The second register established a civilizational hierarchy between developed and underdeveloped cultures. For example, Hayek offers a constitutional design for new nations, which lack traditions and beliefs that "in more fortunate countries made constitutions work". (Hayek, 2013, pp. 443–444 apud Cornelissen, 2020). As we have already seen, this constitutional model restricts popular influence on the law, since new nations would not be ready for democratic government. As Cornelissen points out, in the hierarchical scale of civilizations, democracy is a privilege for the few.

This type of reasoning was used in the neoliberal approach to the problem of apartheid in South Africa and the independence of Rhodesia, in an international context where universal suffrage was demanded. In general, the neoliberal position was to promote equality of formal rights at the socioeconomic level of the market economy, for which it was necessary to maintain a restriction of the freedoms and political rights of Black people.

Perhaps the best-known position on this issue is that of Röpke, who in 1964 wrote a pamphlet defending the regime and arguing that "the South African Negro is not only a man of an utterly different race but, at the same time, stems from a completely different type and level of civilization" (Röpke, 1964, p. 139, apud Cornelissen, 2020, p. 354; Slobodian, 2014, p. 61). For the German, race and underdevelopment were intimately connected.[16] The development that

---

16 These arguments also influence his defense of the right of countries to control migratory flows, not only on the basis of their economic needs, but also on the basis of their race and culture. In a statement that could be subscribed to by today's far-rightists, he pointed out that nations have an essential right to safeguard their populations from immigrants "who may threaten them by their qualities [...] or even by their numbers". The immigration of workers must be qualitatively controlled in order to take care of the spiritual and biological heritage, the political tradition, the ethno-linguistic character and the social structure of the country. (Röpke, 1950 in Biebriecher, 2020, p. 13). Paradoxically, a thinker who opposed the racial policy of Nazism ended up

existed in South Africa was due exclusively to the pioneering spirit of the white population, the country's attractiveness to tourists, its favorable tax structure, and the high returns it offered to foreign investment. If universal suffrage were enabled, the Black people would crush the White people and put an end to this development. For reasons of "racial superiority, economics, and Realpolitik" Röpke "believed that white supremacy had to persist in South Africa" (Slobodian, 2014, p. 61).

However, this racialized defense of Apartheid did not find much support among European neoliberals, but it did among the new American right, in the midst of a supremacist campaign against the civil rights of African Americans. In this framework, Röpke proposed a federation of nations with formal political sovereignty but reduced economic autonomy regulated by the free movement of capital and investment between countries. A "a loose world federation would help prevent mass popular expectations from becoming reality because the ever-present threat of capital flight would curb campaigns of expansionary social policy. Economic actors voting with their feet—and their assets—would be the surest corrective on projects of building domestic welfare states" (Slobodian, 2018, pp. 155–156). The same would be true for interest rates: the further a country moves away from the West, the higher the interest rate it must pay to receive a loan[17] (Slobodian, 2021). In any case, Röpke distanced himself from the globalists of the Mont-Pèlerin Society, holding a "racialized worldview" that led him to become a leading intellectual for the American National Review and the new conservatives of the 1960s (Slobodian, 2018, p. 171).

Another strong opponent of universal suffrage in South Africa was William Hutt, an economist at the London School of Economics and member of the Mont-Pèlerin Society who worked from 1928 to 1966 at the University of Cape Town and wrote *The Economics of the Colour Bar* in 1964. Using arguments borrowed from Milton Friedman and Gary Becker, Hutt argued that "racism is a form of rent-seeking analogous to trade unions defending their own privilege against the

---

justifying the limitation of democracy and the free movement of people on the basis of racialized assumptions.

17 Today, it is enough to deviate from the rules dictated by the global financial market for the "country risk index" to increase and for external financing to become more expensive. As Dardot and Laval point out, "The disciplinary weapons of the financial markets have made it possible to pitilessly punish all transgressors of programmes of wage deflation, labour market flexibilization, privatization, and public expenditure reduction. Should a government take 'bad decisions', it would immediately be penalized by the refusal of loans or a downgrade in the credit rating awarded by the ratings agencies, which would ipso facto raise the interest rates payable to lenders" (Dardot & Laval, 2019, p. 20).

entry of nonwhite workers" (Hutt, apud Slobodian, 2018, p. 173). Since racism was outside the market and opposed to it, Hutt promoted racial equality in the labor arena, but not in the political one, where he promoted weighted voting, first in terms of race and then of income. He also vehemently defended the Rhodesian Republic against "'one man, one vote' tyranny" (Sloboldian, 2018, p. 176).

Sanctions on Rhodesia were also opposed by Milton Friedman. In 1976 he made the puzzling argument that majority rule for Rhodesia was a euphemism for black minority rule, which would surely mean the expulsion or exodus of most whites and a drastic lowering of the standard of living and opportunities for the thousands of black Rhodesians. In a lecture he gave in Cape Town that year he argued that the "one man, one vote" system favored interest groups playing a far greater role than the general interest. In contrast, the economic market was a system of effective and proportional representation. While he agreed with Röpke in pointing out that the isolation of Rhodesia was a sign of Western suicide, his conclusions were not based on race or level of civilization but on a general criticism of the practice of electoral democracy and on the concern that sanctions against Rhodesia would only weaken the system of free markets. In this Hayek concurred. While condemning apartheid, the Austrian expressed his fear that the use of sanctions as an economic weapon would transgress the boundaries separating the world of property—the dominium—from the world of states—the imperium.

According to Slobodian, Southern Africa is the ultimate test of the different neoliberal perspectives on the issues of race, world order and empire in the era of decolonization. Not only was there no single position, but the views of the main actors changed over time. Perhaps the most extreme turn was that of Röpke, who went from opposing imperialism as a story of barbarism and brutality. However, three decades later, with decolonization, he argued that colonialism had brought civilization to the non-Western world.

> Whereas he wrote in 1934 that European imperialism corresponded "to all of the irrational powers in the inner life of nations", by 1965 he was claiming that it was European patrimony that was threatened by "the monstrous forces of chaos and destruction" that opposed it. Most important was his newfound conviction that "Europeanization" had turned the whole earth into a "single colony of the West". Given this reality, stability and relative prosperity would come to the Global South only when they dropped their disavowal of Westernization and embraced it as an ethos, life way, and mindset. [...] Empire was not an era that had ended but a task to be completed (Slobodian, 2018, pp. 180–181).

Indeed, for neoliberals, the end of the Empire confronted populations with a dilemma: the path of development *or* that of democracy. (Cornelissen, 2020). The neoliberal argument of political immaturity is mixed with a series of racialized and colonial assumptions. The idea that racial differences directly influence economic, social, and civilizational development was common in neoliberal writings of the time. For example, in a 1961 article, Louis Rougier agreed with the nineteenth-century belief that race and climate were among the main causes of the stagnation of the 'third world' before asserting that Muslims, Africans, and Indians were prone to fatalism and superstition (Rougier, 1961, p. 187, apud Cornelissen, 2020, p. 354). Mises also linked the history of civilization to racial differences. In his 1922 book *Socialism*, Mises ventured that "races differ in intelligence and will power" and that "the better races distinguish themselves precisely by their special aptitude for strengthening social co-operation" (Mises, 1951, p. 325, apud Cornelissen, 2020, p. 354). In his 1927 book *Liberalism*, he also opined that "European civilization really is superior to that of the primitive tribes of Africa or to the civilizations of Asia" before going on to characterize "Europeans" as "members of a superior race"" (Mises, 1985, pp. 125–126, apud Cornelissen, 2020, p. 354). In *Human Action* he admitted that there is some truth in the racist position that "attributes the great achievements of the white race to racial superiority" (Mises, 1998, p. 90, apud Cornelissen, 2020, p. 354). He continued: "It is vain to deny that up to now certain races have contributed nothing or very little to the development of civilization and can, in this sense, be called inferior" (Mises, 1998, p. 90, apud Cornelissen, 2020, p. 354).

As Cornelissen points out, many neoliberal thinkers considered racial difference as a key analytical category, whether to study economic development or the history of civilization. The critique of the self-determination of decolonized peoples as not being sufficiently mature or developed for democracy must be placed in this framework.

In fact, such arguments were used to justify the absence of democracy in Latin America and later in the Middle East. In a 1986 symposium, Arnold Haberger argued that Latin Americans have a tendency toward romanticism, vulnerability to demagoguery and self-pity. Fortunately, the military governments were counteracting these predispositions. In the same framework, Ramon Díaz, future president of the MPS, argued that Latin Americans were enamored with concepts such as unlimited democracy, sovereignty and revolution as they were inherently contrary to the institution of private property. It was also said there that Latin America had an immature political culture and that the Spanish and Portuguese cultural heritage made Latin Americans averse to commerce and manual labor and that they tended to blame others for their misfortunes. For these neoliberals, cultural and temperamental inclinations not only explained Latin American economic backwardness but also their inability for democratic self-government. (Cornelissen, 2020)

Perhaps the most famous intervention in this regard is that of Hayek, who in the interview granted to El Mercurio in 1981 argued that, unlike the Anglo-Saxon tradition of freedom, the South American tradition was based on that of the maximum governmental power of the French revolution. South America was therefore too much influenced by totalitarian ideologies.

As Cornelissen points out, such claims were also frequent in relation to Islam and were revived in the aftermath of the 9/11 attacks. It was argued that the long history of despotism made it impossible for democracy to triumph in countries like Iraq or Afghanistan. These kinds of arguments were already present in Mises and Rougier, for whom Islam was a dead religion, which encouraged fatalism. (Cornelissen, 2020, p. 357).

According to Cornelissen, both the neoliberal justification of the Chilean *coup* and more recent neoliberal commentary on the prospects for democracy in the Middle East follow the pattern of the neoliberal critique of postcolonial self-determination. Again, the neoliberal argument against democracy is based on a racialized argumentative structure. From this he concludes:

> By casting entire populations as culturally, temperamentally, or historically incapable of enlightened self-governance, neoliberal thought not only reproduces a nakedly racist tradition of thought (as reflected in the writings of Mill or de Tocqueville, for instance) but also fundamentally misrepresents the history of democracy. Indeed, by imagining the lack of democratic stability to only ever be the result of a cultural lack on the part of the population, neoliberals blatantly disavow the long and sinister history of political and economic violence (often spearheaded by the USA) that, in many countries in the global south, has sabotaged many a well-functioning democracy; and by arguing that these countries have no experience in self-governance they commit an act of historical erasure, casually effacing a multitude of rich and long-standing traditions of self-rule and autonomy to which people in the global south have given rise since time immemorial. (Cornelissen, 2020, p. 357)

As we can see, the neoliberal critique of democracy is based on dissimilar arguments, mixing moral, technical, civilizational, political, and ideological aspects. However, a common denominator is the conservative aspect of these criticisms. Democracy is always presented in an unfavorable light, as a movement that promotes egalitarianism and the tyranny of the majorities. In that framework, only a competent minority can rule. In order to better understand this rejection, and its link with certain claims of the new far-right, we now turn to certain conservative aspects of Hayek's thought, given its importance for the neoliberal thought collective and its apparent opposition to the conservatism of Röpke and the National Review.

2.4 Was Hayek a conservative?

As we have been showing, like the ordoliberals, although from a different theoretical and political conception, Hayek's thought is extremely relevant for analyzing the relationship between neoliberalism and conservatism. In the first place, because Hayek has been one of the most influential neoliberals at the global level, having been the main driving force behind the Mont-Pèlerin Society and having participated intensely in the struggle of ideas not only as a professor and author but also as a public intellectual. Secondly, because of Hayek's ability to articulate different ideological currents, which in turn has led him to influence them, like liberal-conservatism and libertarians. Third, because, as Brown (2019) argues, in his conception, morality and the market go hand in hand, both orders being spontaneously generated and grounded in tradition.

As we have seen, unlike Röpke, who declares himself openly conservative and expresses disdain for the masses, Hayek criticizes unlimited democracy precisely because of its conformism. In fact, his defense of the superiority of economic over political democracy, which he recovers from his teacher Mises, is based precisely on generalized ignorance and not on the superior knowledge of the elites.[18] Moreover, towards the end of *The Constitution of Liberty* (2011 [1960]), possibly his most important book, Hayek includes a chapter entitled "Why I am not a Conservative?" to differentiate himself from Russel Kirk and, through him, from Röpke himself, who was being adopted as an inspiration by the new American conservatism of the 1960s, and who towards the end of his life was at odds with the Austrian for his opposition to South African apartheid, which the German supported. Why then should we look to Hayek for elements that allow us to think about this conservative and often reactionary character of the neoliberal project?[19]

As Jeremy Perrin points out, Hayek's argumentation regarding his distance from conservatism develops in an eulogy of reactionary thought and, in turn, attempts to show his liberalism as a sort of *aggiornamento* of his original conservatism. Indeed, Hayek explicitly salutes the influence of reactionary thought on the liberal movement, especially as far as the functioning of institutions outside

---

18 Moreover, in the 1930s Hayek considered the constructivist position of the ordoliberals and of Lippmann and Rougier as too interventionist. In turn, they considered Mises and Hayek as too attached to nineteenth-century liberalism. (Foucault, 2008; Dardot & Laval, 2013; Audier, 2012). **19** This support for conservative policies from seemingly non-conservative neoliberal positions is analyzed by Brown (2019) and Cooper (2017). The latter shows how the Chicago and Virginia schools defend traditional family values from the point of view of the economic costs of its breakdown to the welfare system.

the economy is concerned. According to the Austrian, figures such as Coleridge, Bonald, de Maistre, Justus Moser, and Donoso Cortés gave proof of a profound intuition of the functioning of institutions resulting from spontaneous evolution such as languages, law, morals, and conventions, of which liberals could have taken advantage. According to Perrin, Hayek describes liberal principles as the politically presentable translation of his private conservative views in an era of universal suffrage. (Perrin, 2014, p. 49). In this framework, Perrin highlights nine examples of repressed reactionary thinking in Hayek:

In the first place, Hayek's conservatism would result from his ponderation of the historical role of instincts, values and feelings and his minimization of the weight of reason, which distances him from part of the classical liberal tradition. Indeed, Hayek interprets the course of things in terms of morality or virtue, which is a characteristic expression of reaction, contrary to the progressive view, which, as Brown (2019) points out, is more attentive to the structures that engender aptitudes and morals. For Hayek, reason can admire the work of nature, but it cannot guide it.

The second conservative theme highlighted by Perrin is the hatred of psychoanalysis. Hayek makes a reactionary denunciation of this interventionism of souls by which proud reason seeks to change the spontaneous order of the spirit. For Hayek, psychoanalysis was a haughty and irresponsible questioning of the secular fruits of morality. Towards the end of *Law, Legislation and Liberty,* Freud is singled out as the greatest demolisher of culture: his fundamental aim, which was to abolish culturally acquired repressions and liberate natural drives, opened the most fatal offensive against the basis of all civilization. Freud is thus presented as personally responsible for the "moral confusion" that struck the youth in the 1960s and 1970s.

This distrust of psychoanalysis is combined with a kind of moral authoritarianism and a conservative conception of justice as "reciprocity in frustration". In one passage, Hayek points to moral suffering and guilt as an indispensable basis for an effective society. Unlike unlimited democracy, which treats its members as right-bearers, a healthy society is based on the exercise of discipline, through which the upper classes would have conquered their privileges.

A fourth element of Hayek's moral conservatism manifests itself in statements concerning homosexuality and sexual freedom. In the 1980s he still wonders whether these freedoms are acceptable as spontaneous experiences or whether they are liable to be outlawed because they threaten the birth rate of the group.

The fifth element has to do with the movement of people between countries. A coherent ultraliberal should promote the complete opening of borders, both for reasons of principle linked to freedom and for reasons of efficiency in the localization of labor.[20] However, for Hayek, migration restrictions are inevitable as long as certain national characteristics or ethnic traditions remain, especially differences in birth rates.[21] Hence his support for Thatcher's restrictive immigration policies. If at the beginning this conservative concern for the perpetuation of national cultures was immersed in liberal rhetoric, later he would refer directly to communitarian thought.

The sixth indication of Hayek's conservatism is the disdain for democracy that we have been analyzing. In *Law, Legislation and Liberty*, he promotes a radical restriction of the right to vote. He points out that it is unreasonable that civil servants, retirees, the unemployed, etc. should have the right to vote on the way they are paid out of the pockets of the rest.

This liberal rejection of the exercise of power by the people is accompanied by a seventh conservative motive: fascination with the elites. His teacher Mises, for example, exalts the caste of entrepreneurs, considered as individuals superior to the masses in energy and mental power. Hayek, for his part, in chapter 11 of *Law, Legislation and Liberty*, quotes Ortega y Gasset, presenting liberalism as an elite thought, reserved for the elite, and which finds it difficult to impose itself because the masses do not deserve it intellectually and morally. In this quotation appears the image of a ruling class naturally different from the people and which has a vocation to lead it in the name of its nobility and refinement. Mises puts forward a similar idea when he points out that "the masses do not think [...] the spiritual leadership of mankind belongs to the small number of men who think for themselves". (Mises, 1951 [1922], p. 527) However, neoliberals, like conservatives, distinguish between good and bad elites. It is always a matter of devaluing progressive elites and positively valuing liberal-conservative ones.

The eighth element highlighted by Perrin has to do with the contempt for intellectuals, as elites who talk, but do not act, and the ninth with the fascination for the countryside and the aristocracy, as realms where social cohesion reigns as opposed to the discord that prevails in urban society (Hayek, 2013).

---

20 However, several of the Vienna and Geneva globalists argued that, while the movement of goods was desirable, the same was not true of population. One of the arguments, outlined by Haberler, had to do with the fact that freedom to migrate would result in the concentration of people at one point and total emptying at others. The important thing was that goods and prices should be able to circulate freely, which is why it was necessary to tear down the tariff walls. **21** The birth rate argument was already used by Hardin in "Lifeboat ethics" to justify why aid should not be given to poor countries and why the emigration of poor populations to rich countries should not be allowed. For his part, while Röpke used racist arguments to oppose migration or defend Apartheid, Mises points out that the problem is given by the racist resentment that the immigration of people of color can generate in white men. (Slobodian, 2018, p. 330, n. 159).

Perrin summarizes the above in a brief synthesis:

Valorization of instincts in history, hatred of psychoanalysis, repressive view of social justice, latent homophobia, fear of cultural mixing, limited enthusiasm for democracy, fascination with classical elites, denigration of intellectuals, attraction to the countryside and the aristocracy: without doubt Hayek's liberal ideas did not always succeed in covering the reactionary background on which they unfold [...] the least one can say is that the father of neoliberalism was not particularly libertarian or modern from a moral point of view. (Perrin, 2014, p. 71)

According to Perrin, at the conservative heart of Hayek's neoliberalism lies an echo of the anti-Enlightenment thinking of the nineteenth century. The Frenchman highlights the existence of a symbiosis between the nobility and the bourgeoisie in the pre-war period, from which liberal-conservatism emerges. In fact, Hayek would take up the central values of reaction and inscribe them in a new theoretical framework. For both reactionaries and liberals, property and existing wealth are sacred. Indeed, Hayek justified full inheritance without succession rights as a healthy measure capable of providing society with a perennial upper class. This privileged caste would exercise a vanguard role that is useful to all.

In line with anti-Enlightenment thinking, Hayek points to the inability of human reason to grasp the meaning of history and to master its evolution as a means of organizing political life, society, and the state in the service of the individual. He stresses the spontaneous and haphazard character of human evolution, which resembles the blind fate that, according to Herder, dominates human affairs. Similarly, Hayek expresses his own ultra-Darwinian view of a spontaneous and unintentional order in the origin of the wealth of the moderns. He points out that we have not invented our economic system because we would not be capable and that we have been guided by chance.

According to Perrin, this same challenge to reason arises in the cultural realm. Culture consists of a complex set of practices and rules of conduct that have not been adopted intentionally because it was known that they would produce the desired effects. While this is obvious, the problem lies in the political conclusions to be drawn from such a finding. In the case of Hayek and his acolytes, this ends up serving as a justification for not taxing the wealthy. (Perrin, 2014)

Following a line of historicism and anti-Enlightenment, Hayek denounces those who have the "fatal arrogance" of wanting to change the world without fully knowing its mechanisms—which is impossible. This resembles the Herderian view according to which human pride pretends to judge the divine work but cannot understand it. Submission to impersonal market forces would have made our civilization possible, building something greater than we can comprehend. In line with this debased view of human capacities, Hayek apprehends the world as the unintended result of decentralized efforts of partially unconscious actors. Following Herder and Renan, for Hayek social change must remain spontaneous, i.e. non-political, and the mutations of law must result from the obscure work of jurisprudence. Something similar was raised by Burke, for whom reason had a subordinate place in history, which was a blind process. The rejection of reason thus appears as one of the conservative invariants in Hayek's thought, who praises fatalism and tradition, which the rationalists would have denigrated. *"Man is not and never will be the master of his fate"* (Hayek, 2013, p. 507).

Like conservatives such as Burke or Renan, Hayek expresses a fear of reason that does not concern the individual who trades but the one who votes and governs. Hayek does not believe that the human species can make progress in its political capabilities, but only in its mercantile skills. Most interestingly, for Hayek progress is not desirable unless it helps to reinforce the norms inherited from the past. Therefore, Perrin concludes that, in Hayek's ultra-Darwinism, the existent is confused with the legitimate.

In this sense, Wendy Brown affirms that Hayek's thought allows us to glimpse that neoliberalism is not simply an economic project, but also a moral one. Traditional morality would make it possible to unite liberty and tradition, family and free market, and would establish the possibility of *dethroning politics* in order to *dismantle society*. According to Brown, only by recognizing the existence of the social can we visualize the differences in power and try to correct them. If, as Thatcher asserted, "society does not exist", neither can there be social policies that seek to remedy inequalities. For Hayek, the myth of social justice would only serve to legitimize the advance of totalitarian or unlimited democracy over liberties.[22] That is why he proposes a model of limited democracy that, as we shall see, in the Chilean Constitution of 1980 will be translated, through the liberal-conservative synthesis of Jaime Guzmán, into tutored democracy, combined with economic liberalism (Mansuy, 2016). According to Brown, neoliberal reason, as formulated by Hayek, presents "markets and morals as singular forms of human need provision sharing ontological principles and dynamics. Rooted in liberty and generating spontaneous order and evolution, their rad-

---

22 In *The Origins of Totalitarian Democracy*, Jacob Talmon distinguishes between the liberal way, which implies individual freedom as the absence of coercion, and the totalitarian, Rousseaunian and Jacobinian way, which grants absolute power to popular sovereignty.

ical opposites are any kind of deliberate and state-administered social policy, planning, and justice". (Brown, 2019, p. 11)

As we shall see in chapter 5, this conception of any state intervention as distortive and potentially totalitarian, which confuses the totalitarian state and the welfare state as part of the same unstoppable evolution, will be taken up by the paleolibertarianism of Murray Rothbard and his current admirers. In this sense, Brown studies "how neoliberal formulations of freedom animate and legitimate the hard Right and how the Right mobilizes a discourse of freedom for its sometimes violent exclusions and assaults, for resecuring white, male, and Christian hegemony, and not only for building the power of capital". Brown points out that such idea of freedom conceives social justice defenders "as tyrannical or even "fascistic" [...] and at the same time as responsible for disintegrating moral fabrics, unsecured borders, and giveaways to the undeserving". (2019, p. 10)

This type of discourse, which has become hegemonic since the 1970s, has made it possible to transfer the responsibilities of the social state to families and individuals. As Melinda Cooper has shown, morality and the market, family values and entrepreneurship, accountability and efficiency, are conceived as inseparable projects. In that sense, Brown points out that rather than a project of expanding the sphere of competition and the market that entails the economization of everything, "Hayekian neoliberalism is a moral-political project that aims to protect traditional hierarchies by negating the very idea of the social and radically restricting the reach of democratic political power in nation-states" (Brown, 2019).

Now, if it is a matter of denying the scope of democracy in favor of a liberal-conservative project, another milestone we must highlight is that of the Trilateral Commission.

2.5 The Trilateral Commission and the ungovernable democracy

In addition to being reflected in the writings of theoreticians such as Hayek, this anti-democratic and conservative character of neoliberal thought is reflected in a paradigmatic document that influenced the massive application of neoliberal public policies in the world, especially in its "combative stage". I am alluding to the first report of the Trilateral Commission (1975), which warned about the excess of democracy—excessive involvement of the governed in political and social life, the rise of egalitarian demands, the political participation of the lower classes—which led to the ungovernability of political systems.

Indeed, just as the Walter Lippmann Colloquium (1938) and the Mont Pèlerin Society (created in 1947) can be considered key moments in the theoretical re-founding of liberalism and the political beginnings of neoliberalism, we could say that the Trilateral Commission, created at the initiative of David Rockefeller in 1973, represents a significant precedent in the implementation of neoliberal governance on a global scale.[23]

As we know all too well today, many of the major guidelines of world government are taken behind closed doors by big businessmen, politicians and intellectuals behind the backs of citizens. Although the Davos forum has become the most publicized face of this logic, the Trilateral Commission has had a decisive influence on the transformations that took place in the transition to neoliberal globalization and still plays a fundamental role in the government of the main democratic states in the West. This commission represents just one example of the great centers of production of ideas and decision-making, which stand out for their anti-democratic character, both in their form—a small elite imposing its interests on the rest—and in their content. And by content, we are not only referring to economic measures but also to the political proposals and the overall political vision that sustains them.

Already in the initial 1975 report Crozier, Huntington and Watanuki argued that political democracy could only function with a certain degree of "apathy and noninvolvement on the part of some individuals and groups" and that there are "desirable limits to the indefinite extension of political democracy. Democracy will have a longer life if it has a more balanced existence". (Crozier, Huntington & Watanuki, 1975, pp. 114–115).

---

23 This commission was created as a private policy-making organization between the United States, Europe and Japan and has 170 members in Europe, 100 in Asia and 120 in North America. It brings together leaders of multinational companies, bankers, politicians, academics and experts in international politics with the declared aim of discussing the pressing issues affecting our planet, which translates into measures to protect the interests of multinationals and to influence the decisions of political leaders. For this elite, democracy is an obstacle to good international governance. In its experts' annual and thematic papers, the TC addresses global problems that transcend national sovereignty and supposedly require global intervention by the rich countries: reform of international institutions, globalization of markets, environment, international finance, economic liberalization, regionalization of trade, indebtedness of poor countries, and so on. According to this Commission, the liberal democracies would be the "vital center" of the economy, finance and technology and the other countries would have to join this center and accept its self-appointed leadership. The TC expresses the neoliberal credo according to which the globalization and liberalization of economies, financial globalization and the development of international exchanges would be at the service of progress and the improvement of living conditions for the majority of people, calling into question national sovereignties and protectionist measures. (Boiral, 2003)

On the one hand, they identified contextual challenges to democracy that did not come directly from the functioning of democratic government itself but from the environment in which it operates. In this sense, one of the groups that would undermine democracy in advanced liberal societies would be the "value-oriented intellectuals" who question leadership and authority, delegitimizing established institutions, representing a challenge potentially as serious as aristocracies, fascist movements and communist parties in the past. Opposing them are the technocratic and policy-oriented intellectuals, who play a central role in the commission.

In any case, the most serious challenges to the viability of democratic government are intrinsic, since, far from functioning in an automatic equilibrium, democratic government can give rise to forces that, left to their own devices, can undermine democracy. Democratic processes seem to have generated a breakdown of the traditional means of social control, a delegitimization of political authority, and an overload of demands on the government that exceeds its capacity to respond, making the situation ungovernable. (Crozier, Huntington & Watanuki, 1975, pp. 8–9) Due to the broadening of political participation and the increased demands on government, material welfare giving rise to new lifestyles and political values, etc. an anomic democracy emerges, where democratic politics is more an arena for the assertion of conflicting interests than for the construction of common purposes. (Crozier, Huntington & Watanuki, 1975, p. 161).

In short, for the authors of the report, the extension of democratic government gave rise to the tendencies that impede its functioning: 1) the pursuit of the democratic virtues of equality and individualism has led to the delegitimization of authority in general and loss of confidence in leadership; 2) the democratic expansion of political participation has created an overload on government and encouraged the unbalanced expansion of government activities, exacerbating inflationary tendencies in the economy; 3) political competition, essential to democracy, has intensified, leading to a disaggregation of interests and the decline and fragmentation of political parties; 4) the democratic government's search for answers from the electorate and social pressures foster nationalistic parochialism in the way democracies conduct their foreign relations. (Ibid.)[24]

The whole report tends to point out that democracy is a threat to democracies. It is claimed that the democratic ethos is egalitarian, individualistic, populist, and impatient with class and rank distinctions and that it threatens social

---

24 As Slobodian (2018) shows, neoliberalism emerges in the framework of a globalist militancy that not only opposes democracy but also the nation, especially with regard to economic nationalism and the idea of autarky.

bonds such as family, enterprise, and community, which must be recovered. Not only would some measure of inequality of authority and functional distinction be necessary, but the weakening of authority in society would contribute to the weakening of the authority of government. In other words, for democracies to be governable, a disciplined society is necessary.

In this atmosphere, and after the crisis of the 1970s, the programs of Thatcher and Reagan, the IMF and the World Bank were naturally presented as a set of responses to a situation that was considered impossible to manage and where the answers were taken for granted. Monetarist policies transferred the drain produced by the stagflation crisis to the purchasing power of wage earners for the benefit of companies and the states behaved as builders and auxiliaries and ultimately victims of globalized financial capitalism. (Dardot & Laval, 2013) All this was legitimized by the knowledge of this type of technocrats and policy-oriented intellectuals who today continue to swarm in the major decision-making centers.

Since then, every time "governance problems" appear, the first thing to be sacrificed is the democratic popular will. For neoliberalism, government is legitimized not by popular election but by good governance, an expert government that does not contemplate the participation or the opinion of the governed. Governance thus implies the total emptying of popular sovereignty and of any idea of democratic government.

In this sense, the installation of neoliberalism not only implied a process of upward redistribution of power and income that resulted in growing social inequalities, but also instituted a way of doing politics where a small elite of technocrats decides for all and for the benefit of the small minority that controls key resources. When democracy is not aligned with the demands of the great economic powers, so much worse for democracy. We saw this, for example, with the bailout by the states to the same banks that produced the last great crisis and with the referendums on the European Constitution or the absence of popular consultations in Latin America on issues that clearly concern the collective future. Should not such strategic decisions as what to do with the public debt, with natural resources, with the production model, the use of pesticides, the protection of glaciers and wetlands, etc., be subject to popular consultation?

Therefore, neoliberalism, as a worldview and as a governmental rationality, and democracy, both in its face of popular sovereignty and in its promise of self-government, have become highly incompatible: "Forty years of neoliberal policies have undermined already weak representative institutions and the crisis has strengthened all the political systems the Greeks considered opposed to democracy. Choices and decisions concerning whole peoples have been made by an oligarchy, a plutocracy, and an aristocracy". (Lazzarato, 2012, p. 159)

2.6 From the critique of democracy to the defense of authoritarianism

As we have seen, neoliberal contempt for democracy from elitist, conservative, and even reactionary and racist positions has been formulated in different ways since the 1920s. In fact, neoliberal globalism emerges as a project to neutralize democracy and protect the economic sphere of the *dominium* from the advancement of the *imperium*. (Slobodian, 2018).

In this framework, neoliberals who accept democracy only do so in formal terms, recognizing the people as the source of sovereignty or of the election of representatives, but never as a form of government. In fact, they maintain that dictatorships or monarchies can be more liberal than democracies that seek to exercise political control over the economy or propose redistributive measures. Hence the support for regimes such as Salazar's, Franco's, or Pinochet's among various neoliberal intellectuals. The favor enjoyed by the Chilean regime is evidenced in the well-known support of Friedman and Hayek, in the advice of the "Chicago boys" and in the fact that the congress of the Mont-Pèlerin Society was held there in 1981, where the prevailing diagnosis was that the liberal dictatorship of Pinochet saved Chile from a communist dictatorship, establishing a freer regime than the one that existed during 40 years of "socializing" policies in the country. For example, Reed Irvine celebrated the coup promoted by his country against Allende, and pointed out that, instead of focusing on human rights violations, the U.S. press should have highlighted Chile's economic progress. Criticism of the media accused of "leftism" is also found in Erik von der Kuehnelt-Leddihn. This ultra-conservative Austrian Catholic member of the Mont-Pèlerin Society, underlined the violence that would be consubstantial to democracy, considering that "in the last two hundred years, real or supposedly privileged minorities were expropriated, persecuted, exiled, repressed or assassinated. Of course, the principle of majority rule favored such developments [...]" (Solchany, 2016, p. 53).

In different ways, in the same year in which Reagan assumed the presidency of the US, those present at the congress applauded the Chilean regime and denounced, on the contrary, the unlimited democracy prevailing in the North. In that context, the theory of public choice developed by James Buchanan, a leading figure at the congress, appeared as a kind of denunciation of bureaucracies and interest groups, which, following their own agendas, give rise to the growth of a Leviathan that must be curbed.

In this context, Wolfgang Frickhöffer pointed out that the reforms promoted by Ludwig Ehrhard in occupied Germany would not have been possible under a parliamentary democratic regime. Such necessary reforms would only be possible under an authoritarian regime, as in Chile. If a democracy would never be willing to establish such reforms, and if a free regime could only exist under a market society, it follows that a pro-market dictatorship will always promote greater freedom than a democracy.

As Solchany points out, this praise of authoritarian regimes does not cease with the fall of the USSR. In 1992, economic journalist Gerhard Schwarz points out that democracy, for example, leads to the sanctioning of confiscatory taxes to be paid by the rich, while an authoritarian dictatorship has many advantages in the transition to a market economy. In fact, by imposing a market order, a dictatorship would be placing extensive limits on its own power. Schwarz thus proposes an authoritarian democracy, ruled by a leader with broad support among the population and imposing an authoritarian constitution.

This type of anti-democratic and state-phobic thinking is supported in the USA by Hans-Hermann Hoppe, a follower of Mises and Rothbard (see infra, chap. 5). For Hoppe, democracy, "The god that failed", would be responsible for moral degeneration, state power and criminality. Hoppe aspires to a liberal-libertarian revolution which establishes small-scale communities that will be separated and governed only by freely consensual exchanges between private property owners. The libertarian order will be undemocratic, hierarchical and elitist, and guided by a natural authority.[25] Indeed, while monarchy was better than democracy, since a monarch has incentives to preserve the long term capital of its kingdom, it is a matter of returning to a natural order, based on the traditional family and the unrestricted defense of private property in the face of the democratic impulse to larceny implied by the welfare state and the moral degeneration it entails, especially in its tolerant and multicultural drift. The defense of property implies the possibility of exclusion and therefore of discrimination, which makes it possible to determine who can be part of a community and who must be expelled. Within this framework,

> There can be no tolerance toward democrats and communists in a libertarian social order. They will have to be physically separated and expelled from society. Likewise, in a covenant founded for the purpose of protecting family and kin, there can be no tolerance toward those habitually promoting lifestyles incompatible with this goal. They—the advocates of alternative, non-family and kin-centered lifestyles such as, for instance, individual hedonism, parasitism, nature-environment worship, homosexuality, or communism—will have to be physically removed from society, too, if one is to maintain a libertarian order. (Hoppe, 2001, p. 218)

---

25 As we will see in chapter 5, there is an increasingly fluid transition from this type of paleo-libertarian positions to the neo-fascist and supremacist extreme right.

This type of thinking is taken up in Europe by Frank Karsten and Karel Beckman in *Beyond Democracy*, a pamphlet translated into ten languages, which seeks to explain—following Mises, Hayek, Rothbard and Hoppe—why national parliamentary democracy necessarily leads to the tyranny of majorities and the loss of freedoms (Karsten and Beckman, 2013). According to the authors, democracy is a collectivist system in which all social ties tend to be controlled by the state. Therefore, they suggest that bureaucracy, government intervention, parasitism, crime, corruption, unemployment, inflation, low educational levels, etc., are not due to the lack of democracy, but to its existence. Democracy is conceived as the dictatorship of the majority through the State, while a free society can only be achieved through a political system based on the self-determination of the individual, characterized by decentralization, local government, and diversity (Karsten & Beckman, 2013).

As Solchany points out, because of its phobia of the masses and of parliamentarism, and because of its aspiration for elite power freed from the constraints of universal suffrage, neoliberalism partakes a long tradition of liberal distrust of egalitarianism. The insistence on the elitist dimension of liberal thought gives a certain neoliberalism a conservative, even reactionary, connotation.

Now, if neoliberal contempt for democracy enabled a diagnosis of its dangerousness and a series of policies that tended to limit it; if neoliberalism reveals itself as an ademocratic and even demophobic rationality: how to characterize current neoliberalism, whose greatest exponents come from a far-right that unambiguously affirms white, male, and heterosexual superiority? Are we facing a new type of fascism, neoliberal in nature, as some current theorists and activists maintain, or is it something else?

In what follows, I will try to conceptualize an authoritarian spirit and praxis in neoliberalism. I will discuss the notion of neoliberal fascism and the debate on authoritarian neoliberalism, bearing in mind the violent origins of neoliberalization and the strategic character of neoliberal thought. If we have devoted so much space to the reactionary and antidemocratic roots of neoliberalism, it is because we consider that the rise of authoritarian neoliberalism and neoliberal right-wing populism is not alien to the thinking of the very popes of neoliberalism from its birth to the present day. In the genealogy of anti-democratism and neoliberal conservatism it is better understood why this shift towards punitive neoliberalism is not unprecedented, and why "authoritarian neoliberalism" runs the risk of becoming a pleonasm.

3 The new neoliberalism: neoliberal fascism or neoliberalism reloaded?

In the first part of the book, we have commented on neoliberalism as a governmental rationality, and some of its combative, reactionary, and undemocratic features. In the next three chapters, we will analyze the intensification of the authoritarian traits of neoliberalism and their relationship to the emergence of new right-wing political movements—a process that many scholars and political activists have described and conceptualized as *neoliberal fascism*. By the notions of *authoritarian, punitive* and *reloaded neoliberalism,* we will understand a moment of neoliberal capitalism in which governments enforce undemocratic legal measures and policies that tend to punish, discipline, control and marginalize groups of people that do not adjust to the norm of competitiveness and initiative-taking market behavior. Those sovereign, biopolitical and disciplinary apparatuses not only produce a sense of failure in those subjects who make their best to adjust to the norm of competitiveness, creditworthiness (Feher, 2019), and performance, but also force great parts of the excluded subjects to an entrepreneurial management of their own precariousness. Therefore, authoritarian neoliberalism evidences a twofold logic of the production of *homo economicus* and an *entrepreneur of the self.* On one hand, neoliberal governmentality involves the production of situations of choice through incitements and positive stimuli linked to the promise that individual effort and investment in human capital will be rewarded by more access to goods, services, wellbeing, and enjoyment. On the other hand, it entails an abandonment of every human being to a ruthless *bellum omnium contra omnes* and to the pressure of precarization, indebtedness, exclusion and, in some cases, punishment of those who fail (Wacquant, 2009; Callison & Manfredi, 2019).

This ugly face of neoliberalism showed its teeth in the aftermath of different financial crisis, first in Latin America and Africa, during the 1980s, and later in Europe and the United States, following the 2008 crisis. After decades of promoting private and public debt, through tax cuts, deregulations, free trade and capital flow, loss of social entitlements and public services, mixed with a moralizing discourse of individual and familial responsibility and unlimited growth possibilities, governments have been applying policies that tend to transfer the costs of systemic failures to precarious populations instead of trying to build consensus or co-opt the working classes with new incentives to support neoliberal governmentality. According to neoliberal reason, the state should not help its citizens—or foreign populations—without asking for anything in return. A "nanny state" that intervenes in this way not only distorts prices and favors in-

https://doi.org/10.1515/9783110723939-005

flation but also encourages an ethics of laziness and the dissolution of familial responsibility, which is not acceptable according to the moral and economic philosophy of neoliberalism. Furthermore, as we have already seen in the previous chapters, according to neoliberals, the dangerous myth of social justice not only leads to more poverty; it also endangers freedom. From these core ideas derive the transition from welfare to workfare, debtfare and prisonfare that most countries have experienced in recent decades, especially since the 1990s.

This situation of abandonment, exclusion, and punishment was aggravated with the austerity measures that followed the 2008 financial crisis in different parts of the world. While during the first years after the crisis there were social movements that had put neoliberalism and national governments into question, the discontent with the ruling classes has not given birth to a new form of society nor to any serious threat or alternative to neoliberal capitalism. On the contrary, after years of protests and uprisings against inequalities and the violence of authoritarian neoliberalism, a new political far right which promises to dissolve the contradictions generated by neoliberal capitalism and globalization through the erection of new scapegoats has become increasingly influential. While part of it promises to address social unrest by limiting the power of financial capital and enforcing protectionist and unorthodox economic measures to shield the "legitimate" citizens against globalization and migrants, the other branch promises to provide better economic opportunities for the "national workers" through more deregulation, tax-cuts and competition while limiting immigration and reestablishing traditional hierarchies. In the next chapters, we will distinguish between *social-identitarians* and *neoliberal authoritarians* or *national-neoliberals*. However, we will pay more attention to the latter since many scholars and activists linked their political success to a fascist moment of neoliberalism. Indeed, by the notion of *neoliberal (neo)fascism*, an increasing number of pundits and activists seek to characterize political movements and parties that combine ultraliberal economic ideology with a discourse of hatred and policies of exclusion towards immigrants, racialized people, LGBTQI collectives, women, the poor, etc. It comprises the recovery of "our country", with its traditional hierarchies between gender, races, and classes, the restoration of traditional moral and familial values and—in some cases—a twisted notion of meritocracy. Hence, humiliated manhood and whiteness, and the ressentiment derived from lost entitlement, have become key elements of this authoritarian liberalism (Brown, 2019). In order to understand these phenomena, we will try to historicize it and also to clarify very vague and widely used concepts such as "fascism", "neofascism", and "populism" that can be very useful in political discussions but, at the same time, may be very imprecise for research in social sciences when they are not clearly defined. Hence, even if we recognize the potentialities of some political uses of these terms and the risks of underestimating the far-right's threat for a pluralist society, we expect to arrive to a proper conceptualization of these new political movements, recognizing their genealogy but also their novelty. That is why, even though we will need to use these terms in this book, we prefer the notion of *punitive* or *authoritarian neoliberalism*, or even *neoliberalism reloaded*, since they enable us to put at stake *the authoritarian nature of neoliberalism itself, to distinguish different phases of neoliberalism and to link them to their historical and ideological roots*. In this sense, we will seek to inscribe neoliberal reason in its political and intellectual sources and in the moment of its violent landing in South America, and then in the United States and Europe. Through this brief genealogy, we expect to show, on the one hand, that neoliberalism can acquire different political forms—be they democratic, liberal, conservative, progressive or authoritarian—provided they enforce pro-market and pro-competitiveness policies, and, on the other hand, to be able to analyze what forms of violence and social conservatism are inherent to neoliberalization itself.

In this account, we will try to bear always in mind the strategic nature of neoliberalism and, therefore, to inscribe it in the wider history of capitalism itself and its domination over racialized, feminized, and impoverished populations that were part and parcel of its birth. In this sense, another way of understanding the ongoing process of dispossession and today's neoliberal violence is *the becoming black of the world* (Mbembe, 2017). In a new moment of crisis of capitalist accumulation, the war towards racialized people, women, gender dissidents, former colonies, and the poor—and also the war towards nature—returns in the form of neoliberal reshaping and normalization of society. And once again, like a century ago, finance becomes a key element of capital's war machines.

Therefore, neoliberal discourse and politics should always be situated in concrete historical and political terms. To begin with, neoliberalism has changed its *field of adversity* (Foucault, 2008). During the last century, neoliberals were still fighting socialism, Keynesianism, and the Welfare State. While the former was conceived by Western intellectuals as a threat that came from the influence of the Socialist bloc, the latter was blamed of undermining the basis of a free society from within. After the victory of Liberal Capitalist Democracy over the Socialist World, which can be dated back to 1991, neoliberal capitalism has no longer being defied by an alternative global political or socio-economic system. After the crisis of 2008, the enemies seem to be, on one hand, those social subjects that were already punished by neoliberal policies and financial capitalism and, on the other hand, the political movements that seek to promote political alternatives or redistributive measures. In this sense, while neoliberal governmentality is focused on making unviable any alternative to market rule and the commodification of everything, the punitive, xenophobic, misogynist, and racist populism that characterized the interwar fascisms returns under new guises, not only to build an imaginary community, but also to discipline and punish impoverished and precarized subjects, who suffer the consequences of, and are targeted by, the policies of austerity and repression.

In this context, as we have seen in the previous chapter, both liberal democracy and the rule of law enter into crisis: while people cannot decide on their own future, at the same time the Law, far from placing a limit on power, is revealed as an instrument of domination, which ensures the extension of private property and capital accumulation to new domains while restricting the political freedoms and civil and social rights of populations.

Finally, far from being compensated with greater well-being, growing inequalities have proliferated in a context of lower economic growth, less freedom and greater suffering for the subjectivities that pay the costs of financialization and the commodification of life. In fact, in its paranoiac defense of private property and market rule, neoliberal governments are targeting precarious populations, even though they do not represent a threat to them, as the revolutionary movements of the past century.

In this section, taking into account what has been already pointed out, we will discuss whether we are facing a fascist moment of neoliberalism, as if it were a mixture between two radically heterogeneous political rationalities, that were opposed in their respective origins, or whether these elements that we see unfolding today are drifts enabled by the authoritarianism contained in neoliberal rationality itself, that is, by a government of populations that seeks to adjust the totality of our lives to economic rationality and competition. In this sense, although various theorists use the term *neoliberal fascism* to characterize the politically reactionary and economically commodifying wave that is sweeping over liberal democracies, our hypothesis is that we should reflect on the novelty and specificity of neoliberal capitalism as a regime of accumulation and government, and on the political and subjective forms that it produces and with which it is interwoven. For that reason, with the notion of *neoliberalism reloaded* we name a *radicalization of neoliberalism itself, articulated with reactionary political-cultural currents, in which the anti-democratic, anti-collectivist and anti-egalitarian component that its principal promoters have rarely hidden stands out.*

3.1 Towards a periodization of 'actually existing neoliberalism'

To give a proper account of the authoritarian and undemocratic roots of the neo-liberal project, we need to consider not only its ideas but also how they were implemented, a process that in many cases was overseen by neoliberal thinkers themselves. However, neoliberal policies are not a straightforward application of a theoretical framework. That's why—paraphrasing the distinction between actually existing socialism and Marxist theory—some scholars distinguish between neoliberalism as a utopian and a political project and the neoliberal state in theory and in practice (Harvey, 2005). Other scholars differentiate between neoliberal ideas and neoliberalism as we know it. In that sense, Peck, Brenner and Theodore propose the notion of '*actually existing neoliberalism*' in order to account for "*constitutive* discrepancies between the utopian idealism of free-market narratives and the checkered, uneven, and variegated realities of those governing schemes and restructuring programs variously enacted in the name of competition, choice, freedom, and efficiency". (Peck, Brenner, Theodore, 2018, p. 3) However, if we consider the theoretical elements that favor an authoritarian and undemocratic rule of society and the personal preferences and militancy of many neoliberal thinkers, the discrepancy between idealistic narratives of a pluralistic society in which anybody is "free to choose" and variegated governing schemes should be put into question, since neoliberalism should always be read in strategic terms.[1]

In this chapter we will focus on the second aspect in order to name and characterize different periods of actually existing neoliberalism. Of course, any periodization is imprecise since neoliberalism has not developed worldwide at the same time and under the same conditions. However, we will try to propose a periodization to understand the evolution of neoliberalism from a theoretical project that promised to increase freedom and wellbeing of individuals to a political one that, after defeating its external enemies, shows little regard for building consensus and for the fate of important parts of the population. To do so, we should bear in mind the legitimizing discourses of the different stages of neoliberal enforcement.

For instance, William Davies, who focuses on the Anglo-Saxon experience, marks relevant milestones for understanding the transformations of neoliberal-

---

1 Indeed, this strategic feature was stressed during the Walter Lippmann Colloquium by Rougier, who maintained that neoliberals should fight with spiritual weapons and Hayek, according to whom the war of ideas was to be fought also by mediators, secondhand dealers in ideas, like intellectuals, journalists, think tanks and politicians. (Dardot et al., 2021, p. 21)

ism at the global level, bearing in mind the ethical and philosophical orientations that accompany neoliberal policies and regulations (Davies, 2016): combative neoliberalism (1979–1989), normative neoliberalism (1989–2008) and punitive neoliberalism, initiated in 2008, in which "systems and routines of power survive, but without normative or democratic authority" (Davies, 2016, p. 132).[2] In a similar sense, Neil Davidson distinguishes between vanguard neoliberalism (1979–1997), social neoliberalism (1997–2007), and crisis neoliberalism (2007–), a defensive "attempt to preserve the now decaying order through ever-more generalised attacks on the subaltern classes [...] as permanent aspects of the political regime" (Davidson, 2017).[3] Bob Jessop adds more complexity to this picture by distinguishing different types of shifts towards neoliberalism: neoliberal system transformation in post-Soviet successor states, neoliberal regime shifts like those of Thatcher and Reagan, neoliberal economic restructuring and regime shifts that occurred in response to inflationary and/or debt crises in (semi-)peripheral economies in parts of Africa, Asia, Eastern and Central Europe, and Latin America; pragmatic and potentially reversible neoliberal policy adjustments like in the Nordic social democracies and Rhenish capitalism. (Jessop, 2019). From Argentina, Carlos Hoevel explores different strands of the Mont-Pèlerin society and then distinguishes four historical phases of application of neoliberal ideas: the Chilean experiment, the alliance between neoliberalism and neoconservatism in the '80s in England and the US, the Third Way, and the Washington Consensus and Latin-American neoliberalism.

---

2 However, in recent years, especially after the crisis of 2008, we have witnessed at the global level an accelerated growth of political forces that contain unmasked authoritarian, reactionary, and xenophobic components, both politically and socio-culturally. In that sense, if the commodification of everything seemed to go hand in hand with the vanishing of singularities into the icy waters of competition and the wet dreams of mass consumerism, today we are witnessing the rebirth of strongly exclusionary social identities and a consolidation of different forms of war (military, psychological, financial, commercial, legal, mediatic) whose declared or implicit targets are immigrants, women, sexual dissidents, the poor, the precarious, peasants, terrorism, Muslims, Indians.

3 According to Davidson, crisis neoliberalism "has no strategy for restoring general levels of profitability" since it is not able to address long-term issues. This situation enabled *the revival of the far right* "as a serious electoral force [which] is based on the apparent solutions it offers to what are now two successive waves of crisis, which have left the working class in the West increasingly fragmented and disorganised, and susceptible to appeals to blood and nation as the only viable form of collectivism still available [...] Here we see emerging a symbiotic relationship between one increasingly inadequate regime response to the problems of capital accumulation and another increasingly extreme response to the most irrational desires and prejudices produced by capital accumulation. (Davidson, 2018, pp. 65–66)

Indeed, it would be unconceivable to start analyzing the process of neoliberalization without taking into consideration the Chilean dictatorship presided by Augusto Pinochet, a genocidal regime that was supported by key neoliberal figures such as Friedrich Hayek, James Buchanan and Milton Friedman and in which former students at the Chicago School of Economics played a decisive role.

3.1.1 Combative neoliberalism: from the Chilean experiment to Thatcher and Reagan

In line with what we have been arguing regarding the strategic and combative nature of neoliberalism, it is worth remembering that in its beginnings its main target was socialism, establishing a dichotomy between a market society and everything else (Davies, 2016). Although this antagonistic and strategic character of neoliberalism manifests itself early on, its triumph in the contest against socialism and Keynesianism is gestated in the 1970s, when the conditions of stagflation crisis become propitious for a change of economic and governmental paradigm.

As we know, most historizations of neoliberalization processes place the Chilean case as a decisive precedent which, in many cases, is chronological: Chile would be the first country in which, after the *coup d'état* led by Augusto Pinochet against the democratic government of Salvador Allende on September 11, 1973, the economic policies recommended by the Chicago Boys were explicitly and systematically implemented. Starting in 1975, they inspired a new Constitution that combines conservatism and neoliberalism, and which today is being reformed after decades of struggles and the popular insurrection of October 2019. In turn, this background is even more important if we take into account the violent and authoritarian character of the regime that imposed neoliberal policies.[4] Hence, many critical perspectives on neoliberalism and its violence have taken

---

4 As Foucault (2008) points out, many crucial neoliberal reforms took place in the implementation of the social market economy in the German Federal Republic, with an ordoliberal-inspired Economic and Social Council, where a new state had to be built and legitimized by the market. However, the implementation of a systemic change project that would overthrow Keynesianism, democratic socialism, and the welfare state, where the different neoliberal currents converge, occurred for the first time in Chile. (Hoevel, 2014)

the Chilean case as a model, laboratory or experiment (Klein, 2007)[5] while neoliberals tend to highlight the success of the model in terms of economic growth, financial stability and freedom of enterprise.

Although each process of neoliberalization is singular, certain dynamics that will signal the neoliberal implementation in the rest of the world were present in Chile. On the one hand, the incremental and non-linear character that the neoliberal revolution had at the beginning. This can be seen in the fact that at first there was no clear definition by the military junta regarding the economic course to be taken, although there was a clear definition of its conservatism and anti-communism. Based on a political society devastated by repression and the search for the reestablishment of Western and Christian values, the economic proposal of the Chicago Boys and the blessing received from the great theoreticians of neoliberalism were able to prosper.

In effect, the current Chilean society is a product of the encounter between the military, neoliberal intellectuals, and national and transnational business-people (Moulian, apud Fagioli, 2020, p. 17). The military were the ones who disciplined not only the opposition to the regime but also the workers and discordant sectors of the bourgeoisie itself, which they forced to compete with foreign capital. As in other latitudes, the rise of neoliberalism in Chile meant the end of the policy of import substitution and industrial promotion. Initially, the economic area was left in the hands of the Navy, which was the one that ended up calling the Chicago boys, who had already prepared themselves for the fall of Allende and had devised an alternative economic plan, formalized in the document known as "the Brick", whose head was the then Dean of the Faculty of Economics of the Catholic University and future minister, Sergio de Castro (Fagioli, 2020, p. 20–21). Within this framework, Chilean economists trained in Chicago conducted institutional and economic reforms, especially after 1975. Both in the first monetarist stage and in the second stage of the 7 reforms, Austrian and Friedmanian ideas and some from the Virginia School were applied. (Hoevel, 2014, p. 54).

In this framework, the line of the military linked to the Christian Democracy, which at first were oriented to restore the 1925 Constitution and outlaw the UP, was quickly relegated by a foundational or revolutionary line. The liberals, who considered that fundamental institutional changes were needed to change the Chilean mentality, prevailed over the nationalist sector. Like Thatcher, with her

---

5 In the context of the popular revolt that led to a referendum and a new Constituent Assembly, a banner in the streets of Santiago stated that *"Neoliberalism was born in Chile and will die in Chile".*

apothegm "Economics are the method; the object is to change the heart and soul.", the Chilean military and neoliberal intellectuals were aware that it was not enough to apply savage repression on their political antagonists, but that, in addition, institutional changes could have profound and lasting effects on the subjectivities to be governed.

These changes occurred first with a series of Constitutional Acts that came to modify the 1925 Constitution. However, the meeting of the aspirations of the different parties was sealed in the 1980 Constitution, in the drafting of which Jaime Guzmán, who personally experienced a transition from "gremialismo" to neoliberalism, played a key role.[6] This Constitution expresses a synthesis of Catholic conservatism and neoliberal rationality. Although it was submitted to referendum, the fact that it was promulgated in the context of a bloody military dictatorship cannot be ignored. It was drafted with the idea of laying the foundations of an institutional and economic model that could not be modified and where democracy and government were limited in their spheres of action (Fagioli, 2020, p. 32).

This constitution is not only the institutionalization of a model of limited democracy, guarded by the military high command, through lifetime positions in the senate—which is compatible with the distrust shared by Guzmán and Hayek towards a democracy for which the country would not have been ready —[7]but also, and more fundamentally, of what is called a constitutionalization of economic policies, something that also occurred progressively in the European Union. The Chilean Constitution of 1980 not only guarantees private property and economic freedom, but also limits the role of the state in this area, subjecting it to private law, prohibiting it from implementing redistributive policies and constitutionalizing competition.

This idea of constitutionalizing neoliberal economic policies to neutralize the vicissitudes of democracy is one of the fundamental features of what several theorists define as authoritarian neoliberalism (see below). This is what Wolfgang Schäuble would later express with respect to the elections in the framework

---

6 As Hoevel points out, "Jaime Guzmán would be a key intermediary in introducing neoliberal ideas into the military government, making a skillful transition from a Catholic corporatism, which was shared by most of those in uniform", to a 'new' type of liberalism that combined the free market with a strong and largely paternalistic state as espoused by the German ordoliberals. Guzmán would have been inspired by Hayek and Rüstow, "in defending the possibility of authoritarianism as an exceptional but necessary regime for founding a free society". (Hoevel, 2014, p. 55)

7 As we have seen in chapter 2, this immaturity of certain peoples for democracy or for freedom is one of the imperialist and racist presuppositions shared by several great neoliberal theorists.

of the EU, where the economy is not subject to the popular will, and above all Thatcher in the famous acronym T.I.N.A. (there is no alternative). At this point, beyond the singularity of the Chilean case, it establishes a fundamental precedent for the foundational moments of neoliberalism in general. As Hoevel points out, the Chilean case combines

> the first concrete application of its eclectic economic-institutional praxis, which includes the practically complete list of the four major points of convergence between the three dissimilar neoliberal schools (pro-market macroeconomic policies, institutional framework, regulations and social engineering for competition, justifying ethical discourse and authoritarian *enforcement*), and it is also the only case in which this praxis did not experience an extreme crisis. (Hoevel, 2014, p. 56)

Regarding the genealogy outlined here, the Chilean case also stands out for the aforementioned confluence of conservatism, neoliberalism and far right authoritarianism, which today are increasingly common in many parts of the world. In the articulation of these three elements was key the political intervention of Jaime Guzmán with his doctrine of a subsidiary state that guarantees the maximum possible economic freedom, combined with a tutored democracy that would keep away the Marxist danger.

Now, it could be said that these objectives were shared by what is usually recognized as the second milestone of neoliberalization: the cases of Great Britain under Thatcher and the United States under Reagan. Although in these cases institutional regime change was not necessary, here too the combative nature of neoliberalism is evident as well as its moral aspect, in its quest to regenerate individuals, families and the national community (Giddens, 1994). Indeed, in this combative (Davies, 2016) and neoconservative (Hoevel, 2014) stage the moral dimension is revealed as more fundamental than that of economic efficiency.

The development of think tanks related to the Mont Pèlerin Society—such as the Institute of Economic Affairs in England or the Heritage Foundation in the United States—responded to the battle of ideas. However, as we have been pointing out, the neoliberal revolution did not come about through the weapons of criticism alone. In fact, the scope of this war was evident for Hayek. In a famous interview during his stay in Chile, the Austrian maintained that he was very optimistic about the possibilities of the triumph of neoliberalism in the United States under Reagan, but not so much in the United Kingdom, under Thatcher. The reason was that the war against trade unionism was much more difficult to win in a country with a stronger trade union tradition linked to socialism (Hayek, 1981).

However, the Iron Lady considered that the implementation of her program and her model of society had to be conceived as a decisive struggle. After winning the Malvinas war and facing the miners' union conflict, Thatcher maintained: "We had to fight the enemy without in the Falklands. We always have to be aware of the enemy within, which is much more difficult to fight and more dangerous to liberty".

Indeed, without resorting to a military dictatorship, Thatcher and Reagan's combative neoliberalism destroyed the power of the organized working class, reduced taxes for the rich and wages for workers, and commodified public goods to preclude any alternative to neoliberalism.

As Davies points out, in its applied form, combative neoliberalism included various tactics aimed at undermining the possibility of socialism. Anti-worker legislation and violent confrontations with labor unions. Monetarist anti-inflationary policies and high interest rates that raised unemployment to unprecedented levels. The Reagan administration's accelerated military spending that imposed unsustainable strains on the Soviet economy, while masking the lack of growth in the U.S. private sector.

For Davies, Marxist explanations such as Harvey's, which see political change as an expression of class power, fail to capture the *cultural and ideological orientation of combative neoliberalism*, which sought to demolish non-capitalist paths of political hope (Davies, 2016, p. 126). In that framework, Davies recovers David Graeber's observation: "Given a choice between a course of action that would make capitalism seem the only possible economic system, and one that would transform capitalism into a viable, long-term economic system, neoliberalism chooses the former every time." (Graeber, 2012, p. 31). In fact, while, from the economic point of view, the neoliberal policies of the '80s failed, from the strategic point of view of destroying the labor movement as a political force and socialism as a horizon of expectations they were highly successful.

This vision coincides with one of the definitions of strategy given by Foucault, as "the procedures used in a situation of confrontation to deprive the opponent of his means of combat and to reduce him to giving up the struggle" (Foucault, 1982, p. 793). Combative neoliberalism, both in South America and in the center of global capitalism, managed to destroy any alternative and lay the foundations of a new hegemony, which would reach its most successful moment in the 1990s.

3.1.2 Normative neoliberalism

According to Davies, "normative neoliberalism" emerged after the fall of the USSR and the rise of a neo-liberal globalization accompanied by a multiculturalist opening promoted by governments that—like those of Blair, Clinton and

Schroeder—had come to power with a center-leftist discourse and brought the politics of privatization, commodification and the culture of narcissistic and meritocratic individualism to its ultimate consequences. Indeed, Thatcher would recognize the New Labour Party as her greatest achievement.

In this framework, a "normative neo-liberalism" appears in the 1990s, that is, a type of governance that seeks to establish a norm of justice based on the measurability of everything. The logics of investment in human capital, of economic maximization and of competition, already commented on by Foucault in *The Birth of Biopolitics*, will allow institutions and people to distinguish as something fair that some people win, and other lose. "Normative questions of fairness, reward and recognition become channelled into economic tests of efficiency and comparisons of 'excellence' [...] the ideal is that of meritocracy, of reward being legitimately earned, rather than arbitrarily inherited". (Davies, 2016, p. 128)

This legitimacy was built on the basis of measurement and evaluation systems that became transversal to all social spheres and human experience, from financial agencies to scientific research and educational institutions. However, according to Davies, it entered crisis when it became clear that the rating agencies that evaluate the financial situation of countries responded to economic-financial interests and the inequalities generated by this society began to be questioned.

However, it cannot be said that the sources of legitimacy of this hegemonic neoliberalism have functioned in the same way in all geographies. While in Europe and the United States its implementation was due to a combination of the combats carried out by Thatcher and Reagan and the victory of certain ideas that had been developing in the previous decades to the point of transforming social democracy into the neoliberal credo, in Latin America these policies were imposed in a situation where the economic crisis obliged governments and societies to accept neoliberal reforms as inexorable. Indeed, the debt crisis orchestrated at the end of the 1970s, the absence of economic growth and the hyperinflationary crises that hit countries such as Argentina, Bolivia, Mexico, Peru, and Brazil during the 1980s, enabled the Washington consensus to be imposed without having to legitimize itself in a deep moral or societal project. As Hoevel recalls, it was not great theoreticians like Hayek or Friedman but IMF and World Bank technocrats like Jeffrey Sachs who were advising Latin American governments. Moreover, debt refinancing, such as the Brady Plan, was conditional on the implementation of structural adjustment measures that would later become part of the neoliberal decalogue. The absence of an underlying project would have allowed neoliberal reforms to impose themselves rapidly, but also meant that their legitimacy was highly questioned. In fact, in line with neoliberal contempt for democracy, these reforms were carried out behind society's back by governments that had emerged from the popular vote and whose leaders betrayed their voters, such as Fujimori in Peru, Menem in Argentina, or Paz Estenssoro in his fourth presidential term in Bolivia. These reforms generated substantial changes in society and obtained their legitimacy at the beginning from the efficiency shown in the fight against inflation, achieving macroeconomic and price stability unknown for decades in the region and allowing access to new imported consumer goods. At the same time, their legitimacy also came from the process of modernization and technological transformation that capitalism was undergoing at that time with economic and financial globalization, which seemed to offer great benefits, especially to consumers.[8] Access to new information and communication technologies was perceived not so much as a product of global technological change but as an immediate effect of the privatization of state enterprises, which had been accused for decades of being inefficient and expensive. However, privatizations and the abandonment of the internal market logic led to higher rates of unemployment, poverty, and inequality, which, over the years, gave rise to great discontent and new forms of resistance against neoliberalism. Thus, at the beginning of the new century, the Latin American map was partially tinged with what in the Anglo-Saxon world was called the "pink tide", an attempt to leave behind many of the measures of the Washington consensus, which made it possible to improve income distribution, although less successful in terms of reversing the extractivist model of accumulation and the processes of neoliberal subjectivation. As in the center of global capitalism, although more belatedly, this experience ended up leading to what Davies calls punitive neoliberalism.[9]

---

8 According to Catanzaro and Stegmeyer (2019, p. 138) "Menemism sustained itself through the simultaneous deployment of a cold economic rationality and a style of charismatic leadership that encouraged a festive consumerism in a carnavalesque and utopian dimension projecting a horizon to be achieved: the total deregulation of the market; the image of a world devoid of hierarchies, fully horizontal and rid of bureaucracy; and the opening of borders to hyper-communication in a technological revolution still to be realized".

9 As with the combative stage of neoliberalism, it is also not so clear that in the global north this normative stage lacked violent and authoritarian features. This was observed not only from collectives such as Midnight Notes, which showed the loss of labor rights as a consequence of the new enclosures and the incorporation of cheap labor from other countries into global competition, but also from certain versions of political economy that already identified a *disciplinary neoliberalism*, two decades before the notion of *authoritarian neoliberalism* was widely used. In an article written by Stephen Gill in 1995, this notion referred to a macro and micro behavioral power that reconfigures the state and society to serve the interests of capital, secured by new constitutional measures: "'disciplinary neoliberalism' is a concrete form of structural and behavioural power; it combines the structural power of capital with 'capillary power' and 'panopticism'". (Gill, 1995)

3.1.3 Punitive neoliberalism

As we have seen in the first chapter, combative and hegemonic neoliberalism saw an exponential increase in debt, first public and then private, which led to a speculative bubble that exploded with the 2008 crisis. As a response, instead of helping citizens that were defrauded, many western countries decided to give support to financial institutions and enforce austerity measures that privilege the rights of the creditors. In that moment, *punitive neoliberalism* arises. According to Davies, it is a moment of neoliberal rule that no longer seeks to build consensus to legitimize itself. Rather, it punishes the parts of the population that are already victims of cuts on social spending, the privatization of welfare, the divestment in health care and education, the growing rates of unemployment, etc. In this framework, instead of critically reviewing the policies that produced the financial crisis, ordinary people who in many cases was deceived by financial institutions, is treated as if they were guilty of spending beyond reasonable limits and thus forcing the authorities to impose austerity measures.[10] Although many of this policies reissue the measures of the previous stages—such as housing policies, austerity measures or public audits—they now adopt a punitive logic and seem to obey to an irrational desire for revenge. According to Davies, the enemy is no longer the socialist but the poor and the failed[11] who are not a threat to neoliberal system, "yet somehow this increases the urge to punish them further". (Davies, 2016, p. 132)

What is striking about this new 'post-hegemonic' stage is that it no longer seems necessary to give any rational justification for the measures taken by governments[12]. For example, even though for four decades austerity measures have

---

10 This type of discourse was very present in the electoral campaign of the former Argentinean president Mauricio Macri. Before his mandate, he promised a "revolution of joy". Once he took office, he argued that it was necessary to sincere the prices of the economy (i. e. increase tariffs, devalue the currency, raise interest rates, etc.) and that Argentines were living too well for the country's fiscal situation. Then, after asking Argentines to fall in love with Cristine Lagarde, hence director of the IMF, who gave the country the largest loan in the history of the organization, and a brutal adjustment program, he ended up challenging his fellow countrymen, calling them "ungrateful" and saying that because they had voted wrongly, now they had to pay the consequences.

11 Although it is true that there is no socialist enemy outside the neoliberal world, as we will discuss later, the new right will denounce as "communist" or "socialist" any governmental measure that can disturb the smooth functioning of markets.

12 In fact, as Foucault and Villacañas after him remind us, any political hegemony, any government of the living, must be based in alteurgia, a manifestation of the truth (Foucault, 2010; Villacañas, 2020). However, neoliberalism considers "that politics no longer disposes of an aletur-

produced the opposite effects to those declared to be desirable (promoting growth, allowing debt to be reduced, diminishing public deficits, etc.) they are being applied with greater insistence. In this regard, Lazzarato (2021) and Dardot and Laval (2019) suggest that it is a matter of perpetuating the crisis as a form of government.

Within this framework, social policies aimed at disciplining vulnerable populations have become equally incredible. (Davies, 2016) This has to do with the shift from welfare to workfare (not to mention debtfare here). This system means that the unemployed must lend their labor force for free in order not to lose unemployment benefits and house-rental assistance. In that framework, not only millions of citizens have lost their social and disability benefits, but also those who are on workfare are subject to "dubious behavioral activation techniques, from neuro-linguistic programming to self-marketing slogans" in which people must read statements such as "My only limitations are the ones I set for myself". (Davies, 2016, p. 123)

While Lazzarato maintains that the economy of debt redefines the functioning of sovereign, disciplinary and biopolitical power in order to produce the indebted man, for Davies, this redefinition of public policies based on the rule of austerity and the payment of public debt to creditors casts doubts on the productive rationality of biopower, which seems to be turning to sovereign forms of the exercise of power, i.e., aneconomic forms, not based on any scientific evidence, excessive and circular (Davies, 2016). For instance, if we take the case of immigration, while governmentality seeks to manage the flow and circulation of populations to improve economic outcomes and says yes to the desire of the subjects, sovereignty imposes restrictions on the freedom to move, defending territorial identity and integrity, and therefore, restricting immigration. (Davies, 2020) In that sense, punitive neoliberalism would be a manifestation of the irrationality of current sovereign power and of its definitive distancing from democratic-liberal rationality and "the rights of the majorities". (Ramírez Gallegos, 2019)

---

gy". That is why, as we have seen in chapter 2, its imaginary "is not that of egalitarianism and democracy"; it's just the one of "individual freedom, but not that of political freedom" (Villacañas, 2020, p. 71). As we have already commented in chapter 1, for liberal rationality the market becomes a space of veridiction. According to Gary Becker, "neo-liberalism would be "a rational art of governing" if it succeeded in making the governed accept its truth" (Villacañas, 2020, p. 71). However, with punitive neoliberalism the government of the living does not seem to recur to any pretension of truth that should be accepted by economic agents. Therefore, power seems to transform itself into ruthless domination.

3.2 Neoliberal fascism?

As we have already seen, after the outbreak of the 2008 financial crisis, we are turning to increasingly authoritarian and violent forms of government. This reality is aggravated with the rise of nationalist and xenophobic right-wing political movements and with the reactionary turn taken by governments that claim to be defenders of globalization. For some scholars, before the financial crisis, neoliberalism could build consensus despite the rise of inequalities because it promised that economic growth would benefit everyone and would reduce poverty. At the same time, part of the middle classes benefited from the post-Fordist production system while the poor would expect that the fruits of economic growth in developing economies would trickle down to them. However, after the financial crisis and the widespread rejection of neoliberal policies, corporate capital has shifted from a promise of expansive freedom and wellbeing to neoliberalization through violent and authoritarian means.

As Alliez and Lazzarato point out, the era of deterritorialization of the 90s and 2000s is followed by the racist, misogynistic and xenophobic territorialization of Trump, "who has already become the leader of the new fascisms" (2016, p. 12). In fact, this situation leads some pundits to characterize this combination of authoritarianism and neoliberalism as *neoliberal fascism*. By this term critics do not refer to the neo-fascist parties or movements that exist in Europe since the end of the Second World War, which include paramilitary violence against immigrants, and which vindicate historical fascism, but to the promotion of ultraliberal policies combined with xenophobic, misogynist, chauvinist and aporophobic discourses and practices, especially with the rise of a neoliberal far-right. This link between neoliberalism and (neo)fascism is explored in a recent collective book in the preface of which it is stated that, beyond the anti-establishment rhetoric of leaders like Trump or Bolsonaro,

> the new fascisms maintain a strong link with the markets, financial power, and global capitalism. The ravages caused by neo-liberalism (inequality, impoverishment, intemperance, fear, resentment, distrust of democracy) have prepared the ground for the emergence of a new fascism which, far from fighting the neo-liberalism that caused it, offers itself to it in order to carry its hegemony even further. A capitalism that in its last phase no longer needs democracy and can function without it. A market that has given for liquidated the great post-war social pact, and whose dominance finds less resistance through the scrapping of democracy, opting for authoritarian formulas to ensure that dominance (Guamán et. al., 2019, Foreword).

Henry Giroux refers to Trump's rise and government as a synthesis of fascist and neoliberal practices. Giroux understands neoliberalism as the most predatory form of capitalism, marked by the quest to consolidate power in the financial elite and to ensure that no alternatives to its form of governance can be imagined. For Giroux, the neoliberal hatred of democracy, the common good and the social contract has unleashed elements of a fascist past in which white supremacy, ultra-nationalism, misogyny, and hatred of immigrants combine in a toxic mix of militarism, state violence and the politics of disposability. Social bonds and moral barriers are eliminated, enabling new forms of violence and cruelty, such as that exercised against immigrants caged at the southern border of the United States (Giroux, 2018). According to Giroux, 'fascism' is not something fixed in history but an authoritarian ideology and political behavior characterized by a series of mobilizing passions (Paxton) that include the attack on democracy, the appeal to the strong leader, a disregard for human weaknesses, an obsession with hypermasculinity, an aggressive militarism, an appeal to national greatness, a disdain for the feminine, a language of cultural decadence, the withdrawal of human rights, the suppression of dissent, a propensity for violence, contempt for intellectuals, a hatred of reason, fantasies of racial superiority, and eliminationist policies aimed at social cleansing. "In this mix of economic barbarism, political nihilism, racial purity, economic orthodoxy and ethical somnambulance, a distinctive economic-political formation has been produced that I term neoliberal fascism". (Giroux, 2018)

This new fascism would have been simmering in the US, not only from the inequalities generated by the destruction of the welfare state but also from Bush and Obama's war on terror, where the rule of law was finally overthrown. Instead of brown shirts, purges or mass state violence, 'fascism' would have been reborn enabled by casino capitalism, which unleashed a series of political, economic, religious, and educational fundamentalisms. (Giroux, 2018). In line with Davies' point, Giroux argues that this corporate state imposed incomprehensible cruelty on the poor and vulnerable Black populations.

According to Giroux, a premonitory aspect of this new fascism is the use of language, as fascism would always begin with language before moving to physical violence. Early in his presidency, the Trump administration suggests to officials at the Centers for Disease Control not to use words like 'vulnerable', 'entitlement', 'diversity', 'transgender', 'fetus', 'evidence-based' and 'science-based'[13]. In the immediate aftermath, references to climate change and the greenhouse effect were deleted from official websites[14] as well as information about LGBTQI citizens[15].

---

13 See https://edition.cnn.com/2017/12/16/health/cdc-banned-words/index.html
14 https://www.independent.co.uk/news/world/americas/us-politics/trump-climate-change-government-websites-global-warming-a9020461.html

In addition, dehumanizing language reminiscent of Nazism has been used, such as calling 'animals' or 'criminals' undocumented immigrants who 'infest' the southern border of the USA. Moreover, Trump has downplayed the violence of white supremacist and neo-Nazi marches, thus implicitly encouraging racial hate crimes. Likewise, he has been responsible for not assuming his electoral defeat and provoking the assault on the Capitol, which could have unleashed a tragedy. This also impacts on the terrain of public memory, where there is an attempt to eliminate the memory of genocidal violence against Native Americans, Black slaves and African Americans.

According to Giroux, in the neoliberal context, freedom is transformed into an obsession with self-interest, part of a culture of war that pits individuals against each other in a framework of indifference, violence and cruelty that rejects any sense of moral and political responsibility. "Neoliberal fascism" insists that everything must be remade in the image of the market and all the problems of human capital must be solved by the individual himself. (Giroux, 2018)

In the same vein, from France, Éric Fassin (2018b) argues that we are witnessing a fascist reconstruction of neoliberalism and also refers to Macron's government as illiberal liberalism. The Frenchman points out that in Europe economic decisions seem to be too important to be left to the discretion of the people, which renders democracy irrelevant. That is why he wonders how to think about the rise of the extreme right and the authoritarian drift of neoliberalism together. On the one hand, the rise of a sexist and xenophobic white supremacism. On the other hand, democratic *coups d'état*, through the banks, lawfare, etc. To this is added the violent repression of any kind of protest. For Fassin, illiberal liberalism is not reduced to the anti-European extreme right, but perfectly characterizes Europhiles like Macron, who seek to save the French from the extreme right by imitating their policies. For Fassin, it is not enough to call this a right-wing populism (vid infra, chapter 5). It is a neo-fascist populism which, like historical fascism, promotes racism and xenophobia, a blurring of the boundaries between right and left, the veneration of the charismatic leader and the celebration of the nation, the hatred of the elites and the exaltation of the people, contempt for the rule of law and the apology for violence. In this framework, an anti-fascism is needed to hold neoliberalism accountable as responsible for the fascist drift we are witnessing. (Fassin, 2018b)

From India, several analyses insist on characterizing the current government of the most populous democracy on the planet as a form of neoliberal neo-fas-

---

15 https://www.playgroundmag.net/cultura/trump-esta-eliminando-informacion-lgtb-de-sus-webs_30727984.html

cism. As in other latitudes, neoliberal reforms started strongly in India in the 1990s and after three decades, there was an increase in inequality and poverty —which is measured in the level of access to 2100/2200 calories per day per person—from 57% in 1993–1994 to 68% in 2011–2012. Modi's government emerges from a Hindu nationalist movement with a strong xenophobic and authoritarian component, but at the same time—as in the cases of Bolsonaro, Trump, and others—it has a pro big capital orientation. Since faith in the possibility of the "spillover effect" was lost, the neoliberal regime is sustained by an alliance between globally integrated corporate capital and local neo-fascist elements (Patnaik, 2021). Although there were many who saw in this type of leadership a move away from neoliberalism, none of these governments put controls on the free flow of financial capital, but they did put controls on the free flow of people. According to Patnaik, neo-fascist elements exist on the margins of all societies, but only take control when they are supported by corporate capital. Their strategy is not to talk about economic crisis but to blame some other—racial or sexual—for all ills and to regain the self-respect that this other would have taken from us.

In an interview, Ajay Singh Chaudhary offers an operational definition of fascism that would relate it not only to the old cases but also to several current movements and governments:

> Fascism is a tendency toward a mass, right-wing political formation—authoritarian in character, nationalist in its promotion of class and social harmony in the context of cultural or ethnic homogeneity, and presenting a vision of a hierarchical society as utopian. Fascism offers a thorough critique of liberal society from the right. Although fascism is often imagined as a unified, all-powerful, all-encompassing state, in practice it often works more like a handshake deal. Fascism is able to offer capital a mobilized base in exchange for supporting its particular program. (Singh Chaudhary, 2021)

In this framework, neo-fascism would be a response to the crisis of capitalism and liberal democracy, where climate change and secular stagnation put pressure on capital. (Chaudhary, 2021). At the same time, neo-fascism would resemble classical fascism by attacking all its critics, calling them anti-national and equating criticism of the government with treason. Neo-fascism creates an atmosphere of fear in society.

> by putting people in jail without trial; by browbeating or weaponizing the judiciary; by abrogating constitutional rights of the people; by terrorizing opposition politicians to defect to the neofascist party in places where they lose elections; by unleashing gangs of thugs on the streets and on social media to attack opponents; by making fake charges against dissenters; by subverting the independence of state institutions; and so on. In all this neofascism is helped by a pliant and docile media. And through it all, it uses its ascendancy to

help the corporate sector attack the rights of workers won through decades of struggle. (Patnaik, 2021)

Patnaik points out that, in other respects, neo-fascism departs from its predecessors. For example, classical fascism arises in a national context and in the framework of an inter-imperialist rivalry where capital supports its own nation-state to divide the world into economic territories. In contrast, today's neo-fascism takes place in a globalized financial regime. The Indian case would be a clear illustration of the relationship between neoliberalism and neo-fascism. On the one hand, Chaudary argues that the Bharatiya Janata Party is quite similar to classical fascism since Prime Minister Narendra Modi emerges from a fascist movement such as the Rashtriya Swayamsevak Sangh (RSS). The BJP adopts an extreme right-wing ideology in Hindutva and introduces it into everyday life, commanding both security forces and irregular street forces that commit acts of violence with impunity. (Chaudhary, 2021) On the other hand, the Hindu supremacists coming to power in 2014—who had already combined neoliberal reforms with attacks on Muslims in their previous government (1998–2004)—did not participate in the anti-colonial struggle and even had a militant of theirs assassinate Mahatma Gandhi. They are arch-neoliberals, whose economic policy is based on keeping the fiscal deficit at bay so as not to obfuscate global finance, even during the covid-19 pandemic. The government seeks to privatize public enterprises and give aid to corporations while seeking to involve them in agriculture, which already comes from years of neoliberal reforms. (Patnaik, 2021). Unlike classical fascism, which revived employment through fiscal deficits, today's neo-fascism cannot end mass unemployment, because it would imply higher public spending, and that would imply taxing capital or increasing the fiscal deficit. Both options are ruled out under neoliberalism. (Patnaik, 2021)

Also María Galindo argued, in her polemic review of the 2019 coup d'état in Bolivia against the government of Evo Morales by extreme right-wing forces, that we are witnessing a fascist stage of neoliberalism. Galindo maintained that Bolivia was witnessing a dispute between two fascisms, that of the oligarchy of Santa Cruz de la Sierra and that of the Movement towards Socialism (MAS), which are inscribed in the emptying of liberal democracy and the privatization of politics produced by neoliberalism, of which the "caudillista" politics of Evo Morales would be an expression. For Galindo, this is related to a crisis of democracy, where political agreements and dialogue to reach solutions are no longer sought. On the contrary, there would be a "generalized fascistization" and terror "to turn legitimate solutions and social questions into scenarios of violent contraposition of forces. This is what I call the fascist phase of neoliberalism" (2019).[16]

3.3 Post-fascism?

The perspectives of historians such as Enzo Traverso or Robert Paxton, who reflect on the present after having studied the genocidal and totalitarian violence and the anatomy of classical fascism, are more nuanced. For Enzo Traverso, in a characteristic tension between history and memory, one cannot speak of fascism without further ado to characterize the rise of the radical right, which shares racism, nationalism and xenophobia, but neither can one discard this term, insofar as public memory brings it up. Therefore, considering that the context has changed radically with respect to a century ago, but that democracy is once again threatened from within, he proposes the term post-fascism. One of its central characteristics is that the myths about the past are not aimed at instituting a new society but at restoring an imaginary past. It is as if the horizon of expectations were blocked not only for those who wanted the end of capitalism but also for neoliberal forces.

In line with what we have commented on punitive neoliberalism, the enemies of this post-fascism would no longer be communism or the workers' movement, but ethnic-religious minorities, immigrants, etc. In this context, Traverso considers France as a case study to observe the proliferation of this phenomenon at the European level. In post-fascism, as verified in France, Judeophobia has been replaced by Islamophobia and racism has become culturalized, marking an incompatibility between the Judeo-Christian world and Islam. As was the case with the Jews, who made it possible to define German identity negatively in the 1930s, nationalist groups today seek to define French or European identity by its opposition to Islam, with reference to the Enlightenment. Indeed, in several European countries, while opposing what it calls "gender ideology", the radical right in turn points out that Islam does not respect the rights of women and gay people. Thus, enlightened universalism becomes (once again) a vector of

---

16 Galindo not only banalizes the term fascism, but also does not specify in what sense the MAS government would be neoliberal. García Linera theorized the construction of an Andean-Amazonian capitalism as an alternative to such a model and as a transit towards a socialist horizon, within the framework of a type of model that bears similarities with developmentalism. In any case, from a Foucauldian point of view that focuses on government rationality, the subjective effects compatible with neoliberalism, as recognized by the former Bolivian vice-president, could be noted.

xenophobia. Moreover, this Islamophobia has a colonial matrix, but it is no longer a matter of conquering and colonizing the other, but of expelling him.

In a similar vein, in the months prior to Trump's election as US president, Robert Paxton preferred to speak of quasi-fascism or proto-fascism, to differentiate Trump from historical fascism, because although there were important analogies in style, in his campaign themes and techniques, such as the fear of national decline, for which he blames the immigrant as an internal enemy, the need for a strong leader, an aggressive foreign policy, his disdain for the rule of law, etc., he also emphasized differences in his fundamental purposes: while classical fascism promised to unite the nation fragmented by class struggle and subordinated individual will to the national interest, Trump promoted unabashed individualism and plutocracy. At the same time, Trump was not seeking to replace existing institutions, nor was he confronting the threat of a communist revolution. However, Paxton himself hesitated with the storming of the Capitol by white supremacists with Trump's acquiescence to disregard the outcome of the presidential election, since it would have been a step in the direction of a form of fascism by the Republican leader. (Paxton, 2021)

For his part, the day after Trump was elected as president, Alain Badiou (2019) denounced a "democratic fascism" that contains racist and chauvinist components and is sustained by a discourse that scorns rationality and argumentation in favor of the production of emotional reactions. In that framework, Badiou stated that the current situation is characterized by the dialectic between four factors: The blind violence of contemporary capitalism; The fall of the classical political oligarchy, i.e., the end of an educated ruling class and the emergence of democratic fascism; The frustration and disorientation of the people in the face of the brutality of contemporary capitalism; The absence of an alternative strategic direction, i.e. the fragility of a communist Idea. (Badiou, 2019)

Linking "neo-fascism" to the neoliberal present, Diego Sztulwark (2019) points out that a common feature of all forms of neoliberalism is its intolerance towards forms of life that do not conform to the ways of life proposed by the market (standardization) and towards the creation of singular forms of life. In this framework, he argues that, if in its optimistic stage, neoliberalism operated through *coaching*, after the loss of control over basic social balances, its fascist features are highlighted, targeting everything in the social field that appears as symptomatic or abnormal, seeking its own truth outside the commodity and setting limits to the accumulation of capital and the control of capital over life. For Sztulwark, the basis of the "neo-fascist becoming of neoliberalism" has to do with an existential and political hatred of the symptom. "The phobia of the symptom—of sexual, racial, class difference—expresses the neoliberal horror at the threat of collapse represented by the tendency towards the autonomization of forms of life." (Sztulwark, 2019, p. 69) However, this is not a repetition of historical fascism. Marking continuities in historical discontinuity, Sztulwark argues that it is possible to speak of a postmodern fascism that functions in alliance with the absolutization of corporate values over life (2019, p. 89) and that can be defined as "a specific type of vitalism that asserts itself in a certain ethnic, class, or national essence or purity by means of intolerant violence and through the inferiorization of entire populations, be they migrants, blacks, women, or homosexuals". (2019, p. 78)

As we see, where Giroux speaks of neoliberal fascism, Fassin of neo-fascism and Galindo of a fascist moment of neoliberalism, Traverso, Badiou, Paxton and Sztulwark argue that the concept of post-fascism, proto-fascism, or democratic or postmodern fascism would allow us to inscribe certain continuities in the historical discontinuity. However, beyond its potential for political mobilization, and some analogies with classical fascism, one might ask whether "fascism" is the best way to conceptualize movements that combine neoliberalism with political authoritarianism or reactionary culture.

Obviously, the analogies are tempting, but the differences are apparent. Fascism emerged historically to save capitalism after the first post-war crisis and that of 1929 by means of nationalist, xenophobic and authoritarian political regimes. The fascist solution was given in the context of the threat of a communist revolution, which later motivated the imposition of the welfare state in the West and was accepted by the owners of the great corporations of the time. In contrast, today the major economic powers do not look favorably on the trade war promoted by Trump or the current Russian invasion of Ukraine. Today, capitalism can produce all kinds of social, economic, and ecological disasters, but it has no major rival political movement that can call its continuity into question. It is therefore paradoxical that counterinsurgency policies are applied at times and places where there is no insurgency at all (Harcourt, 2018). While it is true that these new political movements promote fear, hatred and violence against specific populations, even enabling expressions of street violence, vigilante justice, use of weapons, etc., from our point of view, the ultimate goal of the current radical right is not to produce the permanent mobilization of the people against their enemies, nor the framing of society in organizations controlled from the state-party, but to guarantee that the entrepreneurialization of existence and competition at all levels leads to better living standards for what they consider as the true national community. In fact, many of these leaders and movements use social networks as vehicles for the propagation of hatred and not the large mobilizations acclaiming the leader. To conclude, the foreign war policy does not seem to be marked by motives of expansion of one race to the detriment of the others nor territorial annexation but by the dispossession of strategic resources, the creation of markets for transnational corporations and the expansion of capitalism itself. Therefore, from a historical point of view, the analogy with fascism is inaccurate.

3.4 Reflecting on the specificity of current neoliberalism

As we have seen, although the notion of fascism warns us about the danger of the rise of this new radical right, there are those who discard it as a key to interpret the present. For example, Atilio Borón (2019), professor of political theory at the University of Buenos Aires, argues that it is a mistake to qualify Bolsonaro as a fascist, because fascism does not have to do with a psychological but a specific sociohistorical issue. Fascism would be "an exceptional form of the capitalist state" which took place as a product of the interwar crisis of bourgeois democracy.

Skepticism towards the "fascist hypothesis" has also been expressed by Wendy Brown (2019). For her, the novelty of the present lies in the fact that neoliberalism has promoted an undemocratic freedom and a strong idea of authority. As Nancy Fraser pointed out, Trump's election was the *coup de grâce* to a progressive and multicultural neoliberalism carried forward by social democratic governments, which encouraged the financialization of society and produced a resounding increase in inequality (Fraser & Sunkara, 2019). Thus, the heir and the result of "progressive neoliberalism", which destroyed all links of collective solidarity and public welfare, would be "libertarian authoritarianism". (Brown, 2018)

The characterization of the new neoliberalism by Dardot and Laval could be inserted in this line. These theorists have not only given continuity to the Foucauldian research on neoliberal rationality, but have also marked, in tune with Brown, how neoliberalism undoes the people and democracy in favor of economization by a plutocratic and expertocratic oligarchy (Brown, 2015; Dardot & Laval, 2016). For the Frenchmen, democracy has become an obstacle to neoliberal domination, which today mobilizes the resentments of populations against new scapegoats. They argue that, in what we have called its hegemonic phase, neoliberalism had often been associated with openness, progress, individual freedoms, the rule of law. Today it is combined with the closing of borders, the construction of walls, the cult of the nation and the sovereignty of the state, the declared offensive against human rights, accused of endangering security. In this framework, it is essential to understand that the nationalist, authoritarian and xenophobic tendencies of Trump, Bolsonaro or Salvini "governments in no way challenge neoliberalism as a mode of power. Quite the reverse, they light-

en the tax burden on the wealthiest, reduce social benefits, and speed up deregulation, particularly in financial or ecological matters. These authoritarian governments, of which the Extreme Right is increasingly a component, in reality accept the absolutist, hyper-authoritarian character of neoliberalism". (Dardot &
Laval, 2019, p. xiv). In this sense, authoritarian is not only the political or discursive form adopted by these governments but the neoliberal power apparatuses
themselves. For the French, a social order based on competition carried to all
spheres, the destruction of collective solidarity, the entrepreneurialization and
precarization of existence gave rise to a profound crisis of the liberal and social
democracy that had been built in post-war Europe, and which neoliberal theorists attacked early on. Far from the once promised market democracy, we are
witnessing a de-democratization (Brown, 2015), where the exploitation of
anger by the far right gives rise to a more aggressive and militarized neoliberalism: "Basically, it is as if neoliberalism were using the crisis of liberal-social democracy it has generated, and which it constantly exacerbates, the better to impose the logic of capital on society". (Dardot & Laval, 2019, p. xx)

In this new state of legality (Harcourt, 2018) that sanctions what were emergency measures in the face of economic and social crises, the law no longer functions as a limit to neoliberal power but as an instrument that it uses against democracy.[17] In that framework, "the Rechtstaat is not abolished from without, but
destroyed from within to make it a weapon of war on populations in the service
of the powerful". (Dardot & Laval, 2019, p. xxviii).

3.4.1 Reactionary neoliberalism in the Latin American context

After a long division between nationalists and liberal-conservatives, since the
late 1970s the most influential Latin American right-wingers have been characterized by being neoliberal in economic matters, and at the same time conservative
or reactionary in cultural matters, as we have seen in Perrin's (2014) characterization of liberal-reactionaries. This radical right openly questions legacies of
the liberal tradition itself such as human rights and even the rule of law,
which they see as defending criminals to the detriment of crime victims, corrupt
politicians, or subversive subjects against the forces of law and order. These
right-wingers question the right to legitimate defense in court, the principle of

---

17 In that sense, Harcourt (2018) points out that the transformation we are living through is not
from the rule of law to the state of exception but from a model of governance based on large-
scale warfare to one based on tactical counterinsurgency strategies.

innocence or even the opposition to the arbitrary actions of the security forces when others are affected by them.

At the same time, the radical right is on a crusade against abortion, feminism and "gender ideology", strongly articulated with the rise of religion as a political and electoral force. The most significant case is Brazil, due to its geopolitical and population importance, where evangelical sectors have a prominent political and cultural role and where crimes against members of the LGBTQI community are commonplace. With the presidency of Bolsonaro, whose first campaign act after the impeachment of Dilma Rousseff was to convert to evangelicalism without abandoning Catholicism, the central government assumes the task of openly combating feminism, communism, cultural Marxism and "gender ideology". His slogan, repeated in his inaugural discourse as president "Brazil above all and God above all", not only reminds the "Deutschland über alles" chanted during Nazism but is also inscribed in the nationalist, authoritarian, anti-communist, and religious tradition of the last military dictatorship (1964– 1985), which Bolsonaro revindicates. Paradoxically, just as we have a counterinsurgency without insurgency and a counterrevolution without revolution, so we have a revival of anticommunism without communism (see infra, chap. 6).

These tendencies have been verified in the *coup d'état* against the former Bolivian president Evo Morales, conducted with a bible in one hand and a rifle in the other. Its promoters asserted the need for the bible to return to the Palacio Quemado and to expel the Indians and the Pachamama from power and Bolivian Constitution. As in Brazil, religion is mixed with racism as a decisive political factor, reediting scenes and speeches typical of the conquest of America. During the presidency of Jeanine Áñez and the popular uprising generated against her appointment, the repressive forces had license to kill without legal consequences, transforming opponents into *homines sacri* (Agamben, 1998). The political, police and military forces deployed a counterinsurgency war against a constitutional government and against a part of the defenseless population, which they do not hesitate to qualify as subversive, with the silent approval of the international community.

The Bolivian case is not an isolated one. In the face of the new cycle of protests that have been taking place in recent years against governments of different political-ideological matrix, the ghost of an internal enemy whose contours and origins nobody could define appears once again. While Bolsonaro declares war on communism and *gender ideology*, the right wing in Argentina declared war on an imaginary Mapuche terrorism that would threaten national sovereignty, the reactionary sectors in Bolivia declare a war against "Indians and thieves" who have contaminated the institutions with the paganism of Pachamama, while former Chilean President Piñera's declaration of war against a powerful enemy which, according to his wife, would be composed of aliens, is symptomatic of the need to establish an antagonist and to declare war on any possibility of attenuating the advance of neoliberal capitalism. The Chilean case is the one that best explains a silent war that neoliberalism has been winning for four decades in its attack on social rights, on the possibility of a well-paid job with labor rights, on the right to education, health, housing, and the environment, today replaced by the right to go into debt (Lazzarato, 2012). It could thus be said that neoliberalism comes, with its entrepreneurial, competitive, precarious and dispossessive logics, to complete a picture of violence against the American populations that begun with the conquest and primitive accumulation, but that never ceases to be updated. At the same time, as we shall see, the Chilean case also exhibits the power of resistance to the neoliberalizing offensive: by the intensity of the popular struggles from the Penguin revolution of 2006 onwards, by the conquest of a Constituent Assembly that will end the cycle inaugurated by the 1980 Constitution, and by the recent electoral victory of Boric, whom Piñera refused to receive in 2011 as a student leader and is now forced to consecrate as the new president.

3.5 From neoliberal fascism to authoritarian neoliberalism

As we have seen, broad political sectors and critical intellectuals warn that current neoliberalism is characterized by a constant attack on democracy, human rights, and the rule of law itself, even in the countries where these traditions originated. In this framework, political movements are emerging that openly vindicate xenophobia, sexism, aporophobia, and ethnic supremacism. As we have seen, it is this rise of a radical and openly authoritarian right that leads some theorists to argue that we are witnessing a new fascism that, despite its anti-globalization rhetoric, is articulated with neoliberalism and its vocation to expand the market to all geographical and existential terrains.

Without ignoring the specificity of the present moment, we attempt here to outline the hypothesis that there are authoritarian elements inherent to neoliberalism itself and that, in this framework, the notion of neoliberal fascism can lead to confusion. The wars that neoliberalism has been waging for decades against the populations in which it is implanted do not seek to aggrandize a nation or to frame populations around a mythical Palingenesque project. Rather, it is a matter of eliminating any possibility of collective action and solidarity, since neoliberal society must be governed by the logic of competition and performance, installing new forms of discipline through the increasingly accentuated precarization of living conditions, indebtedness, and the commodification of everything (Harvey, 2005). Indeed, the control that debt exerts over our lives was deepened during what Davies (2016) calls the normative stage of neoliberalism and is now what allows us to foster a punitive rationality of governance.

Thus, while notions such as neo-fascism, post-fascism, or neoliberal fascism have an unavoidable critical and political potential, we believe it is necessary to understand the authoritarian and violent dynamics of neoliberalism itself, beyond its multicultural or ethnocentric, progressive or reactionary versions. Now, if we are not facing a new fascism, how can we characterize these new radical right movements that are on the rise today, and what is the relationship they establish with capitalism and neoliberal rationality? To elucidate this, I now turn to explore some discussions on authoritarian neoliberalism and its relationship with the rise of the new radical right or right-wing populism.

4 Authoritarian neoliberalism and the rise of the new radical right

As I have pointed out in the previous chapter, in recent years, especially after the global financial crisis of 2007 and the response of various Western states to it—from the bailout of banks, evictions of debtors, structural adjustment programs for indebted states, repression of protests and the tightening of workfare and debtfare—several theorists have pointed to the emergence of an authoritarian (Bruff, 2013; Tansel, 2017; Ryan 2018; Harrison, 2019; Fabry, 2019) or punitive neoliberalism (Davies, 2016).

For some scholars, this represents a new stage in neoliberal capitalism, which can be clearly differentiated from its hegemonic period (Davies, 2016), characterized by an attempt to build consensus around the legitimacy and necessity of neoliberal policies (Davies, 2016; Bruff, 2013; Tansel, 2017). As we have pointed out, the radicalization of the crisis with the same neoliberal remedies that had generated it—such as the austericidal responses developed mainly by the Troika in Europe or the cycles of indebtedness and adjustment in Latin America—has been the breeding ground for what several authors have called "neoliberal fascism" (Giroux, 2018; Fassin, 2018b), "neo-fascism" (Lazzarato, 2020; Sztulwark, 2019; Gago & Cavallero, 2019; Guamán et. al., 2019), "post-fascism" (Traverso, 2019) or "libertarian authoritarianism" (Brown, 2019). This authoritarian moment of neoliberalism would find its apex in the electoral consecration of Trump and Bolsonaro as the most prominent representatives of national-neoliberalism (Sauvêtre, 2019; Slobodian & Plehwe, 2019) and the radical populist right (Antón-Mellón & Hernández-Carr, 2016; Mudde, 2021; Acha, 2021) which will be discussed in the next chapter.

As we anticipated in the previous chapter, it is thus possible to recognize two concomitant phenomena that must be analyzed in their singularity and in their reciprocal relationship. On the one hand, there is the authoritarian evolution of neoliberalism and, on the other, the rise of a new radical right capable of winning elections and exercising political power, thus shifting the axis of current politics towards increasingly reactionary and violent coordinates.

Regarding the first aspect, without ignoring some empirical differences between different stages and geographies of neoliberalism, we would not want to exaggerate the discontinuities between a supposedly consensual, democratic, globalist, open, multicultural, plural and progressive neoliberalism and this new reactionary neoliberalism (Fraser & Sunkara, 2019), as it would give rise to a predominantly Eurocentric (Ryan, 2018) or Atlantic view and would ignore its violent political origins in the genocidal dictatorships of the Southern Cone, in

https://doi.org/10.1515/9783110723939-006

the structural adjustment programs imposed through debt blackmail on Latin American and African countries, in the privatizing shocks of former socialist countries (Klein, 2007), not only in Europe but also in Asia, and in the "authoritarian populism" (Hall, 1990) of Margaret Thatcher and Ronald Reagan, which, as we have commented in the previous chapter, have been the central figures of the combative stage of neoliberalism (Davies, 2016). It would even entail forgetting the imperialist roots of the financial, biopolitical and disciplinary power apparatuses that had their origins in the domination of colonized peoples (Alliez & Lazzarato, 2016; Lazzarato, 2021; Mbembe, 2017) and the persistent reality of accumulation by dispossession (Harvey, 2005).

With regard to the rise of new right-wingers, we will differentiate, in the field of the far-right (Mudde, 2021; Acha, 2021), the extreme right, with little electoral relevance, from the radical right, which is the one that has best capitalized on popular discontent in various countries in the face of the crisis generated by authoritarian neoliberalism itself and the opposition of conservative sectors against left-wing experiences that have been defeated, such as the so-called "pink tide" in Latin America or the Syriza coalition in Greece. In this framework, we will distinguish between radical national-liberal or authoritarian neoliberal rightists, who reject global institutions as a hindrance of socializing bureaucracies for the development of national capitalism, and a social-identitarian right, critical of the austerity policies recommended by neoliberal governance, and ready to promise a defense of the social rights of national workers and traditional values, excluding immigrants.

Now, if we accept that financial capitalism remains the hegemonic mode of accumulation and that neoliberal reason establishes the rules that govern our behavior, we must insist on the distinction between the policies of these new rightists, marked by a defense of the hierarchies of race, class, gender and nation, and the authoritarianism and violence inherent in neoliberal rationality itself, which seeks to transform human beings into economic agents in permanent competition and where only some can triumph. However, contrary to the claims of certain theories of human capital, *homo oeconomicus* can never be fully deanthropologized, insofar as racial, national and sexual hierarchies are maintained between those who can be employed and those who must be discarded and between those who can govern themselves and those who must be governed (Cornelissen, 2020; Elyachar, 2019; Salzinger, 2019). In what follows, we will delve on these analytical distinctions in order to understand not only the continuities and ruptures within neoliberal capitalism but also how to characterize the new right-wing political movements.

4.1 Neoliberalism and authoritarianism

Although the concept of authoritarian neoliberalism began to circulate in the social sciences especially since the global crisis of 2007, it also serves to mark a profound continuity with the very roots of the neoliberal project and its political materialization. Indeed, as we have already pointed out in the preceding chapters, in order to understand neoliberal authoritarianism, one cannot take a purely theoretical view of neoliberalism, nor reduce it to a class-based political project. In previous chapters, we have commented that the elitist and antidemocratic vision of society led central figures of neoliberalism to promote or accept authoritarian regimes such as the dictatorships of Chile, Brazil, Uruguay, and Argentina. In this context, when we speak of authoritarian neoliberalism we have in mind the very reflections, preferences, and interventions of those who thought of themselves as defenders of freedom as opposed to socialism, Keynesianism, and the welfare state and who, to this end, did not hesitate to place limits on popular sovereignty. Indeed, as we have seen in chapter 2, neoliberal thought itself contains authoritarian, reactionary and anti-democratic elements, since some of its advocates consider that racial, cultural, class, and gender hierarchies are immovable and that in order to establish the free market it is necessary to have a government of experts opposed to the whims of the majorities, which makes a liberal dictatorship preferable to an illiberal democracy. As we have pointed out, Perrin considers that in many cases this is due to the socio-cultural background of its promoters, where the defense of neoliberal freedom ends up being the most presentable face of a reactionary, authoritarian and sometimes racist way of thinking. As Biebricher points out, the link between neoliberalism and authoritarianism arises to a large extent from the theoretical assumptions of neoliberalism itself, where the conditions of actually existing democracy are described in such a way that "neoliberal thought inadvertently comes to yearn for authoritarian political actors who paint themselves as destroyers of the established status quo. Only they can cut the Gordian knot of mass democracy and dissolve the iron triangles that enchain any kind of transformational dynamic for the better" (Biebricher, 2020, p. 14).

In fact, for a long time it was thought that it was not possible to conduct a neoliberal transformation without resorting to political repression and authoritarianism. However, when we speak of authoritarian neoliberalism, we refer not only to the forms of state authoritarianism that were necessary to implement neoliberal policies in different geographies, but also to the violent mode of operation of the neoliberal apparatuses in the transformation of the modes of management of everyday life. In that sense, Ryan (2018) notes that research on authoritarian neoliberalism can focus both on the intertwining of authoritarian statism and neoliberal reforms and on processes of neoliberalization occurring in key social spaces for capitalism such as homes, workplaces, urban spaces, etc. The latter also takes place in democratic regimes, whose practices seek to further protect the spaces and circuits of capitalist accumulation (Ryan, 2018, p. 8) In this sense, it seeks to mark different modalities of subordination of society to the increasingly demanding imperatives of capital accumulation through neoliberal mechanisms of governance and disciplining behaviors.

In this framework, when we speak of authoritarian neoliberalism, we must distinguish at least three dimensions.

a. A historical period after the 2007 crisis that ends with what would be the hegemonic and consensual moment of neoliberalism and that we defined above as punitive neoliberalism (Davies, 2016). Moment that, in turn, is inscribed in a deeper logic of implementation of neoliberal policies (Ryan, 2018) that recall its own birth or combative stage (Davies, 2016).

b. The authoritarianism inherent to neoliberal rationality itself and its vocation to produce a society of enterprise units in competition with each other, which exacerbates pre-existing inequalities, intersubjective violence, and the need for state coercion.

c. A current within the "reactionary international" following the 2007 crisis, and in particular an important part of the new radical right.

4.1.1 The concept of authoritarian neoliberalism

Drawing on the notions of authoritarian statism outlined by Nicos Poulantzas in the 1970s and of authoritarian populism used by Stuart Hall to characterize Thatcher's policies, Ian Bruff (2013) envisioned the emergence of an authoritarian neoliberalism, which has its roots in "the reconfiguring of the state into a less democratic entity through constitutional and legal changes that seek to insulate it from social and political conflict". (Bruff, 2013, p. 113) After the 2007–2008 crisis, and in the absence of alternative proposals from the center-left, permanent austerity policies, which had already shown their devastating effects in Latin America and Africa, were imposed without difficulty in Europe, even at a time when neoliberalism was strongly discredited intellectually. In this sense, Bruff (2013, p. 15) argues that post-crisis policies, with their changes in legality and criminality, no longer seek to build hegemony and that, in this framework, they are not apt to win the consensus of the governed. Legal and constitutional changes seek to reform the purpose of the state and associated institutions in the name of economic necessity, appealing to material circumstances as a reason for the state's inability to reverse processes such as economic inequality and dislocation and to recalibrate the kinds of activities that are appropriate for its involvement. (Bruff, 2013, pp. 115–116)

Indeed, once the idea that "there is no alternative" becomes commonsensical, the dominant groups no longer seek to neutralize the resistance of the governed through concessions, but favor the exclusion of subordinate social groups, through changes in legality that neutralize the scope of democratic institutions and through practices that seek to marginalize, discipline and control dissident social groups. In this context, it is worth mentioning the centralization of power in the executive power at the expense of popular participation, the repression of oppositional forces, the restructuring of the redistributive mechanisms of the state and the transfer of the costs of the crisis to households. (Bruff & Tansel, 2019, p. 4)

As we can see, the notion of *authoritarian neoliberalism*, like that of *punitive neoliberalism* elaborated by Davies (2016), does not necessarily refer to a particular political form but to the exercise of political power by various governments worldwide since long before the advent of Trump or Bolsonaro. In fact, Bruff finds antecedents of authoritarian neoliberalism in 1970s England, where a narrative of crisis emerges from a radical populist right that opposes the people to the unions and the nation to the class. In that framework,

> [...] rhetorical attacks on the "welfare dependency culture" and the "overloaded state"—combined with appeals for greater self-reliance and family values—resonated with parts of the population that would otherwise lose out under a Thatcherite government. This building of a populist, "moral" common sense made it possible for Thatcher to appear to be with the people and against the state and its intrusions/failings, despite the fact that moves against welfare and organized labor would inevitably lead to the reorganization of class power along considerably more unequal lines, with only a minority of "the people" benefiting. (2013, pp. 117–118)

While Thatcherite rhetoric is anti-statist, a strong state is needed for the moral, economic, political, and punitive reform implied by its appeal to traditional values and moral panic. This was evidenced in a law-and-order discourse that demanded "more policing, tougher sentencing, better family discipline"—all of which are still part of the mantra of a "new" radical right. The notion of authoritarian populism thus refers to a shift from above to authoritarianism, "pioneered by, harnessed to, and to some extent legitimated by a populist groundswell below" (Hall, 1985 apud Bruff, 2013, p. 118).

> Now, if already in the 1970s the scapegoats were the trade unions and the welfare state, with the 2008 crisis the intensification of neoliberalism goes hand in hand with a shift of blame from financial institutions to individuals and states, for allowing the excesses of the financial sector, which implied that they should bear the burden of putting capital-

ism back on track. For example, welfare programs were accused of embodying "the same morally questionable values that the state allowed to develop in the financial sector", and to remove such "poison", "a whole host of highly regressive changes and developments have been pursued and enforced: sustained falls in real income; attacks on public sector pensions, unions, and workers; drastic cuts in welfare spending; and the accelerated dismantling of the "nonmarket" core of public services, all as part of the overall "necessary" act of cleansing" (Bruff, 2013, p. 122).

These moralizing narratives have been accompanied by the drive to subordinate the state to constitutional and legal rules that are deemed necessary to achieve prosperity and that make neoliberal policy measures such as fiscal austerity achieved through cuts in the provision of public goods mandatory. This logic is as valid for Europe as it is for the United States or Brazil, especially with the government of Michel Temer, who, after staging a parliamentary *coup* against Dilma Rousseff, succeeded in reforming the constitution to freeze public spending for twenty years. This line was later followed by Jair Bolsonaro, who left the economy in the hands of the Chicago boy Paulo Guedes and who, faced with the covid-19 pandemic, which he minimized for putting the economy at risk, called in November 2020 to "stop being a country of faggots" (Reuters, 2020). In the same vein, in 2011 Spain constitutionalizes austerity and budgetary priority to debt repayment, even though its debt ratio was not so high, and the following year the same happens in Italy and Austria. In the European case, this becomes more emphatic with sanctions against members that do not meet fiscal targets and the alignment of tax and fiscal policies supervised by the Troika, with little or no democratic participation of the citizens concerned. Of course, the most emblematic case is the Greek one, where several administrations were forced to resign for not being able to comply with the measures imposed by the Troika, reaching its climax with the referendum called by the Syriza government that had no effect on the decision of the European bureaucrats. (Alliez & Lazzarato, 2016; Davies, 2016).

Now, although the concept of authoritarian neoliberalism attempts to distinguish it from previous forms of authoritarianism and neoliberalism, the differences of this stage with what we have analyzed as combative and hegemonic stage should not be exaggerated, since in these it was also necessary to deploy significant doses of violence to liberalize society.

4.1.2 The authoritarianism inherent to neoliberal rationality

After carrying out one of the most exhaustive genealogies of neoliberal governmental rationality, Pierre Dardot and Christian Laval analyze current neoliberalism, studying the characteristics of the neoliberal *homo economicus* and the disciplinary and violent modalities by which it is produced. In addition to showing that neoliberal rationality has been anti-democratic from its beginnings, in the last five years they have observed that current neoliberalism is undermining the rule of law itself. However, as we have already pointed out, the authors stress that this authoritarian character of neoliberalism should not be confused with the rise of the new far right, which in any case is a drift enabled by it.

For Dardot and Laval, current neoliberalism, as a system of power that governs our lives, secretes a political form that combines anti-democratic authoritarianism, economic nationalism, and expanded capitalist rationality (Dardot et al., 2021). Such a situation derives from a crisis of liberal-social democracy produced after four decades of neoliberalization that led the losers of the competitive order to take refuge in a far right that has been able to echo this resentment. Taking advantage of this situation and the crisis of liberal-social democracy that it has provoked and continues to aggravate, the new neoliberalism radicalizes the war against the population and the domination of capital over society.

While it is true that leaders like Emmanuel Macron, Angela Merkel and Justin Trudeau, have continued to defend, at least verbally, human rights, division of powers, tolerance and equality before the law that the radical right openly questions, Macron himself, who claims to be the defender of liberal democracy and the republic against the threat of *Rassemblement National*, has not hesitated to implement a strongly repressive "corporate Bonapartism". In this sense, the economic and police war waged by neoliberalism against liberal-social democracy does not occur within the framework of a permanent state of exception (Agamben, 2003), but begins to form part of the new state of legality (Harcourt, 2018), emptying democracy and the rule of law from within. (Dardot & Laval, 2016)

From such emptying, and from the discontent generated by recurrent crises and their neoliberal solutions—and the absence of a leftist alternative (Bruff, 2013)—a radical right gains strength, which does not hesitate to appeal to the hatred of the immigrant, the poor, women, transgender people, etc. as a way to mobilize the electorate and to impose its ideology.

4.1.3 New radical right, authoritarianism, and neoliberalism

In recent years, there has been a debate about the new far-right parties and their electoral growth within the framework of authoritarian neoliberalism (4.a). In this sense, it is worth differentiating the traditional conservative and liberal right-wing, which continue to represent the political-electoral mainstream, from the *far-right* (Mudde, 2019; Acha, 2021), and, within this heterogeneous group, the *extreme right* from the *radical right*. Indeed, neo-fascist movements, nostalgic for the interwar period, who support biologistic racism and are prone to expelling foreigners from their countries, remain marginal. However, today a *radical right* is on the rise, combining nationalism, nativism, authoritarianism, xenophobia, culturalized racism, misogyny, etc. but without glorifying the fascist past or claiming to expel foreigners, except illegal ones (García Olascoaga, 2018).

In this sense, Cas Mudde explains that in the twenty-first century we are witnessing not so much a new wave of neo-fascism, but rather a new wave of "the mainstreaming and normalization of the far right in general, and the populist radical right in particular" (Mudde, 2019).[1] Indeed, what only three or four decades ago was a cause for scandal and protest mobilizations—such as the appearance in Europe of leaders or parties with a xenophobic or anti-immigration discourse—today is not only gaining support, but also beginning to form part of the agenda of the traditional center-right parties.[2] As sociocultural issues and identity politics become more and more central, the radical right gains more political power and the ability to set the public agenda and to shift the frontier of the sayable and the practicable. In this context, nativist, xenophobic, misogynist, and authoritarian discourse becomes commonplace.[3] In this sense, Mudde (2019) argues that if the extreme right is a *normal pathology* of liberal democracies—a pre-modern phenomenon of a minority disconnected from reality—the centrality of the radical populist right is a *pathological normalcy*, insofar as it represents an authoritarian radicalization of the values of the prevailing political system.

According to Mudde, unlike the extreme right, which rejects popular sovereignty and political pluralism, the radical right accepts democracy, although it opposes central aspects of liberal democracy such as the rights of minorities,

---

1 Mudde (2019) traces three previous waves of post-war far-right to analyze the fourth wave that would have begun with the new century. These would be neo-fascism (1945–1955), right-wing populism (1955–1980), and the radical right (1980–2000).

2 A well-known example is the Austrian FPÖ. In 1999, under Haider's leadership, it won 27% of the vote in the parliamentary elections and was then incorporated into the government. In response, there were demonstrations and an international boycott. In 2018, that party returned to the government without generating any protest. (Mudde, 2019)

3 The open vindication of fascist dictatorships or state terrorism in the public space is a clear example of this. From Abascal in Spain, Bolsonaro in Brazil, Trump in the USA, Kast in Chile, to the libertarians in Argentina. This rupture with the "Nunca Más" consensus was recently seen with the act of swearing in of the libertarian c Victoria Villarruel in Argentina, who in her speech denies the existence of state terrorism and treats the victims of it as terrorists.

the rule of law or the separation of powers. This radical right is often populist in the sense of proposing itself as a genuine expression of the people in the face of corrupt elites (both political and economic), who—according to this discourse—only seek their own benefit and corrupt the nation with their postmodern, progressive ideas or their "cultural Marxism". (Mudde, 2019)[4] At the same time, it tends to advocate an *ethnocracy*, closing borders to immigrants and accepting only those resident aliens who manage to assimilate culturally. This gives rise in Europe and the United States to a strong Islamophobia, since for these new rightists Muslims want to destroy Western culture and replace the white and christian population. This xenophobia is reinforced by an obsession with security, the absence of which is associated with the presence of foreigners—who are accused of being criminals—and multiculturalism. This obsession with security—and the correlative punitivism, with tougher laws and higher incarceration rates —has not stopped growing even though in most Western countries the crime rate has fallen, in what Didier Fassin (2018) has called the *punitive moment*. In terms of foreign policy, the far-right distrusts supranational organizations, such as the UN or the EU, accusing the "globalist elites" of disregarding the sovereignty of nations (see below, chapter 5). Likewise, religion plays a fundamental role in many of these groups, as another way of separating 'us' from 'them' and of rescuing the true values of the nation in the face of discourses that question the hierarchies of gender, ethnicity, or nation. In that sense, Mudde points out that these movements are authoritarian to the extent that for them even personal problems are perceived as "essentially law-and-order issues which can only be countered by a tough punitive approach and prevented by reintroducing "moral" or "traditional" education in schools". (Mudde, 2019, "Ideology").

This new authoritarian wave is also addressed from a biographical, analytical, and journalistic approach by Anne Applebaum. The author highlights the transformation of what the right-wing was in 1999—conservative Atlanticist liberalism favorable to globalization—and the difference with what is happening twenty years later, in societies absolutely polarized by these new forms of authoritarian, xenophobic and reactionary nationalism and where the radical right is becoming central. The author especially analyzes the trajectories of several leaders, journalists, and intellectuals, many of them personally known to her, who, coming from intellectual circles of that liberal-conservative elite, have ended up promoting the authoritarianisms currently prevailing in Poland

---

4 For his part, Biebricher (2020) points out that the notion of authoritarianism captures what "right-wing populism" really is and does not give it the semi-democratic credentials of the term populism.

and Hungary, as well as Brexit. At the same time, Applebaum links these experiences with the threat posed by other current far-right movements to liberal democracy.

Indeed, the Law and Justice (Poland) and Fidesz (Hungary) governments have shifted from liberal conservatism to the radical populist right. In the process, they have destroyed the division of powers, an independent judiciary and press, a professional civil service and non-party aligned cultural and educational institutions, and the possibility of expression of political dissent. Despite the limited real influence of those who form their field of adversity, they have promoted Islamophobia, anti-Semitism and the fight against the left and the LGBTQI movement.[5] All this is legitimized through conspiracy theories, fake news, hate speeches and memes which recall the American alt-right. This movements seek to rewrite the past to modify the future—through what the author calls *restorative nostalgia*[6]—and have been building a parallel reality in which many of its promoters and followers feel more comfortable.

Applebaum stresses that, to explain the success of authoritarianisms, it is necessary that part of the intellectual, political, cultural and media elite help to build the legitimacy of those leaderships, and that is what is happening today in different geographies. In any case, for Applebaum, the new right-wing is not conservative but revolutionary, to the extent that it wants to: "overthrow, bypass, or undermine existing institutions, to destroy what exists." (Applebaum, 2020, p. 20)

Now, although the political centrality of socio-cultural aspects has given impetus to the various far-right currents, there are programmatic differences within this universe in the socio-economic field. Within this framework, we can distinguish between a sector that questions elements of global neoliberal capitalism—but does not modify them when it has the opportunity, as in the case of Fidesz—and a radical ultra-liberal right. In this sense, Clara Ramas San Miguel distinguishes between authoritarian-neoliberals and social-identitarian right-wingers. The former would be heirs of Anglo-Saxon neoliberalism and combine

---

5 In fact, empirical studies show that on many occasions anti-immigration parties obtain more votes in places where immigrants are not abundant. (Acha, 2021)

6 Applebaum points out that, unlike *"reflective"* nostalgics, restorative nostalgics seek not only to remember and learn from the past but to reinstate it, constructing myths that are functional to new nationalist projects. The mythologizing of a pure national identity or a seamless community is part of this kind of nostalgia, as is the conspiratorial accusation of others—immigrants, elites, supranational organizations—that through their attacks reduced the nation to a shadow of its former self. (Applebaum, 2020, p. 58)

[...] a fierce defense of the free market and the development of unrestrained capitalism, with reactionary moral values. It is thus the sum of two vectors. Firstly, ultra-liberal economic positions: deregulation, the rule of meritocracy, a deep-rooted hatred of the poor, tax cuts, dismantling of the social state, extreme individualism. On the other hand, reactionary positions in the moral sphere: return to traditional values, recovery of religion in its most fundamentalist versions, as the governing body of society, total reform of customs, hostile positions towards immigration and minorities, hatred of feminism, rejection of abortion and the LGBT movement. (Ramas San Miguel, 2019, p. 72, my emphasis)

This current has as "implicit or explicit" referents Thatcher, the Tea Party, the evangelical church, Christian fundamentalist lobbies and Steve Bannon as an organic intellectual. They are politically represented by Bolsonaro and Trump in the Americas, and by Vox in Spain, the Freedom Party of Austria (FPÖ), the Dutch Party of Freedom (PVV), etc. in Europe. (Ramas San Miguel, 2019, p. 72) This conservative current finds its sources in the 1970s in the United States, in reaction to a set of social movements—student protests, counterculture, Black movement, feminism, environmentalism—and certain government social policies to alleviate poverty (Ramas San Miguel, 2019, p. 72; see also Cooper, 2017).

However, these new right-wingers do not form a homogeneous group. For example, in the United States, the alternative right has been developing with an extremist discourse on social networks, and gamers' communities, using memes, a millennial aesthetic, etc.[7] In Europe, on the other hand, this trend is closer to traditional conservatism. In any case, these currents combine anti-communism, free market fundamentalism and social reactionaryism. (Ramas San Miguel, 2019, p. 74) They were very important to produce the victory of Trump and Brexit, finding their antecedents in Thatcher's criticisms of the European Union (see below, cap. 5).[8]

The second group would be formed by the social identitarians (Ramas San Miguel, 2019) who incorporate elements of traditional anti-modern and anti-liberal conservatism mixed with some traditional demands of the left, such as the defense of Welfare and redistributive policies for those who have suffered the consequences of economic adjustments, as long as they are considered legitimate national citizens—which excludes immigrants. They also tend to criticize

---

7 The alt-right can be defined as a heterogeneous set of far-right currents—white nationalists, paleolibertarians, neo-Nazis, etc.—that has an anti-establishment discourse and is very active on the internet (Stefanoni, 2021). They are characterized by the belief that "white identity" is under attack by multicultural forces that use "political correctness" and "social justice" to undermine the white population and "their" civilization (Mudde, 2019).

8 However, Applebaum (2020) believes that Thatcher would never have supported Brexit, as Britain played a key role in the European common market.

the economic and monetary policies of the European Union and defend environmentalism as a way of preserving traditional ways of life in the face of modernizing and predatory capitalism, but also in the face of the demographic growth of non-European populations, even going as far as to promote *eco-fascism* (Stefanoni, 2021).

Basically, it could be said that these currents, while raising a critique of the financialized global economy, on the other hand, like the national-liberals, do not address the root causes of the economic crisis and social unrest, but seek to use immigrants as a scapegoat. To this end, some propose openly xenophobic discourses and practices (Alternative for Germany (AfD), Golden Dawn, etc.) and others criticize globalization for expelling people from their homelands and ways of life. There can also be a mixture of both, as in Matteo Salvini's discourse, where such defense is used as a pretext to prevent the entry of immigrants.

As for their intellectuals of reference, while the national-liberals found inspiration in the impulse and strategies of Steve Bannon, a key player in Trump's victory and advisor to various right-wing populists, the social-identitarians are inspired by the Russian Alexandr Dugin, the French Alain de Benoist, respectively founders of national-Bolshevism and of the French *Nouvelle Droite* or the Italian philosopher Diego Fusaro.[9] Precisely Dugin, the philosopher of *The Fourth Political Theory*, largely inspired by the philosophy of the conservative revolution, considers that liberalism is today economically right-wing and morally left-wing. In a 2018 interview he maintains that globalization combines abortion, progressivism, and big capital, while the populism he promotes is the opposite:

> economically to the left, coupled with traditional conservative values. These two aspects have been abandoned by liberals. In Modernity, the left was cultural progressivism coupled with social justice, and the right was traditionalism and free markets. With today's liberalism, the traditionalist part and social justice are abandoned and demonized. The establishment does not recognize the traditional right of values, which it demonizes as fascism; nor does it recognize the struggle for social justice, which it demonizes as Stalinism. Populism must unite the right of values with socialism, social justice, and anti-capitalism. This is the position of my Fourth Political Theory, of my proposal of "integral populism". (Dugin, 2018, apud Ramas San Miguel, 2019, p. 77).

---

9 The French "new right" emerges as a neo-fascist movement but then adopts the idea of a struggle for cultural hegemony and proposes itself as a meta-political discourse, distancing itself from party politics. Its xenophobic ideas are based on a "right to difference", which defends the European peoples from being subsumed under a logic of population replacement and from being acculturated by global multiculturalism. (García Olascoaga, 2018) As Mudde points out, the ethnopluralism of this current is a central element of the majority of the relevant right-wing formations in Europe today (2021).

In that sense, the Russian saw in the alliance between the *Movimento Cinque Stelle* (Five Stars Movement) and the *Lega* an attempt at integral populism, as it brought together the moral right-wing with the social left-wing. In contrast, Trump and Bolsonaro are considered part of the neoliberal right-wing. Indeed, Trump mounted his campaign on unease with globalist elites, whom he accused of having "spent billions helping other countries—notably China—get rich. Protectionist tariffs, a border wall and a massive infrastructure programme would make America great again" (Riley, 2018, p. 21) However, as we said, most of Trump's policies sought to realize conservative goals (Riley, 2018) and benefited the wealthiest, especially with the largest tax cut to this sector since the Reagan era.

In this example, nationalist rhetoric and the appeal to reactionary cultural and moral values are subordinated to the accumulation of capital, regardless of environmental and human consequences, as demonstrated by the treatment of the covid-19 pandemic by leaders like Trump and Bolsonaro, or of the *laissez faire* in the face of the fires in the Amazon by the latter, even going so far as to generate a diplomatic conflict with France and Germany. Indeed, neither authoritarian neoliberals nor social-identitarians propose alternatives to the neoliberal power system, but reaffirm it. At the same time, both share their authoritarian, nationalist, xenophobic and misogynist vocation. In this framework, after decades of neoliberal globalization that has produced an unprecedented deterritorialization and precariousness, the defense of the nation is once again transformed into a way of responding to social conflicts. Instead of changing the rules of the game that produce ever greater poverty and inequality, the aim is to redistribute these inequalities. In this framework, the immigrant becomes the scapegoat to be sacrificed in exchange for restoring wage, racial and patriarchal privileges.

4.2 By way of conclusion

Throughout this chapter we have analyzed different dimensions of the notion of authoritarian neoliberalism. Recovering the strategic nature of neoliberal rationality, we have pointed out that the belligerent and authoritarian aspects of neoliberalism are far from being a novelty produced by the latest financial crises. Firstly, because from their own intellectual and political origins neoliberals were characterized by their opposition to democracy, in a crusade against Keynesianism, communism, the welfare state and economic planning to which the tyranny of the majorities would inevitably lead. In this framework, they considered that certain nations and peoples were not able to govern themselves and that market society requires a strong and often authoritarian state. Secondly, because, once in power, they did not hesitate to endorse the violent repression of opposition forces as a step towards the reform of society, going as far as to participate in state terrorism, as happened in the Southern Cone. Indeed, to produce the subject governed by neoliberal rationality as *homo economicus* and *entrepreneur of the self*, he had first to be defeated (Lazzarato, 2021) and then indebted, impoverished and precarized.

In this framework, despite the centrality of the South American experiment, we were careful not to consider authoritarian neoliberalism as a characterization of a watertight historical period or of a geographically delimited reality. This notion refers not only to authoritarian forms of statehood that have imposed neoliberal policies, but also to the use of repressive forces and legal rules by the liberal democracies of developed countries themselves, to reform different social spaces under a neoliberal norm, without seeking the consensus of the governed. Therefore, more than a type of political regime, the notion of authoritarian neoliberalism refers us to a series of practices that only reinforce the authoritarianism inherent to neoliberal rationality itself. This is what we call, in the concluding chapter, *neoliberalism reloaded*.

In this sense, we have argued that authoritarian neoliberalism should not be confused with a kind of neo-fascism, insofar as it is the very rationality of neoliberalism that contains authoritarian elements. This is as true for those who present themselves as bastions of liberal democracy and multiculturalism as it is for those who promote an openly reactionary policy in their attack on immigrants, gender dissidents, welfare state aid recipients and racialized subjects.

Therefore, we have situated the rise of the new right and new forms of political authoritarianism in the authoritarian evolution of neoliberalism itself, distinguishing a social-identitarian right, less influential at the global level and more critical of neoliberal globalization, from an authoritarian neoliberal current, which aims to push the domination of capital over every aspect of our lives even further, while combating immigrants, racialized subjects, the LGBTQI movement and even rational argumentation and Western science. In the following chapter we will dwell more specifically on these currents, proposing a brief genealogy of current right-wing populisms.

5 Towards a genealogy of contemporary right-wing populism. An approach to the national-(neo)liberal trend in Europe and the United States

As we have argued in previous chapters, the proliferation of the radical right and the authoritarian evolution of neoliberalism find an important antecedent in the violent origins of neoliberalism in the 1970s and 1980s in Latin America as well as in England and the United States (chapter 3). However, the mainstreaming and rise of the radical populist right (Mudde, 2019), which has been taking place during the last two decades in Europe, the United States and Latin America, has intensified after the successive crises following the 2008 financial crisis (chapter 4).

Since the term populism is often attacked for its vagueness and indeterminacy (Laclau, 2005) and for being controversial and denunciatory (Mudde, 2017), it is necessary to make some clarifications before analyzing right-wing populisms. Following Laclau, we consider populism as a political construction of the people that takes place in a socio-discursive space traversed by antagonism and the struggle for hegemony. The populist moment takes place when a *chain of equivalences* is formed between different social demands that are articulated around an empty signifier, and where one of these identities can precariously represent the name of a communitarian plenitude that is necessarily absent (Laclau, 2005). From this point of view, populism does not refer to a particular political content but to a form of politics. However, in order to approach our problem, this ontological definition of populism must be completed with a socio-political view. In this sense, Mudde and Rovira Kaltwasser define populism as "a thin-centered ideology that considers society to be ultimately separated into two homogeneous and antagonistic camps, "the pure people" versus "the corrupt elite", and which argues that politics should be an expression of the volonté générale (general will) of the people" (Mudde & Rovira Kaltwasser, 2017, p. 6).

According to Hans-Georg Betz:

> Populism is a political doctrine that holds that society is divided into two antagonistic blocs: the vast majority of ordinary people and a relatively small elite that acts in its own interest. Populism is essentially about mobilising ordinary citizens—the "low"—around a common set of grievances and resentments that provide them with a shared notion of identity and pit them against "those above" held responsible for all their grievances (Betz, 2021, p. 10).

https://doi.org/10.1515/9783110723939-007

This means that populism is always associated with other types of ideologies, such as liberalism, socialism or fascism. However, what gives it its specificity is that it differs from pluralism and elitism. For populism, the people (whether as sovereign, as nation or as common people) are opposed to the elite. This labile and ambivalent character means that there can be both left-wing and right-wing populisms (Laclau, 2005; Mudde, 2017). In this sense, María Esperanza Casullo points out that if left-wing populism combines a personalist leadership and a mythical and antagonistic discourse with policies focused on economic redistribution "downwards",

> right-wing populism maintains a very similar strategy combined with "upward" distributive policies, to which it adds a strong emphasis on the need to maintain certain social hierarchies it considers "natural" and a xenophobic obsession with defending the boundaries of the political community against factors designated as contaminating the purity of the "true people" (among them, immigration of all kinds, Islamic religion, African-American or Afro-European population, gypsy population, feminists, people with diverse sexual orientation and gender identity). (Casullo, 2019, pp. 129–130)

In this sense, if left-wing populism is binary, by opposing the people to the elite, right-wing populism is triadic, in that it defends the people against the elite, accused of defending, in turn, a third group made up of immigrants, feminists, etc. (Judis, 2018). In this framework, we will characterize the *radical populist right* or *right-wing populism* as a political current that conceives and tries to mobilize the people against the elites who are considered as corrupt, foreigners, destroyers of harmony and community pride. They are accused of being progressive or leftists, given that they would support social policies against owners and entrepreneurs and in favor of the lazy people and immigrants. At the same time, they would finance abortion and "gender ideology", conspiring against the values of the nation and even favoring population replacement where immigrants would come to displace the authentic citizens of the nation (Camus, 2002). In this way, right-wing populisms promote a solidarity exclusively directed at members of their own *ethnos*, which is generally the most privileged in society. In this sense, Mudde argues that political parties of this tendency gained relevance in Europe since the 1990s and are characterized by combining populism with authoritarianism and nativism. While authoritarianism

> refers to the belief in a strictly ordered society, and is expressed in an emphasis on "law and order" issues, the latter alludes to the notion that states should be inhabited exclusively by members of the native group ("the nation") and that non-native ("alien") elements are fundamentally threatening to the homogenous nation-state. Hence, the xenophobic nature of current European populism derives from a very specific conception of the nation, which relies on an ethnic and chauvinistic definition of the people (Mudde, 2017, p. 34).

As I have pointed out in the previous chapter, a distinction is usually made within the radical right between national-liberals and social-identitarians (Ramas San Miguel, 2019). Here I will focus especially on the first group, which is the most influential on a global scale. In this framework, I seek to identify two foundational moments of national-neoliberal right-wing populism in England and the United States. One has to do with Thatcher's authoritarian populism (Hall, 1985) and her critique of the EU and globalism in favor of a Europe of corporations and nations. The other refers to the confluence in the United States of libertarian and paleoconservative currents in their criticism of big government and liberal elites that promote multiculturalism and social justice. In this framework, we will briefly refer to the "paleo alliance", led by Buchanan and Rothbard in the 1990s, also stressing the differences between both currents. Finally, we show certain continuities between *paleolibertarianism, paleoconservatism* and the current extreme *alternative right.*

5.1 From Euroscepticism to Brexit

In recent years, several genealogies of national-neoliberalism show the connections between the current radical right-wing populist parties in Europe and the position expressed by Thatcher in the late 1980s, for whom the European Union should respect national traditions and the nation should be a key element for economic globalization.

How can we understand this anti-globalist stance in a staunch defender of the free market? How can we interpret her attacks on an institution such as the EU, which is often perceived as a bastion of neoliberalism, especially in its ordoliberal variant? In this regard, Quinn Slobodian and Dieter Plehwe warn that, although the results of the European Union have been clearly neoliberal, it cannot be characterized as an entirely neoliberal project either. In fact, as we shall see, a number of neoliberal intellectuals, think tanks and political entrepreneurs have been critical of the EU. In that sense, while the left tends to regard the EU as a neoliberal artifact, many neoliberals have criticized it as a framework for socialist expansion. (Slobodian & Plehwe, 2019, p. 90) Thus, in the '90s, different neoliberal groups formed Eurosceptic think tanks such as the Club of Bruges (1989), the European Constitutional Group (1992) and the Center for the New Europe (1993). They also organized the European Forum for Science and Environment, against the Union's environmental policies. Within this framework, Slobodian and Plehwe mark a progressive alienation of these currents from the EU. While they considered European federalism to be left leaning, in the early 1990s the neoliberal Eurosceptics believed that the European institutions could be reformed to favor their vision of free trade, full mobility of capital and services, and competition between currencies. This changed after the Maastricht Treaty (1992) and the resolution to introduce the Euro (1999). In that framework, many neoliberal Eurosceptics began to ally with nationalist parties and movements and even to promote secession from the European Union. This national-neoliberal alliance is finally galvanized by the bailout operations following the 2008 debt crisis and the arrival of one million migrants to Central Europe in 2015. Allying with anti-immigrant political forces, the neoliberal Eurosceptics gave shape to a hybrid of libertarianism and anti-immigrant xenophobia, as is the case of Alternative for Germany (AfD), UKIP, Vox or the Austrian Freedom Party.

As we said, this nationalist and neoliberal right wing contains transnational, and post-national dimensions (Solobodian & Plehwe, 2019, p. 91) and finds a decisive antecedent in the formation of the Bruges group, inspired, in turn, by the speech delivered by the then British Premier Margaret Thatcher at the College of Europe. In her speech, Thatcher recovers the British cultural legacy as part of Europe, the Roman heritage, the rule of law and Christianity "with its recognition of the unique and spiritual nature of the individual, on that idea, we still base our belief in personal liberty and other human rights". She establishes as the first guiding principle for a successful European Community the "willing and active cooperation between independent sovereign states" without suppressing national identities (Thatcher, 1988). This requires work among nations and not a centralized power in Brussels. In this context, implicitly criticizing the positions of Jacques Delors, then president of the European Commission, Thatcher pointed out that while the Soviet Union was learning to decentralize, some in Europe wanted to move towards centralization and the creation of a superstate. Hence the best-known phrase from that speech: "We have not successfully rolled back the frontiers of the state in Britain, only to see them re-imposed at a European level with a European super-state exercising a new dominance from Brussels" (Thatcher, 1988). Secondly, the Iron Lady raises the need to address European problems in a practical way and criticizes the Common Agricultural Policy. Thirdly, she promotes policies that encourage enterprise, opposing personal initiative, deregulation, and the elimination of trade barriers to planning and control. She also advocates financial and labor deregulation and the free movement of goods and capital, but not of people, to prevent the entry of drugs, terrorists, and illegal immigrants. Finally, she highlights the role of NATO, Atlanticism and the conception of Europe as a family of nations.

On the one hand, Thatcher's policy and discourse in reference to the EU can be inscribed in a traditional Euroscepticism in the United Kingdom, whose integration into the European Union was late, partial and full of controversies (for example, Great Britain did not adhere to the Schengen Treaty or the Euro). Hence, the Bruges speech is seen as a precursor of UKIP and Brexit. On the other hand, Thatcher's speech affirms the unconditional attachment to free trade, free enterprise and open markets and condemns the "protectionism" and "bureaucracy" of the socializing elites in Brussels. (Sauvêtre, 2019).

In this sense, Thatcher opposes the idea of Europe with the greatest possible freedom of enterprise to the socialist Europe of centralized control and regulation. On the other hand, she opposes the legitimacy of British democracy, with its long and unique history, to a bureaucratic European superstate. At the same time, she opposes an abstract European identity to national identity and argues in favor of Europe as a family of nations. For Thatcher, far from being threatened by economic globalization, nations are a platform for the constitution of global markets. On the contrary, the bureaucratic and socializing superstatism of the European Union threatens both economic freedom and national identities. This would be extensible to all supranational entities controlled by global elites. Thus, entering the 1990s, what Sauvêtre (2019) calls national-(neo)liberalism is outlined.

As we anticipated, this discourse proved foundational for the constitution of the Bruges Group, the first neoliberal Eurosceptic think tank, led by Ralph Harris, former director of the Institute of Economic Affairs and the Mont-Pèlerin Society and declared Baron of High Cross by Thatcher (Slobodian & Plehwe, 2019). This group called for a Europe of nations, with a strong but small state, promoting competition and free markets.

Regarding monetary union, a cleavage was established between neoliberals who thought that supranational governance was necessary to defend the economic order and those who felt that this order should be anchored in national states. The disagreement between the two concerned whether the most effective place for monetary management is a European Central Bank or national central banks. In any case, if at the beginning of the 1990s this group was inclined towards an internal reform of Europe, in the second half of the decade they began to point out the need for Great Britain to leave the Union.

The Bruges group was opposed by the European Constitutional Group, which was also made up of members of the Mont-Pèlerin Society. While it was critical of nationalist positions, it also advocated a Europe with less power and a Constitution allowing the right of secession. While this group advocated internal reform, the Bruges group was moving towards a rejection of the EU. A 1996 paper by Brian Hindley, one of its directors, dismissed that Britain leaving the EU would have devastating consequences. The following year, the UK Libertarian Alliance argued that, faced with the unreformable statism of the EU, the only option was to leave the Union.

Another important milestone in this regard is the founding of the Center for a New Europe in 1993. It establishes itself as a base for the Eurosceptic stance in Brussels, emphasizing the need to return to a Europe that promotes competition and avoids regulation and centralization. At the same time, it assumes socially and culturally conservative positions, affirming the ethical substance of a community in the face of relativism and nihilism. In this way, the CNE seeks to resemble U.S. think tanks such as the Heritage Foundation and the American Enterprise Institute, which combined free market issues and traditional morality. In this environment, theories are developed according to which the relaxation of sexual morality is detrimental to the development of the free market, while homeschooling and anti-abortion positions are promoted. A part of this group is even more right-wing, approaching the paleolibertarian, paleoconservative and supremacist positions of the American alt-right (see below). Some have influence on the Vlams Blok, defending the right of secession and anti-immigrant racism, especially Islamic. (Slobodian & Plehwe, 2019)

During his tenure at the CNE, economist Hardy Bouillon became actively involved with the libertarian magazine *Eigentümlich Frei* founded in 1998, whose aim was to create an alliance between libertarians and the New Right, along the model established by Murray Rothbard in the American "paleo alliance" which—as we will see shortly—was formed during the 1990s between paleoconservatives and paleolibertarians centered at the Ludwig von Mises Institute in the United States. In addition, there was a connection between American paleolibertarians and German neoliberals through the German economist Hans-Hermann Hoppe (see above, chap. 2), a disciple of Rothbard, who defines his position as anarcho-capitalist. Through his relationship with Bouillon, he will participate in the CNE and *Eigentümlich Frei*. (Slobodian & Plehwe, 2019, p. 100)

As we can see, while the Bruges group moved towards a Eurosceptic liberal conservatism, the CNE moved towards radical right-wing libertarianism, which, in addition to its xenophobic and anti-democratic positions, questions the existence of climate change. In that sense, Slobodian and Plehwe point out that, by the first decade of the new century, the NEC was looking for a basis for an effective neoliberal populism, whose opportunity would be the Eurozone crisis (2019, p. 101). After it, the European Conservatives and Reformists Alliance was born in 2009, from which in turn would emerge a new think tank called New Direction. This group, sponsored by Thatcher until her death in 2013, argued the need to leave the EU.

As Slobodian and Plehwe point out, the new right-wing neoliberalism benefits from the dislocations of the neoliberal project itself and the inadequate protection provided by the welfare state. This current offers its own form of regressive politics, with an adherence to exclusionary social romanticism, a defense of the traditional family and competition. This is confirmed in some of the current guidelines of the Mont-Pèlerin Society. At the 2017 meeting, Václav Klaus—president of the Czech Republic between 2003 and 2013—points out that the biggest problem is *welfare-state-induced migration coupled with a postmodern ideological confusion connected with multiculturalism, cultural relativism, right-humanism, continentalism, and political correctness*. He defended European right-wing populist parties as powerless people seeking to oppose arrogant political elites and pointed out that we need to re-found thinking in the nation state. Unlike other more formalist neoliberal currents, such as those of the Chicago school, this nationalist-neoliberal position does not see the subject as a one-dimensional *homo economicus*, but grounds it in morality and emotion, in family structures and group identities which, in the European case, are being defined in opposition to the Islamic threat. (Slobodian & Plehwe, 2019, p. 104)

In this sense, Sauvêtre points out that contemporary populism—at least in this national-neoliberal version—does not seek protectionism but a stronger integration to economic globalization through the reaffirmation of the nation. Their anti-globalism consists of a defense of a globalization under the aegis of nations, purged of the "parasitism" of global elites and non-white migrants. These national-neoliberal groups are paradoxically, but without contradiction, nationalist, mundialist (*mondialistes*) and anti-globalist. (Sauvêtre, 2019)

5.2 The American path to right-wing populism. The alliance between libertarians and paleoconservatives

If Thatcher's criticisms of the EU can be identified as an antecedent of European national-neoliberalism and the right-wing populisms that sustain it, whose epitome is Brexit and the government of Boris Johnson, in the United States Trump's right-wing populism finds its antecedents in the "paleo alliance" between the libertarianism of Murray Rothbard and Llewellyn Rockwell Jr. and the paleoconservatism of Patrick Buchanan, who three decades ago opposed the neoconservative and liberal elites who—according to these currents—benefited from big government.[1] In other words, both movements are critical not only of the *liberals* and the Social Justice Warriors but also of the neoconservatives like Reagan and

---

[1] This neoliberal populism is also reflected, in its own way, in Milton Friedman's direct appeal to the common people vis-à-vis Washington politicians and bureaucrats in his TV show "Free to choose". Cfr. Brandes (2019).

Bush, whom they consider to continue with the liberal-democratic and statist heritage of the *new deal*.[2]

Indeed, paleolibertarianism is the result of the confluence of libertarian and paleoconservative currents. It combines traditional cultural and moral values with the quest for a complete privatization of social life, including justice and security forces. At the same time, it promotes a "strengthening of social institutions such as the family, churches and companies as a counterweight and alternative to state power (the true enemy of freedom)" (Stefanoni, 2021, p. 202). As Sauvêtre points out, this movement is referred to as "paleo", in reference to the Old Right prior to Woodrow Wilson and Franklin D. Roosevelt. It is nationalist, isolationist and anti-war, pro-market, pro-minimal government and opposed to federal centralism. The paleo alliance between Rothbard and Buchanan sought to challenge the neoconservatives and the system formed by big government, big business, fiscal and social programs, and military interventionism. Both currents agreed on nationalist, anti-interventionist and anti-immigration positions for the promotion of a bourgeois and Christian moral order, rejecting the legacy of civil rights, egalitarianism and all "false rights" (of women, sexual and racial minorities, affirmative action policies, etc.) seen as attacks on white property and identity. For these currents,

> [...] the old America of individual liberty, private property, and minimal government has been replaced by a coalition of politicians and bureaucrats allied with, and even dominated by, powerful corporate and Old Money financial elites (e.g. the Rockefellers, the Trilateralists); and the New Class of technocrats and intellectuals, including Ivy League academics and media elites, who constitute the opinionmolding class in society (Rothbard, 1992, p. 7).

Rothbard affirmed in 1992 the need for a right-wing populism to mobilize the American people against the government elites who exploited taxpayers.[3] It

---

2 We could draw a parallel here with the criticisms of Argentine libertarian and conservative groups to the neoliberal-conservative government of Mauricio Macri (2016–2020), which they disqualified as "yellow socialism", considering it too committed to sustaining Keynesian economic and social policies and too soft on "cultural Marxism". In fact, Rothbard is one of the main intellectual references for conservative libertarians such as Javier Milei and Agustín Laje, who—as Stefanoni (2021) points out—partake the ideological struggle in the economic and cultural fields respectively. Although the policy of welfare reduction and moral responsibility of families, debated in the 1960s and 1970s, was implemented by the governments that succeeded each other from 1980 onwards in the United States (Cooper, 2017), the excessive public spending linked in many cases to American military interventionism is a point criticized by libertarians, and was even criticized by Hayek during the Cold War.

3 On the contrary, for Rothbard (1992, p. 6), a left-wing populism would be equivalent to the prevailing system: "Leftwing populism: rousing the masses to attack "the rich", amounts to

was no longer a matter of proposing change from above but of appealing directly to the masses against the political, media, bureaucratic, and intellectual elites who were "plundering" them. As Brown (2019) and Cooper (2021) point out, to ignite the flame of far-right populism it was necessary to spread the conviction that the *angry white men* had been stripped of something that rightfully belonged to them. Unlike the Cato Institute, which targeted the elite, the paleolibertarians decided to target the "rednecks" whose experience of economic uncertainty and loss of privilege had generated intense anger against the state. (Cooper, 2021) In this framework, Rothbard's program was summarized in eight points: 1) abolish taxes; 2) abolish the welfare state; 3) abolish the privileges of minority or racial groups; 4) take back the streets and crush the criminals; 5) take back the streets and "get rid of the Bums"; 6) abolish the Fed: attack the banksters; 7) America First; 8) defend family values. (Rothbard, 1992, p. 9)[4]

As Cooper points out, the paleo alliance allowed for the resolution of some logical inconsistencies that plagued the purely economic libertarianism of the younger Rothbard. Insofar as it involved the protection of private property, a free-market order needed some recognition of law and the administration of violence—for which libertarians propose private militias and courts of justice. Paleoconservatives offered libertarians a way out of the impasse by recognizing that freedom from the state implied the need for a lack of freedom in the private or social sphere, where racial and gender hierarchies must take precedence. According to paleoconservatives, libertarians had been wrong to confuse state and social authority since a free society is founded on the latter. In this sense, a distinction should be made between *natural authority* that "arises from voluntary social structures" and *unnatural authority* that is "imposed by the state" (Rockwell Jr. apud Cooper, 2021). Indeed, although it is paradoxical that a so-called libertarian current positively values hierarchical institutions such as the Church or the family, these sectors consider that libertarianism does not consist in a rejection of any form of authority—as was the case with the libertarians of the 1960s and 1970s, who were closer to the new left—but in a rejection of the state as a coercively imposed authority. The family and religion would be

---

more of the same: high taxes, wild spending, massive redistribution of working and middle class incomes to the ruling coalition of: big government, big business, and the New Class of bureaucrats, technocrats, and ideologues and their numerous dependent groups".

4 This alliance between paleolibertarians and paleoconservatives materialized in the collaboration for the electoral campaign of Patrick Buchanan. Buchanan obtained 23% in the 1992 Republican primaries, and this encouraged the independent candidacy of the populist millionaire Ross Perot. Perot obtained 19% of the votes, which otherwise would have benefited Bush, thus facilitating Bill Clinton's victory.

forms of natural authority—and therefore legitimate—from which the individual can defect if he so desires. On the other hand, if the individual leaves one state, he falls inevitably under the sovereignty of another. (Stefanoni, 2021)

In 1995, the Mises Institute held a conference on "Secession, State, and Economy" in which the libertarian principle of freedom from federal government intrusion merged with neo-Confederate demands for states' rights, racial segregation, and a literal interpretation of Christian law (Cooper, 2021). In the years that followed, the Institute would become a hothouse for paleolibertarian scholars and would exchange ideological positions and personnel with the 'alt-right' (Cooper, 2021).[5]

Although Buchanan had already shown signs of moving towards protectionism and economic nationalism, contrary to libertarian principles, in preparation for the following year's election campaign, Rothbard, shortly before his death, was still trying to influence the only candidate capable of embodying the paleo agenda, before the final break between libertarians and paleocons. In this context, he argues:

> We know what Pat should be doing: He is in a unique position to take up the reins of leading a so far inchoate and leaderless grassroots populist revolution against the egalitarian, collectivist, internationalist ruling elites. This is a revolution of white Euro-males, and Pat needs to focus on their grievances and concerns [...] Briefly: high taxes, Big Government regulation (including victimology; affirmative action, anti-human environmentalism); the welfare system and the welfare state; violent crime, including inner-city crime; gun control; foreign aid; foreign military intervention; world government and managed world trade; immigration by hordes of foreigners not assimilated into American culture; the secular attack on the Christian religion (Rothbard, 1995, p. 141)

As we can see, Rothbard's proposal is very similar to that of his European peers. The American points out that we are facing the century of populism, which consists of hatred of the establishment and the action of the masses against the elites, a discourse that will be taken up by Steve Bannon in 2016 and by the various right-wing populist movements of today, from Eastern Europe to South

---

5 As we anticipated in the previous chapter, the alt-right is a heterogeneous set of far-right currents that sustains an anti-establishment discourse and is very active on the internet (Stefanoni, 2021). In the years leading up to Trump's triumph, it gained space in the "conventional" right-wing media such as Breitbart and was on everyone's lips when it was denounced by Hillary Clinton. It includes diverse currents such as the identitarian movement, the neo-reactionaries, the Men's Rights Movement, etc. They are anti-feminist, anti-immigration, anti-Semitic and racist. They reject liberal democracy and the equal dignity of human beings and assert the need for a white, authoritarian ethno-state separate from the other races, something that contrasts with the composition of current Western states. (Summers, 2017; Main, 2018)

America. This hypothesis seemed to be confirmed with the rise of Trump, who not only came to power with a message of hatred towards "minorities", feminists, liberals and immigrants, but also praised several Buchanan editorials, against immigration and in favor of white supremacism. Indeed, important similarities have been noted between Buchanan's campaign in 1992 and 2000 and Trump's in 2016. In that context, there was also a transfer of a part of the paleolibertarians to a national-socialist far right. (Cooper, 2021)

5.3 Rothbard and Rockwell's anti-statism and free-market anti-globalism

The Paleo alliance has had its moments of cracking, partly due to ideological and programmatic differences between its two basic currents, one more pro free-trade and the other more nationalist in the economic sphere. Both currents reject the "world economic government" exercised by institutions such as the WTO, which they denounce as bureaucratic controlled trade.[6] For Rothbard, this rejection is based not so much on the fact that they infringe on national sovereignty as on true free trade, which would not require political institutions but free competition between companies in the world market. Free trade agreements such as NAFTA, by homogenizing legislation, force U.S. companies to adapt to unfavorable environmental and labor standards and take decision-making out of the hands of the American people, reenacting what happens with the "superstatism of the European Community" denounced by Thatcher and the Eurosceptics (See above). The aim of these institutions would not be to promote free trade but globalist and Keynesian policies, in the face of which the new populist coalition must promote a new American nationalism that must abrogate NAFTA, withdraw from all supranational organizations, end development aid, make immigration more difficult, etc.

Like Thatcher, Rothbard and Rockwell adopt a radical free-trade, nationalist, and anti-globalist position. That is, national-neoliberal (Sauvêtre, 2019). In that sense, Rockwell summarizes the main ideas of paleolibertarianism:

I. The leviathan State as the institutional source of evil throughout history. II. The unhampered free market as a moral and practical imperative. III. Private property as an economic and moral necessity for a free society. IV. The garrison State as a preeminent threat to lib-

---

6 Paradoxical result of an institution that emerged from a neoliberal globalism that sought to limit the sovereignty of states through global free trade, thus reaffirming dominium against imperium. (Slobodian, 2018).

erty and social well being. V. The welfare State as organized theft that victimizes producers and eventually even its "clients". VI. Civil liberties based on property rights as essential to a just society. VII. The egalitarian ethic as morally reprehensible and destructive of private property and social authority. VIII. Social authority—as embodied in the family, church, community, and other intermediating institutions—as helping protect the individual from the State and as necessary for a free and virtuous society. IX. Western culture as eminently worthy of preservation and defense. X. Objective standards of morality, especially as found in the Judeo-Christian tradition, as essential to the free and civilized social order. (Rockwell, 1990, p. 35)

In this way, Rockwell sought to reconcile libertarianism with the conservative values of the American people and attacked the discourse of civil rights that would no longer be rights of citizens vis-à-vis the state but privileges "for blacks and other minorities at the expense of the majorities". (Stefanoni, 2021)

Coincidentally, Rothbard considers the state to be a parasitic institution that feeds on the wealth of others and transfers its ill-gotten gains to its various dependents: the companies that live off monopolies and state subsidies, the unions, and the non-productive assisted class, etc. Taxation would be the most obvious form of expropriation exercised by the state. Following the nineteenth century Southern leader John C. Calhoun, he states that the class struggle is between the net producers and the net consumers of taxes and that it is the latter who exploit the former through the state. (Rothbard, 2010)

However, the most insidious method of expropriation is *inflation*,[7] a form of stealth taxation that subtly redistributes wealth from creditors to debtors and from savers to consumers, thus altering its "natural" distribution. For Rothbard, in the absence of hard money and fiscal discipline, "the state can all too easily live beyond its means, funding itself through the extortionary instruments of public borrowing, always ultimately paid for in taxes, and the inflation of the money supply, a sleight of hand that completely reshuffles the natural distribution of income, turning rightful winners into losers" (Rothbard apud Cooper, 2021) Therefore, to move away from the gold standard is to fall into legalized fraud. The sole purpose of central banks is to inflate the money supply and deprive producers and savers of their hard-earned money. In short, inflation and progressive taxation would be the main instruments through which the modern fiscal state transfers the resources of the owners and producers to the parasitic class of the assisted.[8]

---

7 This is widely discussed in the neoconservative movement of the '70s. See Cooper (2017).
8 These positions are currently held in Argentina by Javier Milei, intellectual leader and raising star of the Libertarian Party, who drawing on Rothbard and the Austrian School, has proposed to

For Rothbard, inequality is not only natural but also ethical, because it reflects the different biological capacities to produce and earn money. That is why he distanced himself in the early 1970s from the "new left", with which he shared at the time the affirmation of freedom from any form of authority. At the same time, he disagreed with the Chicago and Virginia schools, which preached the free market, but did not attack state control of money, security, and law. For Rothbard, even the fight against inflation promoted by Friedman's monetarism is too innocuous. The federal reserve should be abolished, and we should return to metallic money. At the same time, defense, security, and justice should be totally privatized. It follows from his theory that, since they have been expropriated, the productive citizens must arm themselves against the state and against the "parasites" who receive aid without producing. These would be the modern beneficiaries of the special privileges once held by the feudal elite (Cooper, 2021). In a typical inversion of right-wing thinking, the truly privileged would not be those who possess the capital or the best income. They are seen as victims of the Black people, the poor, women, gender minorities, immigrants, single mothers, in short, the *undeserving poor* who receive social benefits. From there to justifying violence against these groups, there is only one step.

If at the beginning of his libertarian itinerary Rothbard attacked the traditionalism of the National Review—magazine that, under the direction of Bill Buckley, brought together American conservatives since 1955—later he defended positions of a reactionary communitarianism, strong borders, and a right to self-defense of property owners transformed into racism (Cooper, 2021). In that framework, he pointed out that: "racialist science is properly not an act of aggression or a cover for oppression of one group over another, but, on the contrary, an operation in defence of private property against assaults by aggressors" (Rothbard, 1994 apud Cooper, 2021).

Thus, the reactionary and punitive character of this thinking is evident (Davies, 2016). It seeks to legitimize the exclusion of, and even the attack on, the sectors that will be the most affected by the inequalities generated by capitalism and, recently, by neoliberal austerity policies.

---

set fire to the central bank. From a leftist perspective, debt and taxes are seen as forms of expropriation of populations and their future work capacity to favor the creditors, which would be the real beneficiaries of the neoliberal policies. (Lazzarato, 2013; Cavallero & Gago, 2021; Graeber, 2011).

5.4 Libertarians and the extreme right

With the introduction of a racist and communitarian defense of libertarianism, Rothbard's thought will become increasingly close to other right-wing currents more closely linked to ethnonationalism and white supremacism with neo-fascist features. This confluence will be based on themes such as anti-egalitarianism, anti-progressivism, anti-feminism, xenophobia, and racism. In fact, Rothbard's thought builds a kind of bridge that has been traversed by many young people in their journey from (paleo)libertarianism to the extreme right.[9]

According to Stefanoni (2021), this is explained by the fact that both libertarians and reactionaries hate the "egalitarian lie" and "politically correct" thinking, share their discomfort with democracy, the "demagogy of politicians" and the "statist superstitions of the masses". Both can be part of populist coalitions, such as the one that brought Trump to power in 2016. And, not least, they all hate the aforementioned "social justice warriors", which includes progressives, feminists, civil rights activists, etc.

This is not surprising if we bear in mind that libertarianism and the far right capture the same audience: primarily white, middle-class males, i.e., the most privileged sector of our society who, therefore, would not want to see social change. (Gulliver-Needham, 2019) At the same time, they share a language, systems of ideas and emotions. According to Gulliver-Needham, it is almost impossible to distinguish a libertarian from a neofascist when they complain about feminism or immigration, which in theory should not bother the former. The justification usually given by a libertarian is that policies such as free abortion or immigration favor a larger welfare state and therefore more taxes. At the same time, today's libertarians do not attack the extreme right or racists, but they do attack the left. In fact, in many cases libertarians and neo-fascists use the same expressions. A paradigmatic case is that of Christopher Cantwell, known as the "crying Nazi", who moved from libertarianism to the extreme right, or from denouncing taxes as theft, to arguing that "Jews will not replace us". (Gulliver-Needham, 2019). As Stefanoni points out, Rothbard's ideas allowed this kind of people to move from abstract anti-statism towards racist positions, justified in the name of free association. These ideas take on a reactionary tone reminiscent of the theorists of the conservative revolution in Germany of exactly a century ago. Both libertarianism and the far right share the idea that the West

---

9 This is attested to by several referents of the alternative right such as Richard Spencer, Mike Enoch, or Paul Gottfried himself, the paleoconservative academic who is credited with having coined the term "alt-right". (Cooper, 2021) In Latin America, it is worth noting the influence that this thought has had on young people such as Axel Kaiser or Agustín Laje.

is declining because of progressives who have won the cultural battle by asserting social justice and calling into question racial and gender hierarchies. (Stefanoni, 2021). Rothbard's thought can theoretically and politically unite libertarians, reactionaries, and neo-fascists in a common anti-progressive front, such as the one that is being formed in different parts of the world.[10] Indeed, his ideas influenced the turn of many young people from libertarianism to the far right. (Stefanoni, 2021)

5.5 Buchanan's paleoconservatism and the alt-right

According to Cooper, this shift of libertarianism to the far right could be seen as a shift towards social-identitarian, neo-fascist or outright national-socialist positions, which participated in, and were favored by, Trump's rise to the U.S. presidency. This would have been anticipated by the white nationalist intellectual Samuel Francis at the time of the "paleo alliance", noting that the paleoconservative "resentment of welfare, paternalism and regulation [...] is not based on a profound faith in the market but simply a sense of injustice that unfair welfare programs, taxes and regulation have bred" (Francis, 1994, p. 72 apud Cooper, 2021). Francis, one of the intellectual fathers of the alt-right that conflates elite theory with racism and the rejection of liberal democracy, predicted that, once in power, the paleoconservatives would discard their former libertarian allies and instead become economic nationalists and protectionists.

In a way, this was a position held by Buchanan from the beginning, in line with the protectionist tradition held by the pre-New Deal Republican Party (Cooper, 2021). Buchanan's economic program called for the Republican Party to withdraw from all international free trade agreements, deport all undocumented immigrants, oversee a deeper and wider distribution of property and prosperity based on the return of high-paying industrial jobs, and shift the tax burden

---

10 These movements with a strong youth imprint share "the rejection of progressivism. The rejection of feminists, of politicians who speak of social justice and income redistribution, of those who use inclusive language, of campaigns against sexual harassment, of climate change activists. For them, progressivism won the cultural battle [...]. They see it in politics, in their classrooms, in the media and even in "Netflix series" [...] If that is what is fashionable, any anti-progressive practice will be perceived "as a synonym of rebellion", as "politically incorrect" (Alcaraz et al., 2021).

on labor and production to tariffs on imported consumer goods (Buchanan, 1998, p. 289 apud Cooper, 2021).[11]

As Cooper points out, paleoconservatives saw themselves as reactionaries and revolutionaries. They had a revisionist view of the Civil War in which the focus of the conflict was taxation or states' rights, not slavery. As a result, white Southerners were subjected to a form of "cultural genocide". In that framework, paleoconservatives participate in the Neo-Confederate movement of the 1980s and argue for the legal continuation of nullification and secession doctrines that would give individual states the ability to declare a federal rule unconstitutional or secede from the Union, even though the American Constitution forbids it.

The alliance with the libertarians was based on a shared conviction about the illegitimacy of the state and a willingness to take arms if it threatens their independence. But if libertarians resist in order to gain freedom from the state, paleoconservatives see this as a prelude to forms of domination in the private and social sphere. (Cooper, 2021)

There are also tactical coincidences in Buchanan's critique of economic globalization and the welfare state. In *The Great Betrayal*, he cites Wilhelm Röpke, who, while defending economic internationalism and opposing all forms of protectionism, tries to reconcile economic liberalism with Christian values, necessary for the expansion of the free market under the aegis of a natural oligarchy. Indeed, Röpke was a useful reference for the intention to contain the free market within moral, familial, national, and ethnic traditions. (Cooper, 2021). In particular, paleoconservatives value the German for his support for apartheid in South Africa and his criticism of immigration on racist grounds, and since the international economic order imagined by Röpke is led by the Western powers (see above, chap. 2).

However, in this shift to the far right, has the neoliberal position remained unchanged? As we have pointed out, the turn of the new right towards extreme forms of ethnonationalism goes hand in hand, in many cases, with a defense of greater economic liberalization, while in others it is associated with new forms of protectionism and a welfare chauvinism that excludes migrant, feminized and racialized subjectivities. In this sense, Cooper points out that alt-right militants identify with the visceral paleo hatred of Black people, Jews, Muslims, women, gay people and trans people, but not with their libertarianism, advocating a national-social turn and a white ethno-state. (Cooper, 2021)

---

11 Except for the redistribution of property and prosperity, these measures were part of the Trump administration's recipe book.

With the economic policy of National Socialism as a background, Cooper argues that the transit from libertarianism to the far right may result not only in a loss of liberties and authoritarianism in the private and social realm but also in an economic policy which departs from the neoliberal, free-market-centered postulates that were central to this paleo alliance. However, this far-right anti-capitalism seems irrelevant in the face of the national-neoliberal success in imposing an agenda of radicalization of economic liberalism, political-cultural authoritarianism and social conservatism.

For this very reason, as Sauvêtre points out, we must not lose sight of the neoliberal impulse of the populist critique of economic globalization, whether in Thatcher's, Rothbard's or Buchanan's version. By denouncing the socialist and bureaucratic tendencies of transnational institutions, national sovereignty is transformed into a means of combating the "globalist elite" and stimulating a Western moral and identitarian order that maintains a privileged relationship with the free market and acts as a barrier of containment against non-white populations. Indeed, behind Thatcher is Hayek, behind Rothbard is Mises, and behind Buchanan, Röpke. From there Sauvêtre concludes that the origins of populism and anti-globalism are neoliberal and that national-neoliberalism confronts neoliberal globalism in order to push the general dismantling of society even further. (Sauvêtre, 2019)

5.6 By way of conclusion

Throughout this chapter I attempted a brief genealogy of national-neoliberalism and right-wing populism, which are increasingly successful politically and culturally in the context of the authoritarian becoming of neoliberalism. (Bruff & Tansel, 2020; Dardot & Laval, 2019) On the one hand, we have shown that these currents reject international institutions insofar as they would enable the consolidation of socializing global elites that impose regulations unfavorable to the free deployment of competition and exchange. These elites would favor migration which, together with affirmative action policies towards disadvantaged sectors, destroy free trade, national identity, fiscal balance, and security. As a consequence, "hard-working citizens" would be expropriated through welfare, taxes and inflation. At the same time, these "liberal-Keynesian" elites would disregard the value of traditional hierarchies and the importance of natural forms of authority to achieve a harmonious order, and would favor policies such as abortion, sex education not reduced to biology, feminism, etc.—all of which are part of what they call gender ideology—imposing a progressive vision that would oppose not only the Christian essence of the West but also the wishes of the "true people".[12] From this would follow the need for a right-wing populist strategy that appeals to this white male population disenchanted with globalization to act against the government elites that would be exploiting and oppressing this sector and against minorities favored by "false" civil and social "rights". As we have seen, this often entails an explicit racism that legitimizes not only violence against the state and its agents but also against those who receive aid from it.

The alliance between libertarians and paleoconservatives was a turning point in the spread of such ideas, especially in the United States. Although it was established in the early 1990s, it began to gain ground after the financial crisis of 2008 and the bailout of the banks by the Obama administration, but also in the opposition to Obamacare and the demand for social justice and the rights of "minorities". In that framework, paleolibertarian ideas became increasingly popular, with the rise of the Tea Party and then of Trump, but especially in internet forums and social network militancy. However, the rise of Trump, which meant a posthumous triumph for the paleo alliance, also favored some shifts in the grassroots from paleolibertarian positions to other stances linked to the alternative right, which includes currents that defend economic nationalism and the idea of a white ethno-state. For Cooper, if one takes into account the National Socialist antecedent, in which some of these currents of the extreme right are referenced, right-wing populism could even give rise to a critique of capitalism (Cooper, 2021). However, not only xenophobia and racism were the central components of the vote in favor of these parties (Fassin, 2018a), but so far, no recent government has moved from neoliberal coordinates. In fact, while more and more conservative parties have been adopting radical right-wing policies in their treatment of immigration, women's rights and sexual dissent, undermining liberal democracy and the rule of law from within, this has gone hand in hand with a radicalization of neoliberal policies. We have even seen that the Mont-Pèlerin Society itself has moved closer to far-right populisms. Therefore, rather than the rise of an anti-capitalist right wing, we are facing a turn of societies towards a neoliberal far right which recovers nationalist, racist, patriarchal, colonial and classist motives to strengthen the domination of capital over our lives. For Slobodian and Plehwe, these sometimes-surprising mutations and contortions, which we see even within the neoliberal thought collective, are due to the fact that neoliberalism is not a creed but the injunction to defend capitalism against democracy. (Slobodian & Plehwe, 2019, p. 105) As we have already stated,

---

12 Although we do not have space to develop it here, therein lies a difference between right-wing populisms and alt-right and the Nouvelle Droite and neo-fascist groups in Europe, which in many cases advocate a neo-paganism.

neoliberalism is a strategic rationality that adapts to its different contexts (Dardot et al., 2021).

In this framework, Alex Demirović argues that, unlike popular democracy, authoritarian populism represents an effort to build an alliance from above with petty-bourgeois and working-class groups without the bourgeoisie having to make concessions.

> Following Stuart Hall's distinction, it can be said that popular democracy and populism establish different dividing lines. The former constructs an antagonism between the people and the power bloc, exploited and exploiters, poor and rich, peace and war, sustainability and destruction, difference and normalism. In this case, there are progressive processes of opinion and will formation and a shared worldview at a high and rational level of knowledge. Authoritarian populism, on the other hand, is a plebiscitary strategy that separates and mobilizes along racist, nationalist, religious, sexist or anti-ecological lines, reproducing the strangely distorted common sense and neurotizing subjects. (2018, p. 125)

In a similar vein, Chantal Mouffe (2019), argues that right-wing populism does not deal with democracy, nor equality, nor popular sovereignty and builds a people based on numerous exclusions: of ethnic minorities, women, and immigrants, perceived as a threat to national identity. It also is not opposed to neoliberalism. On the contrary, it can lead to authoritarian forms of neoliberalism that end up weakening democracy.

Indeed, radical populist rightists are far from questioning capitalism. Even in social-identitarian versions, their concern is how to protect the white populations from the effects of neoliberal policies, promoting a welfare chauvinism and an exclusion of non-white populations, but without affecting the core of neoliberal governmental rationality. On the contrary, a popular democracy (Demirović), a leftist (Mouffe, 2019; Casullo, 2019) or progressive (Fraser, 2017) populism, would seek to oppose the oligarchy and orient itself towards the future. This implies establishing a chain of equivalences between demands of workers, immigrants, the middle class undergoing precarization, the LGBTQI community, etc. (Mouffe, 2019). To do so, it should offer answers to the demands for recognition without ignoring the need for a more egalitarian distribution. (Fraser, 2017)

However, Eric Fassin (2018a) rejects the idea that democratic recovery passes through a left populism. First, as we have seen in this text, in Europe and the United States populism has been an eminently neoliberal strategy. Therefore, populism would be a symptom of neoliberalism and not a remedy against it. Moreover, Fassin argues that the passions mobilized by populism and the left differ. In that sense, populist resentment could not translate into egalitarian indignation. Angry white men who vote for racism, xenophobia and against feminism and sex-gender dissidence—and not against neoliberalism as some seem to believe—would hardly be attracted to a left populist alternative. Contrary to what Mouffe argues, for Fassin (2018a), far-right voters are not victims whose suffering should be listened to. They are political subjects, driven by sad passions, which we should fight by relying on other subjects and other passions. Therefore, it does not make sense for a left-wing policy to seek to conquer the electorate of right-wing populisms but those who have not yielded to the "seduction of fascism" (Fassin, 2018a). According to Fassin, it would be necessary to rebuild the left and not populism, because such ideological confusion has always benefited the (ultra)right.

In this sense, it would be no coincidence that the Gramscian notion of hegemony has been adopted by the metapolitical currents of the new French right in the 1970s, intellectually led by Alain de Benoist, or that the young Argentine anti-feminist and anti-progressive theorist Agustín Laje, to whom we will refer in the next chapter, considers Laclau and Mouffe's theory of hegemony as an indispensable tool to reverse a "cultural battle" that would have been won by the left. (Laje & Márquez, 2016)

As we see, right-wing populism proposes a white, patriarchal, ethno-nationalist hegemony, defender of traditional values and of what it considers as natural identities and hierarchies. In the name of freedom, these discourses seek to reinforce cultural and political authoritarianism against liberal democracy and the civil and social rights won after decades of social struggles. As the American case shows, there is a fluid transit between paleolibertarianism and neo-fascism because deep down they seek to represent the same social sector: *angry white men*; and the same passion: *resentment* (Brown, 2019; Betz, 2022).

In this framework, more than conclusions we should put at stake some concerns. Will this authoritarian, patriarchal and ecocidal project of white supremacism be the one that will impose itself in the coming decades as a response to the crises generated by neoliberal capitalism? Can we invent any desirable alternative to this model of society, or will the criticism be monopolized by the new right wing, which can only change it for the worse? Is left-wing populism a propitious alternative to its right-wing opponent or should we act politically under other forms of democratic participation and management?

Although we do not have answers to these questions, it seems necessary to take seriously the warnings coming from different geographies. Rather than appealing to the disqualification of these currents, dismissing them as lacking intellectual depth or being indignant in the face of their cruelty, it would be convenient to ask ourselves why they have so much success, what they propose, what idea of freedom to oppose them and how to think of a project for a fairer, freer and more diverse world that should once again conquer the imagination and desire of the new generations.

To a certain extent, this alternative project is the one presented by the commoners (chapter 7) and also by anti-patriarchal and anti-capitalist feminist militancy, which has proven to be a political force capable of opposing the advance of the far right. This has led to a radicalization of the latter in their attacks on feminism. In the next chapter we will analyze the reasons for this hatred and how it is combined with an anti-communist discourse that seemed to have been relegated to the Cold War era.

6 Anti-communism without communism? The construction of feminism as a strategic enemy of the new radical right and the dilemma of social reproduction

We call communism the real movement which abolishes the present state of things. The conditions of this movement result from the premises now in existence. (Marx & Engels, *The German Ideology*)

As we have been pointing out, in recent decades we have witnessed the rise of new right-wing movements characterized by a strong xenophobic, misogynist, racist, patriarchal, classist and aporophobic imprint. This occurred in parallel to the progressive rise of the feminist movement which articulates both the questioning of neoliberal-colonial-heteropatriarchal capitalism and the forms of violence it provokes, and the production of resistant subjectivities and new forms of life and militancy. In this context, the presence of a sort of anti-communism without communism is increasingly noticeable. By that notion I name a strong anti-communist discourse that takes us back to the Cold War era, at a time when there does not seem to exist a communist alternative to capitalism. This extemporaneous McCarthyism is being verified today in different geographies. For example, in the United States, where any intervention of the State in economic and social life is accused of "communism", from Obamacare to the restrictions on movement during the covid-19 pandemic. Also in Brazil, where Bolsonaro proposed to ban "communism", designating with such term the Workers' Party and leftist movements in general. In Argentina, the Preventive and Obligatory Social Isolation decreed by the government of the Peronist Alberto Fernandez during the pandemic was accused by the political, media and social opposition of being a communist measure or that, somehow, it would be the excuse to enforce a "Castro Chavist dictatorship". What is striking is that the same people who opposes communism have expressed their rejection of "gender ideology", of voluntary interruption of pregnancy, of the possibility of determining one's own gender identity, of feminist militancy and of inclusive language. Even neo-Nazi movements and referents have begun to participate in the mobilizations, in the networks, in the political parties and even in some television programs linked to the new right wing. In fact, this storm of constant hatred against communism and feminism has been articulated in the fight against "gender ideology".

https://doi.org/10.1515/9783110723939-008

In previous chapters, we have commented on this construction of the threatening enemy as a discursive and political strategy that enables a counterrevolution without revolution, which is reflected in new forms of control of populations through the repressive and legal apparatus (Harcourt, 2018). However, beyond an objective analysis of the current relations of forces, one might ask: How to think the relationship between anticommunism and antifeminism in these new right-wing movements? Is feminism a threat like that once represented by communism to capitalism? Is feminism the new communism in the sense of abolishing and overcoming the current situation? Is there something inherently anti-capitalist in contemporary feminisms? Is this hatred of feminism a "merely cultural" manifestation, or is there also an underlying dispute about the costs and modalities of economic and bio-social reproduction?

Based on these questions, in what follows I propose to characterize, on the one hand, this construction of feminism and "gender ideology" as strategic enemies of the new right; and, on the other hand, the potential of anti-capitalist feminisms to be conceived as the communism of the twenty-first century, taking into account both their theoretical and political capacity to understand what is happening to us and to subvert the existing state of affairs.

To this end, first, I will carry out an analysis of discourses that seek to show the danger that "gender ideology" would represent for capitalist, Western and Christian civilization. As an example, I draw on some postulates of *The black book of the new left*, a best seller among the Latin American public, where feminism and "gender ideology" are depicted as screens of neo-Marxism. Although this hypothesis lacks historical and theoretical foundations, I find it interesting to understand the mentality of these far-right sectors and to link their rejection of feminism with a recognition of its subversive capacity. In this framework, the question of social reproduction will be treated as a central element for feminist struggles and for understanding the hatred they generate among the new right-wingers.

My hypothesis is twofold. On the one hand, the need to build an enemy responds to the antagonistic logic of any construction of political identities. Just as neoliberalism emerged as a reaction against socialism, the new rightists mobilize hatred and rejection towards all those who are strangers to the white, heterosexual, patriarchal and capitalist norm and acquire new strength in the face of a widespread economic and reproductive crisis. In this sense, feminisms are under attack because they question the hierarchies that the new rightists seek to defend or restore, especially regarding gender relations, sexuality, family, and modes of labor, foregrounding current forms of producing value through sex-gendered and racialized bodies. Moreover, since feminism is a movement that does not seek to assert an identity but to become transversal to different social struggles, it is presented as a strategic target to destroy. Secondly, beyond the opposition between reform and revolution, and in the absence of a visible enemy that serves to agglutinate the right-wing field itself, feminisms, at least in their most radical versions, currently represent the most powerful resistance movement to neoliberal capitalism since, in addition to making demands to the state in terms of rights, they question the expropriation and exploitation of reproductive labor, which is fundamental for the accumulation of capital. In this context, feminisms can not only shake patriarchy and the traditional family but can also enable the production of forms of life that do not obey the economic, gender and racial hierarchies that the new radical right seeks to sustain at all costs.

6.1 The new radical right and the need to build enemies

As we have highlighted in the preceding chapters, the strategic logic of neoliberalism has led it to coincide and sometimes merge with reactionary currents and, at present, with the new radical right when it comes to constituting a field of adversity. It is well known that the constitution of an "us" always operates through exclusions and in relation to an alterity. In this framework, once the communist enemy was blurred with the end of the Cold War, new sources of conflict unfolded that have favored a radicalization of certain underlying antagonisms in the economic, national, ethnic, cultural and gender fields. Indeed, the overwhelming triumph of neoliberal globalization has led to a dramatic increase in economic inequalities, not only between regions, but also within each geographical space, where competition among the labor force at the global level has favored the position of capital to devalue, subordinate and make labor and social reproduction increasingly precarious. To this must be added the massive immigration that took place after decolonization to the former metropolises of people expelled from their places of origin for economic, warlike, cultural, or political reasons. In turn, this stage coincided with the progressive rise of a LGBTQI movement that has questioned the hierarchies that still exist between genders, sexes, races, nations, and classes on the various planes of existence. As we have pointed out in the preceding chapters, after the outbreak of the financial crisis, contradictions became more acute, and political ideologies that had been condemned to little influence on the public scene became increasingly central, showing not only a kind of "return of the repressed", but also evidencing authoritarian features of neoliberalism itself. In this framework, while new social and political movements who question the neoliberal economic and power system emerged, others have been strengthened in search of new scapegoats to be fought to restore an imaginary past where the true citizens (white, male, propri-etary and Christian) ruled undisturbed. Hence the strategic role, for the radical right, of fear of an Other who cannot be assimilated to "our" way of life and who threatens "our" jobs, "our" property, and "our" enjoyment.

These new rightists contain a motley mosaic of political-ideological tenden-cies. In previous chapters, we have distinguished social-identitarians from na-tional-neoliberals, analyzed the alliance between paleoconservatives and paleo-libertarians, and commented on the relationship of both with the alternative right. As we have seen, although they differ in their positions on globalization, the market, sovereignty, the welfare state, etc., they coincide in the affirmation of traditional moral values—family, property, tradition, ethnocentrism, etc.—a polit-ically authoritarian stance, and the promotion of hatred of foreigners, feminism and the LGBTQI movement. In this context, "feminism" and in particular "gen-der ideology" become privileged targets to be attacked.

6.2 "Gender ideology" as a strategic enemy

As we pointed out, in the last decade we have witnessed the rise of new political and intellectual right-wing movements which have identified "feminism" and "gender ideology" as their strategic enemy, linking the subversion of sex-gender identities and sex-affective practices and the defense of the rights of feminized subjectivities to the proliferation of communism. This hatred towards "gender ideology", which includes a crusade against abortion and comprehensive sexual education, is especially intense in Latin America, where the far right emphasizes the defence of morality and market freedom (Dvoskin, 2019, p. 164).

The first axis is very clearly represented in social movements such as Haz-teOír/CitizenGo in Spain or "Con mis hijos no te metas", which emerged in Peru at the end of 2016 against the inclusion of gender in the educational cur-riculum and spread like an oil stain throughout the Spanish-speaking world. This movement denounces a "gender ideology"—a concept initially developed by the Catholic Church—that seeks to destabilize the heterosexual family, with the aim of establishing a "new world order"—led by figures such as Bill Gates and George Soros—that promotes homosexuality, abortion, sex change, homo-sexual marriage, and population control.[1] We also find this denunciation of the new world order in various groups that believe in conspiracy theories,

---

[1] In fact, the Soros-funded Central European University, which includes gender studies in its curriculum, had to leave Hungary under pressure from Viktor Orbán's government.

such as those who oppose quarantines or vaccines, or the QAnon movement, a prominent participant in the assault on the US Capitol on January 6, 2021, which denounced on social networks the existence of a pedophile network promoted by part of the political and cultural establishment. Precisely in that assault— and in this type of events in general—took part from neo-Nazi groups to others who call themselves libertarians and who fight against the socialism that Trump denounced in his opponents.[2]

To understand some aspects of these new rightists worldwide, we will take *The black book of the new left. Gender ideology or cultural subversion,* by Agustín Laje and Nicolás Márquez as an example of this crusade against gender ideology as a spearhead of communism. In this widely distributed text, those who think of themselves as the intellectuals that the Latin American right lacked, without any reference to the complex and tense historical relations between feminism and Marxism, argue that gender ideology—subdivided into feminism, abortionism, and cultural homosexualism—is a screen for neo-Marxism. They point out that, in 1992, while anti-communist forces were celebrating the end of history, communism was being renewed in indigenist, feminist and ecologist movements and leftist thought, which gradually became hegemonic. In the authors' explanation, the leftist structures had to fabricate NGOs and rearrange their slogans and sources of financing in the face of the disappearance of the USSR, but they maintained their communist, subversive and even totalitarian essence.

In this book, which is reminiscent of the counterinsurgency manuals published by the Argentine Dictatorship in the 1970s[3], the authors make it clear that the communist enemy can never be underestimated, because it never presents itself for what it is, but hides, mimics and infiltrates, waging psychological warfare to demoralize the "free world" through collateral organizations that existed before the USSR and "continued existing after the extinction of it" (Laje & Márquez, 2019, p. 11). The concrete objectives of the ecologist, human rights, feminist, indigenist movements would be fake, since they would respond to communist goals. Behind the multicolored flag of the LGBTQI movement, the green flags of environmentalism or the wiphala would lurk the red flag with the hammer

---

2 It should be noted that, in cases such as Central and Eastern Europe, the rejection of "gender ideology" can be a way of organizing against the neoliberal establishment, which requires women to participate equally in the labor market but does not provide economic and social rights that could facilitate reproductive work. (Zacharenko, 2019)

3 This similarity is perhaps not pure coincidence, if we take into account that the authors, who support state terrorism, were awarded scholarships to study counter-terrorism tactics at the Defense University in Washington, where several Pentagon military officers were trained. (Elman, 2018)

and sickle. In this way, the motley mosaic of social movements that has emerged in the last four decades would be divided into conscious Marxists and useful idiots, a category that would include those neutral or indifferent people who, by their inaction, favor the progress of subversion. In this framework, gender ideology would be key in the dispute for hegemony, moving from class struggle to the "cultural battle", whose real objective would be socialism. Socialist hegemony would be achieved by articulating a series of heterogeneous social movements, amongst which "the feminist and homosexualists [...] euphemistically represented as what is known as 'gender ideology'". (Laje & Márquez, 2019, p. 39)

Laje's strategy consists of separating a humanist and liberal feminism of the first wave, which fought respectably for civil, political, and educational rights for women, from an abominable socialist feminism that would come later, inspired by Engelsian ideas that hold a joint origin of private property and the patriarchal family. If the problems posed by liberal feminism could be solved by "introducing electoral and educational reforms", Marxist feminism "can only solve the question by arranging a violent revolution that ends with private property and family as social institution, this here it lies the evil seed" (2019, p. 51).

Now, this Marxist feminism would not be limited to claiming equality between men and women never achieved in socialist states but would derive in "gender ideology", contrary to any idea of nature. In fact, the authors fully subscribe a warning made by Ludwig von Mises in 1922 in the framework of his crusade against socialism that some incautious libertarians[4], that are functional to neo-Marxism would not be taking into account:

> While the feminist move is limited to equate the legal rights from women and men, to provide security about the legal and economic possibilities of unfolding its faculties and show them through actions according to what she likes, her desires and financial situation, it is only a branch of the great liberal movement that embodies the idea of a free and peaceful revolution. If, by going beyond those claims, the feminist movement believes that it should combat institutions of the social life hopping to remove, through this way, certain limitations that nature has imposed to human destiny, then it is a spiritual son of socialism. Because searching in social institutions the roots of the conditions given by nature and is a distinctive feature of socialism, and pretending, by reforming them, to reform nature itself (Mises, 1922, apud Laje & Márquez, 2019, pp. 46–47)

---

4 Márquez maintains that "it has been known for some time now that libertarians do not have much to do with historical liberals. That is to say, with those crusaders who, in a world marked by totalitarianism, defended individual freedom by layer and sword, without losing sight of the fact that there are limitations and reasonable conditions for it (whether due to impediments to the natural order or to life itself in the community). (2019, p. 196)

Now, what Laje understands as the third wave of feminism, "gender ideology", would not be so much an autonomous development of Western feminist thought but rather the result of a KGB strategy to brainwash the new generations of Americans with the aim of demoralizing and destabilizing Western powers. It would find its origin in Simone de Beauvoir's *The Second Sex*, a text that the authors consider the most important book of twentieth century feminism and would prove that "gender ideology has its origin and development in the center of the ultra-left" (Laje & Márquez, 2019, p. 69) and that gradually shifts the hegemonic dispute from the economic to the cultural sphere, in order to destroy "the current—moral, religious, ideological, legal, family—superstructure". (Laje & Márquez, 2019, p. 74)

This cultural Marxism would invert the causal order of classical Marxism. It would no longer be the changes in the relations of production that influence the forms of life, but rather the forms of life must be modified in order to change the political and economic systems. In this framework, "as something independent of the natural datum, is exacerbated as strategy in order to destroy the social institutions that would be functional to capitalism: monogamous family, incest and paedophile prohibition, heterosexuality, etcetera. Here rises the existing bridge between this third wave of feminism, deconstructive and culturalist, and what began to be known as "queer theory" in the 90s" (2019, p. 82) For Agustín Laje, feminism does not serve women but the leftist cultural revolution. Moving away from its noble liberal and suffragette origins, cultural Marxism established a homology between class struggle and the struggle of the sexes, understanding that the liberation of sexuality, the rupture of social and moral superstructures would be the new key to destroy the system. "Gender ideology", with its deconstruction of the very notion of human nature, would be the epitome of this tendency.

Along with abortionism and feminism, "gender ideology" would promote cultural homosexualism, which is addressed by Nicolás Márquez. In order not to be accused of being intolerant, he clarifies: "we will always distinguish between those who suffer from an inculpable homosexual tendency (which deserves all our respect), from those who dedicate themselves to militant or ideological proselytism at the service of the expansion and consolidation of an agenda that today loyally assists the recycled communist cause". (2019, p. 154)

The word "suffer" is not innocent, since the author maintains throughout his work that homosexuality, which he prefers to call with the biblical term "sodomy", is a curable pathology, which leads to multiple other diseases, especially of the venereal type, and that if psychiatry and psychoanalysis do not consider it anymore as a pathology it is not because of a thoughtful revision of their normalizing assumptions but, purely and exclusively, because of the political pressure of the homosexualist lobby.

However, what is fundamental for the author is that not only is it unhealthy to practice homosexuality—although it can be tolerated as long as it does not harm third parties—but also that gender ideology is dangerous because it is a screen of communism. Like feminism, gay people are also being used as puppets for a foreign cause by a sector that until recently would have severely punished them—if we consider the precedents of the USSR, Cuba, the Khmer Rouge and Maoist China.

As we can see, between these reactionary thoughts and movements and feminisms and sexual dissidence there is an antagonistic frontier that has to do with a dispute over the role of feminized subjectivities in neoliberal society. In this context, it is worth asking: Why do these radical rightists draw this antagonistic border?

On the one hand, because "feminism constitutes one of the major fronts against the advance of neo-fascism, both in the vote, as well as in the street" (Alabao, 2019). Feminist, migrant, anti-racist and popular struggles generate "a destabilization to which conservative forces react with an economic, military, and religious counter-offensive. This reaction is conceived from above and is synthesized in the ultra-right governments, but it also operates from below, disputing the terrain of subjectivities and their production of affects". (Gago & Palmeiro, 2020).

At the same time, while feminism looks to the future, the radical right seeks to restore an imaginary past in which classes, races and sexes lived in harmony based on the acceptance of "natural" hierarchies. Anti-feminism rejects women's autonomy because that struggle threatens to destroy existing hierarchies in society as a whole and, especially, because "feminism attacks at the root the sexual division of labor that is at the base of all the other inequalities that occur between genders" (Alabao, 2019, p. 193).

In a similar vein, Wendy Brown understands the anti-feminist crusade and the rise of the far right as parts of a politics of resentment generated by the effects of neoliberalism, not only in economic terms but also in the dethronement of white masculinity. This double humiliation of race and class, in a nihilistic framework in which the will to power and the pursuit of pleasure are no longer sublimated, gives rise to a type of resentment that no longer arises from weakness, as in the Nietzschean analysis of Judeo-Christian morality, but from the loss of race, gender and class privileges. This would enable two possibilities. First, a resentment and rage that cannot be sublimated and gives rise to a permanent politics of revenge, of attacking those who are held responsible for the dethronement of white maleness: feminists, multiculturalists, globalists, who both unseat and disdain them (Brown, 2019, p. 177). The second possibility is that resentment at the loss of privileges gives rise to the emergence of a new scale of values, which denounces equality and merit in order to assert a supremacy based exclusively on traditional law. This nihilism exacerbated by the crisis of white and male domination generates an apocalyptic turn of events according to which, if "white men cannot own democracy, there will be no democracy. If white men cannot rule the planet, there will be no planet".[5] (Brown, 2019, p. 180)

In this framework, the fight against "gender ideology" goes beyond the traditional Christian opposition to the sexual and reproductive rights of women and the LGBTQI collective, to include homosexual marriage, equality policies, gender studies in academia, egalitarian education in schools, etc. (Alabao, 2019, p. 201). This crusade is due to the fact that the "most radical feminism seeks to reorganize the whole society on new bases [...] starting from the interdependence relations, which are the true foundation of the social" (Alabao, 2019, p. 203). In the field of social reproduction, morality and exploitation are interwoven (Gago & Palmeiro, 2020). At bottom, "family values are the translation and moral justification of privatization and extraction without limits". (Gago & Palmeiro, 2020).

In this sense, feminism somehow inverts what Laje and Márquez point out, taking as a program what they take as a premise. If for these authors feminism and cultural struggles are a facade of class struggle and Marxism, for anti-capitalist feminism the "cultural battle" must be able to make visible the link between the control over feminized subjectivities and the exploitation of reproductive labor, fighting against financial capitalism and its effects. To do so, it must seek answers in the future and not, as the radical right does, in the past.

6.3 Feminism: The Marxism of the twenty-first century?

Although the hypothesis of feminism and "gender ideology" as an epiphenomenon of a Marxism which, in the face of the failure of the class struggle, turns to the cultural battle, is unusual, we must recognize that the anti-feminist right-wing seems to have grasped this link between feminism and Marxism—and between feminism and anti-capitalism—even better than some segments of the left

---

5 Indeed, another highly influential movement that accuses its enemies of being communists is climate change denialism. Here too there is a correct identification of the enemy since, in order to reverse the environmental catastrophe, a change in the socio-productive paradigm is required, which the privileged sectors do not want to accept. Hence, these sectors denounce hegemonic science as part of a socializing ideology. Cfr. Klein (2019).

that do not address the problem of social reproduction adequately. What is there in feminism that makes it so dangerous for the current order and brings it closer to communism and even to Marxism?

First, we must consider that both currents have not only dialogued throughout the twentieth and twenty-first century, but that both seek to understand the relations of power and domination that subject and exploit us in order to transform them. In this sense, just as Marxisms throughout the twentieth century set out to update Marx's diagnosis of capitalism, class struggle, the revolutionary subject and communism, critical feminisms have analyzed the material relationship that exists between capitalism, colonialism and hetero-patriarchy, where exploitation, extraction and domination are combined. In this sense, both Marxism and feminisms can be understood as thoughts of the crisis and the critique of the existing state of affairs, given that neither is detached from concrete political-economic conjunctures nor can separate theory from praxis.

With the neoliberal evolution of capitalism, one of the main debates of materialist feminisms begins to focus on the articulation between capitalism, patriarchy, and colonialism through a re-reading of Marxism, social reproduction, and the tension between reform and revolution, taking into account the transformations of capitalism since the 1970s and their impact on political and social subjectivities. Therefore, Laje and Márquez write in a period that is marked, on the one hand, by the antagonism of Latin American feminisms in the face of a neoliberal, reactionary right, and, on the other, by the multiple theoretical and practical stances that are being set in motion within feminisms themselves regarding the problem of the subject of feminism, of reform and revolution.

Now, if, according to our hypothesis, feminism, like communism, seeks to abolish and overcome the current situation, how they characterize the latter?

6.4 Patriarchal-colonial capitalism and the control of bio-social reproduction

Feminist theoretical-political debates on social reproduction raise central questions on three major interrelated issues. First, they debate the relationship between capitalism, colonialism, and patriarchy. For example, whether it is univocal or intersectional. Secondly, they revisit the question of who the main enemy of feminisms is. And, thirdly, they enable a theoretical inquiry into the value-producing capacity of reproductive labor and thus encompass a question about the composition of the revolutionary subject.

If Marx's critique of political economy showed a hidden dwelling of social production and the social relations it generates in capitalism, which are veiled through a mechanism that understands the market as a producer of value, feminisms descend into the hidden abode of reproduction. There it becomes evident that, on the one hand, in production operates a sexual and international division of labor that is often based on a wage differential for equal work, i. e. in a greater exploitation of female and racialized labor (increased extraction of surplus value) with respect to male and white labor, and that also feminizes and racializes certain types of work that are devalued compared to others (Federici, 2014). On the other hand, if in the capitalist system, the reproduction of the labor force is linked to the subsistence capacity of the workers at a given historical moment, determining its value (Marx, 1906), the question that arises is who performs this —fundamentally feminized and/or racialized—labor and why this work that guarantees the reproduction of the labor force is neither remunerated nor recognized as such, or is performed in situations of greater precariousness and flexibilization than the work considered productive (Lorey, 2016; Federici, 2020). Reproductive work, being feminized and racialized, is constructed as given and natural and subjected to multiple forms of social violence (Segato, 2016; Falquet, 2017). At the same time, reproductive work guarantees the fundamental sustenance through which the very capacity to work and, therefore, life itself, is reproduced.

In this framework, materialist feminisms who focus on bio-social reproduction interrogate the value-producing status of social relations beyond wage labor in general and factory labor in particular, questioning the exclusivity of wages in the valorization of capital. This critical reading of Marxism not only implies challenging a historicist and evolutionist historicization of capitalism, but also enables a debate on the specificity of capitalist relations by questioning the centrality, hegemony or tendency of the expanded reproduction of capital in the face of non-wage, informal, reproductive labor, accumulation by dispossession and violent methods of value extraction.

For these feminisms, the expanded reproduction of capital has been able to be erected in a specific historical moment of capitalism, in a specific space and for a specific type of workers, in the framework of an imperialist capitalism that with fire and blood denied the character of workers to those who lacked rights and wage relations. Accumulation by dispossession runs through the subway and silent lanes of a capitalism that has it as a central part of its profit production and its reproductive process. Racialized, migrant, sexed and gendered bodies are re-produced as components of natural resources, which capital exploits, dominates and destroys in many cases gratuitously. Thus, this diversity of bodies and subjectivities are produced as exploited and dispossessed territories of capitalist accumulation.

For these feminist analyses, the exploitation of feminized and racialized bodies resembles the abuse of nature insofar as they are produced as resources that capital extracts until their exhaustion or destruction. Thus, both the destructive and polluting production of technique, as well as the production of a necro-politics of capital over certain bodies (Valencia, 2018), show that the productive forces of capitalism are at the same time destructive. In making this claim, these feminisms understand that there is an overdetermined relation between the social war machine of capital and the technical machine of the technological production of fixed capital (Lazzarato, 2021). In this sense, they break with the reigning productivism of some Marxist analyses and their positive reading of capitalist development, which unfolded as necessary and independent of class struggle. On the contrary, they argue that the technical production of capital is first and foremost a machine of destruction of bodies, subjectivities, and nature in a differential but global way in the process of capital production and accumulation.

Therefore, these feminisms re-politicize social spaces and relations by reinserting them into the capitalist subjective structuring, modulations, and processes of capital valorization. The materiality that defines the capitalist defense of private property is extended to multiple modes of labor that traverse the sphere of the intimate, family, and intersubjective structures in differential ways, making these differences—of forms of labor and production of subjectivities—the mode of accumulation of profit assembled to a logic of abstract valorization of capital that is already directly social.

6.5 The feminist tide: the movement that transforms the existing state of affairs

For these feminisms, it is necessary to problematize the modes of production of value in patriarchal-colonial capitalism, not only focusing on a theory of the socio-sexual-racial and international division of labor, but also on its incessant relationship with the continuous re-production of society through processes of capital accumulation and commodified production of subjectivities and labor power. These feminisms highlight the importance of making visible a whole series of jobs, links and violence that are hidden and reproduced in a sexual division of labor whose moments can be historicized (Federici, 2021; Fraser, 2016). This naturalizes the role of women, feminized and racialized people producing them as a) subjectivities confined to the world of emotions with determined morals, behavior, sexuality, and as reproductive bodies biologically and physiologically determined in the hegemonic sex-gender binarism; b) second-class citizens, in part because they are the property of both the state and the white males; c) as a labor force that is assigned to reproductive tasks, domestic, affective and care work, which are socially and economically devalued.

If "feminism seems to serve less and less to women and increasingly to the leftist cultural revolution" (Laje, 2019, p. 123), it is because, far from considering the sexual relation as a biological and natural determination, feminisms put it in check. Thus, both from the perspective of queer theories and from materialist and Marxist feminisms, men and women are not biological facts but socially produced roles. Sexes—and not only genders—are reproduced and configured in a bio-social and cultural, performative context. The main enemy of these feminisms is not "the male" but patriarchy and its hegemonic maleness, and, therefore, the subject of feminisms are not women in biological terms but *cis* or *trans* women, lesbians, intersex, etc. as political figures antagonistic to the norm and the system as a social totality. From this point of view, patriarchal heterosexuality is a reproductive political regime that is sustained as a powerful ideological device that ensures and reproduces sexual roles and practices, which are naturally attributed to the male and female genders, as an arbitrary set of regulations inscribed on bodies that ensure the material exploitation of one sex over the other. To question the naturalness of the existing relationship between hegemonic masculinity and femininity is to question the patriarchy that the theoreticians and militants of the radical right ignore in theory to better sustain it in practice.

On the other hand, these feminisms warn us that patriarchal control and the production of feminized and racialized labor are a central part of the systematic logic of capital and cannot be restricted to a specific sphere or space. Thus, putting the focus on a perspective of social reproduction allows us to take the analysis beyond the notions of care and domestic work, by embracing the reproduction of both life and patriarchal-colonial capitalist relations (Mezzadri, 2019). That is, to understand both the reproduction of workers and the labor force in the framework of certain conditions of value production and social-sexual-racial and international division of labor. If labor itself becomes a commodity under capitalism by becoming labor power, it is because it has needed past labor to be able to produce and reproduce itself and needs it every day to be able to work again or to be sold on the market. Thus, the commodity labor power "hides" objectified labor in it and this is one more part that the capitalist absorbs as surplus value and assumes the form of feminized, racialized, informal and/or free labor.

Understanding labor power as a commodity (and not as human capital) implies understanding it as a contradictory process where the physical, cognitive, and affective capabilities necessary at a given historical moment are generated, producing the bodies and subjectivities of the workers. Commodities which, like any other, have value because they have labor time objectified in them, and which capital tries to re-produce incessantly and at the lowest possible cost. However, at the same time, this commodity, as Marx says, is "special" and "unique" since it is that which has the capacity to generate value. This peculiar commodity is the one that today has become feminized, precarious, flexible, indebted, and financialized.

Therefore, these feminisms agree that, in order to keep the revolutionary question alive, that is to say the movement that puts in check the existing state of affairs, it is necessary to expand the very notion of labor, transcending the category of wage and wage-earning subject. In this way, they propose to understand a dynamic of class struggle that includes workers' struggles beyond the wage and broaden the debates on working conditions, because class is already sex-gendered and racially determined. This allows us not only to recover a dynamic present of the notion of proletarian class, but also a history that understands the wage worker as exploited but evidences the privilege of the wage and its coloniality vis-à-vis a racialized and feminized sector of the class, which is taken as an almost natural resource that can be exploited and dominated at will, while at the same time that they function as disciplining the salaried labor force to lower its costs and cut its rights.

Once this perspective is considered, we can affirm that the informality, precariousness, and labor flexibilization that feminists denounced in domestic and reproductive work not only reproduced exponentially during the global neoliberal era, but also found new channels of transmission and spaces of production. This process has become central to the current logics of value production, blurring the line between value-generating activities and spheres and those that do not produce value, rendering obsolete the parameters based on different types of tasks and modes of remuneration. Contrary to the assumption of one reading of Marxism, which claimed that in the development of capitalism gender and race distinctions would disappear by the very development of the productive forces, the opposite is true: these complex dynamics of capital valorization imply the maintenance of sex-gender, race, age, ethnic and national distinctions within the working class, and are affirmed on different reproductive and labor processes.

Specifically, capitalism separates the processes of production and reproduction, while differentially producing the reproduction of the working class. It is therefore necessary to listen to feminisms that broaden the very notion of labor and class struggle to include struggles beyond wages and classical working conditions, hence showing the social valorization of difference that capital accumulation produces.

6.6 By way of conclusion

As we stated in the introduction to this chapter, there is an antagonism between the new radical right—which materializes in certain political movements and current governments—and popular, Marxist, materialist, and queer feminisms. While the former strives to sustain the existing order of things or even return to a past where the hierarchy between genders, sexes, races, and nationalities was unquestionable, the latter seeks to revolutionize it, extracting its power and its poetry from the future. Both anti-feminist right-wingers and anti-capitalist feminisms understand that the problem of bio-social reproduction, and therefore control over the bodies and sexuality of women, is central to the production and valorization of capital, to the exploitation and domination of working subjectivities, and to the maintenance of a patriarchal order where the heterosexual norm and male domination remain in force. In this way, economic-political institutions such as the family, private property, wage labor, the heterosexual regime, social and spatial hierarchies, etc. are fundamental to guarantee the reproduction of patriarchal-colonial capitalism. For this reason, the conflict between these anti-feminist right-wingers against what they call "gender ideology" and feminist struggles is presented fundamentally through issues that are central to bio-social reproduction and in a polemic regarding the desirable economic organization. This includes the role of the state and the law in issues such as abortion, comprehensive sex education, same-sex activity—transformed into "cultural homosexualism"—reproductive health—and "unnatural" sexual practices—male violence—whose existence antifeminism denies—forms of enjoyment and use of bodies and contraception, gender identity, egalitarian marriage, etc.

As we have seen, for these right-wingers it is fundamental to construct both theoretically and politically an enemy that allows the unification of certain social sectors on the basis of a white, heterosexual, gendered identity—sexually determined as male and female—insofar as putting in check these structures and technologies of subjectivation would shake not only the pre-existing social hierarchies but also the productivity and valorization of capital. These rightists thus activate hatred, racism, xenophobia, and sexism through the rejection of all those who are strangers to the patriarchal, colonial and capitalist norm. All those who organize, reject, and dispute the norm are considered not only as abnormal, to be re-educated or excluded, but as the new communists—or useful idiots—to be combated. That is, as subjects possessed by an evil that society must exorcise and eliminate if it does not want to see its foundations undermined.

Regarding this characterization, it should be noted that even from certain left-wing thinkers or militants, there seems to be unanimity that we find ourselves—after the crisis of the communist internationals and the collapse of the USSR—, facing a right-wing anti-communism without a communist alternative in the practices of resistance. However, if communism is *the real movement that annuls and overcomes the current state of things*, feminisms, as we try to demonstrate, and as their most conspicuous detractors fear, put into question not only a partial aspect of our socio-cultural forms but the very institution of culture as we know it (patriarchy) and not only a partial aspect of economic exploitation but its very condition of possibility: the dispossession of reproductive labor. Therefore, as theoretical-political movements, they oppose the destructive continuity of patriarchal-colonial capitalism, and, in this sense, can be considered "communist". Of course, not because they attempt to replicate the organizational forms of historical communist internationals or socialist states, but because they organize international, regional and local modes of resistance to colonial-patriarchal-capitalist domination and exploitation, through an analysis of the social reproduction of capital, and at the same time, they disrupt the limits of the subject of revolution—white, masculine, and heterosexual.

In this sense, it could be said with Federici that, if neoliberal capitalism leads to a privatization and dispossession of reproductive work and of the common goods necessary for the reproduction of life, one of the possible responses has to do with their collectivization. This leads us to ask ourselves about the commons in neoliberal capitalism, since it has been one of the key concepts and spheres for thinking about resistance and the possibility of an alternative. If the revolution is to be feminist, it will also be a reinvention and a revolution of the common.

7 Rethinking the common(s) in neoliberal capitalism

In the last decades, the common(s) has emerged as a key concept both in theoretical and political terms. Not surprisingly, this emergence coincided with the violent imposition of neoliberal reforms and governmentality and the recognition of the failure of socialism during the twentieth century. In that context, while the hegemonic discourse maintains that "there is no alternative" to neoliberal reason and the new right-wing populisms denounce any attempt to limit the reach of the market as communism, the commoners are striving precisely to build an alternative to both neoliberal capitalism and state socialism from below.

In this chapter, I try to think this relationship between neoliberal capitalism and the common(s) in terms of *dispossession, expropriation,* and *configuration.* As we have discussed in the introduction of this book, neoliberalism implies a radicalization of capitalism itself, which from its very beginnings has commodified and expropriated the commons and continues to do so, searching for new realms to colonize, hence producing a second great enclosure of the commons. At the same time, neoliberal governmentality aims at transforming society and subjectivity into a polymorphic enterprise that has competition as a norm for action, hence submitting every form of social cooperation to the expanded reproduction of capital. To do so, the economic realm must be controlled by an elite of experts who should avoid the egalitarian policies to which democracy would inevitably lead. This is precisely the opposite to a kind of politics that strives to create institutions of collective decision-making and production. In order to better understand this tension between neoliberal reason and the common, I will review a few landmarks of the contemporary debate on the commons in social sciences and political thought. First, I will comment on Hardin's theory of the tragedy of the commons, which was later refuted by many scholars, including Elinor Ostrom's neo-institutionalist approach, which also helps to differentiate analytically common goods from commons. Then, I will try to characterize their relationship with neoliberal capitalism in order to discuss to what extent the common(s) are already an alternative form of cooperation and self-government to private property and state sovereignty. Finally, I will try to problematize the role of the state for a politics of the common in order to ask if the very institution that has enabled the expansion of capitalism at the expense of the common(s) can be an ally in their promotion.

https://doi.org/10.1515/9783110723939-009

7.1 Defining the commons and their imaginary tragedy

Contemporary reflections on the commons usually start discussing the famous article published in 1968 by Garrett Hardin, "The tragedy of the commons", either to stress the necessary failure of common property and management of resources (the tragedy) or to show how misguided the article was. Hardin wanted to discuss population growth in a world of limited resources and in which each family is free to decide on breeding. To do so, he uses the metaphor of herders in an open pasture in which the only *rational choice* would be to maximize one's own benefit at the expense of the rest, leading to the depletion of the common resource. More generally, Hardin thought that self-interested and rational individuals will behave towards common resources as *free riders* who will try to benefit from them, making others pay the costs. From that he concludes: "Each man is locked into a system that compels him to increase his herd without limit in a world that is limited. Ruin is the destination toward which all men rush, each pursuing his own best interest in a society that believes in the freedom of the commons" (Hardin, 1968, p. 1244).

Contrary to the providential image of the invisible hand, according to which the common good is the outcome of individual search to maximize self-interest, Hardin shows how individual rational decisions can lead to collective irrational outcomes, like the exhaustion of common goods when no rules for access and use are enforced. Hardin maintains that overpopulation, pollution, or the depletion of natural resources are challenges that have no technical solution and can only be overcome by a change in our behavior that cannot be achieved by appealing to the consciousness of individuals. Hence, the only solutions he envisaged was either privatizing the resource or establishing "mutual coercion, mutually agreed upon by the majority of the people affected", (Hardin, 1968) that for him implied the intervention of the state.

In the following years, this theory has been influential not only in the realm of demography or biology, but also in neoliberal economics and in free market environmentalism, which used Hardin's theory to support privatization and commodification as the only available answer against free riding in the use of common and public resources and against pollution. This comes as no surprise if we consider Hardin's reflections in an article that proposes to avoid both international aid to poor nations and immigration to the wealthiest ones, since, bearing in mind the differential rate of population growth that exists between poor and rich countries, in both cases we will be creating more pollution, more poor people, more need for aid and less wealth for *our* future generations. In that article called "Lifeboat Ethics: the Case Against Helping the Poor" (1974) Hardin opposes the spaceship ethics, which considers that we all share a common fate and have equal rights to available resources, to the lifeboat ethics which implies that only part of us is inside a boat with limited capacity (the wealthy nations) while three fourths of the world's population are swimming around and trying to get in. Hence, he claims that pure justice or the Marxian principle of "to everyone according to his needs" would lead to catastrophe (we will all sink). And he explains again the tragedy of the commons in this way:

> The fundamental error of spaceship ethics, and the sharing it requires, is that it leads to what I call "the tragedy of the commons". Under a system of private property, the men who own property recognize their responsibility to care for it, for if they don't they will eventually suffer. A farmer, for instance, will allow no more cattle in a pasture than its carrying capacity justifies. If he overloads it, erosion sets in, weeds take over, and he loses the use of the pasture. If a pasture becomes a commons open to all, the right of each to use it may not be matched by a corresponding responsibility to protect it. [...] In a crowded world of less than perfect human beings, mutual ruin is inevitable if there are no controls. This is the tragedy of the commons. [...] Only the replacement of the system of the commons with a responsible system of control will save the land, air, water and oceanic fisheries. (Hardin, 1974, p. 38 ff)

In this article, Hardin's penchant for private property guaranteed by state coercion as the ultimate solution to the tragedy of the commons is evident. Although his way of reasoning sounds compelling to those who promote privatization and commodification as the more efficient way to manage public and common resources,[1] his analysis was contested both theoretically and empirically by different scholars.

For instance, 2009 Nobel Prize Elinor Ostrom has studied theoretically and empirically since the 1970s the issues raised by Hardin's theory, even within his rational choice framework. One of these problems is precisely "how best to limit the use of natural resources so as to ensure their long-term economic viability". (Ostrom, 1990, p. 1) In that framework, Ostrom showed that Hardin's theory was fundamentally wrong since social agents do not necessarily act following their immediate self-interest and also since users can make arrangements in order to manage common-pool resources. Ostrom explained that Hardin's assumption of no communication between agents, as in the prisoner's dilemma in game theory, had nothing to do with the reality of common-pool resources, in which conditions of access and use can be agreed and enforced by the participants.[2]

---

1 Interestingly, for Hardin the commons are the realm of freedom and his description of them resembles the Hobbesian state of nature, while private property is what limits freedom in order to avoid the tragedy.

2 Let me clarify that CPR does not necessarily entail communal property. Hess and Ostrom maintain that: "Shared resource systems—called common-pool resources—are types of economic

In fact, apart from ignoring historical and empirical evidence, Hardin confused common goods or common-pool resources with unregulated and open access. Indeed, twentieth century economics distinguishes four types of goods in terms of *exclusiveness* and *rivalry*. A good is *exclusive* when its owner can impede access to any person who doesn't buy it at the requested price and is *rival* when its acquisition or use by an individual diminishes the quantity of the good available to other people. Hence, there are *purely private goods*, which are exclusive and rival (like a privately owned motorbike); *purely public goods*, which are neither exclusive nor rival, like an open park; *club goods*, which are exclusive and non-rival, like a concert in a closed theatre; and *common goods*, which are non-exclusive but rival, like open pastures, irrigation systems or fisheries, in which it is difficult to limit access and usage unless rules are established.

Following this classification, Hardin's text should be called "The tragedy of unregulated open access". In fact, as we will discuss later, the real tragedy of the commons from the birth of capitalism to our days had less to do with their immanent unsustainability than with their expropriation by market forces with support from the state. In this sense, David Harvey (2011), maintains that "If the cattle were held in common [...] [Hardin's] metaphor would not work. It would then be clear that *it was private property in cattle and individual utility-maximizing behavior that lay at the heart of the problem*". Another problem identified by Harvey is that Hardin uses a small-scale metaphor to think a global problem, while the commons and the design of institutions for its successful management varies with scale.

The latter is clear in the empirical research made by Ostrom and her school, who elaborated a theory on the functioning of common pool resources based on several case studies of different commons that survived and still thrive around the world (from lobster fisheries in Maine to open pastures for milk/cheese production in Switzerland, from fisheries in Turkey and Sri Lanka to irrigation systems in Spain and Philippines), seeking to understand the motivations social actors have in order to manage certain resources collectively and which are the institutional arrangements that enable their successful management. In that famous work of 1990, which focuses on natural commons, most of which are of a small scale with a maximum of 15,000 appropriators, she identifies that the design principles of long-enduring CPR institutions are: Clearly defined boundaries; Congruence between appropriation and provision rules and local conditions; Collective-choice arrangements; effective monitoring; graduated

---

goods, independent of particular property rights. Common property on the other hand is a legal regime—a jointly owned legal set of rights". (2008, p. 5)

sanctions: conflict-resolution mechanisms, Minimal recognition of rights of the appropriators to organize; and multiple layers of nested enterprises for larger CPR systems. (Ostrom, 1990, p. 90) To sum up, even if the legal property of a resource can be public, collective, or private, CPRs are managed collectively following a series of rules that are accepted by the participants. At the same time, these principles show the importance of democratic and participative management of CPR to guarantee their sustainability.

Another limit to Hardin's theory for thinking present-day commons is that his theory can only work in a context of scarcity, to which most material or natural commons are subject (finite world, lack of food, depletion of fish, lack of clean air and water, etc.). However, in the last decades, knowledge commons and immaterial goods have become more influential in the economy and everyday life. The main difference with natural resources is that with digitalization these immaterial goods are not depleted by overuse and, even when investment in design and innovation can be high, once these goods are produced, they can be reproduced at almost no cost (Rifkin, 2014). In fact, these kinds of goods seem to tend towards a *comedy of the commons*, which, according to Carol Rose (1986), who was writing before the advent of internet about *inherently public property*, follows the principle "the more the merrier". For instance, the more people take part of production and use of software, music, etc. the more valuable they become. In this area, if there is a tragedy, it is that of private and intellectual property, which, by creating scarcity in an artificial way, hinders innovation and information sharing.

As Hess and Ostrom recognize, knowledge usually "fell into the category of a public good since it was difficult to exclude people from knowledge once someone had made a discovery" (2008, p. 9) However, the introduction of new technologies and juridical rules can enable the capture of what were once free and open public goods. When this happens, the resource at stake is converted "from a nonrivalrous, nonexclusionary public good into a common-pool resource that needs to be managed, monitored, and protected, to ensure sustainability and preservation" (2008, p. 10).

Therefore, even if material and immaterial goods are different from each other, what defines a good as common are not its intrinsic properties, but *the institutional framework, juridical rules, available technologies, and social practices* that make it such (Vercelli & Thomas, 2008).[3] In this sense, Benjamin Coriat

---

3 For example, some Constitutions and Civil Codes recognize the existence of common goods and communal property while others don't. A UN 2010 resolution declares access to water and sanitation as a human right. However, many societies have privatized water supply while others have decided to maintain it as public or even as common. This can be stated about

maintains that a commons exists only when there is: a) a shared resource, b) modes of access and rules for sharing it, and c) a form of governance of the resource that enforces the rights of access to it (Coriat, 2015).[4] Therefore, there is no commons without commoners, since it is collective action that defines the common, the rights attached to it, and their forms of management and conservation. Put otherwise, a common is defined not by a good as such, but by the system of reciprocal rights and obligations between participants and their capacity of enforcement. Hence, one of the flaws in Hardin's argument is that it substantializes the resources and assumes a universal set of needs and behaviors (those of the neoclassical *homo oeconomicus*) that lead to a tragic outcome. However, he says nothing about different types of commons and cultural differences in appreciation, production, distribution, and consumption of common resources.[5]

In this sense, Coriat stresses the importance for a political thought on contemporary commons of Ostrom's research, that includes studies on informational and knowledge commons, and of those of Stallman and the hacker movement on free software, that include works on copyright, open source, and public domain. Even though Ostrom's scope was limited in her political ambitions, Coriat maintains that the movement of the commons can become a form of resistance and an alternative solution to representation and exclusive property rights, coinciding with the movement of free software and free culture, with the creation of rules of General Public License, Copyleft and Creative Commons. (Coriat, 2015). In the latter, the right of property is subverted, since it is used not to exclude but to include people who can access, enrich, and modify the good. As Stallman stated, *copyleft* uses copyright laws so that instead of being a means to privatize software, it is a means for keeping it free (Stallman, 2002, p. 22). Put otherwise, *it excludes exclusion*. These principles of sharing and inclusion have inspired licenses that go beyond software, which for some scholars imply the possibility to reconquer the right of property for the commons. (Orsi, 2015)

---

clean air or clean water: new technologies have polluted them, making them exhaustible and even unavailable to people that live in polluted areas. Something of the sort occurs with Intellectual Property Rights in the knowledge commons. For instance, we can think of the dialectic between digitalization, that make information sharable at cero marginal cost, and Copyleft, Open Access and General Public License that try to overcome exclusion, and juridical rules on Intellectual Property Rights and technical protocols that impede file sharing as a clear example of the struggle between artificial barriers that enclose knowledge commons and the communities that strive to make those goods accessible.

4 These same dimensions can be found in the account of David Bollier (2014) and the Metropolitan Observatory of Madrid.

5 Vandana Shiva (2002), states that scarcity and abundance in relation to water are not facts of nature but a product of culture.

Despite the ethnocentrism one may find in Coriat's classification (why not include, for instance, Indigenous peoples' movements and thought?), this political dimension is essential to understand the struggle between the common and its commodification. In this sense, this renewed reflection on the commons is tantamount to a thinking of politics, cooperation, and production as alternative to both capitalism and liberal politics. (Gutiérrez Aguilar, 2001) Yet at the same time, there is no universal principle to promote and sustain a common. Hence, only the stakeholders can decide how best to manage common resources.

To sum up, the distinction between commons and common goods clarifies the importance of institutions and practices (the commons), and hence of politics, to struggle for the institution, protection, and autonomous management of common goods. In that sense, Sandro Mezzadra (2008) proposes that we should not conceive the common as something given and assume that "the common must be produced by a collective subject capable in its own making of destroying the bases of exploitation and reinvent the common conditions of a production structured around the synthesis of freedom and equality". This goal is clearly opposed to neoliberal capitalism which relation to the common we will now seek to conceptualize.

7.2 The real tragedy: the common(s) in neoliberal capitalism

To a great extent, the politics of the commons reemerged with such impulse in neoliberal era as a response to the new wave of *enclosures* and the multifarious subsumption of life to capitalism that took place in the last three decades. Following some of the main perspectives developed in the last decade, I synthesize the relationship between neoliberal capitalism and the commons in terms of *dispossession, expropriation,* and *configuration.*

Dispossession names a form of wealth *accumulation* that privatizes public and communal resources and commodifies realms that were exterior to the market, through violent means like armed force, police repression and juridical coercion. This form of accumulation, which was theorized by Marx as primitive accumulation and described as the original sin of capitalism, has been widely discussed in recent years (De Angelis, 2001; Mezzadra, 2008; Federici, 2014; Harvey, 2003; 2005, Alliez & Lazzarato, 2016) as an ongoing process that reenacts the enclosures of the commons (their real tragedy) under new conditions. The first great movement of enclosures, famously described by Marx, introduced into the emerging capitalist production the lands that were open to communal use by declaring consuetudinary rights of commoners (to harvest fallen branches of trees and wild fruits or using open pastures to feed their animals) as robbery.

Most importantly, they enabled the production of producers, since the *bills of enclosure* of lands and *clearing of estates*, together with the harsh laws against vagabondage obliged peasants to populate the cities and incorporate to the nascent industrial production, giving birth to the modern proletariat (Marx, 1906).

Actualizing Rosa Luxembourg's reflections on Imperialism and the continuity of primitive accumulation[6], Massimo De Angelis (2001), Silvia Federici (2014) and David Harvey (2003; 2005) maintain that far from being a superseded historical stage, primitive accumulation is inherent to capitalism, in which the separation of producers from their means of production is constantly reenacted.

> Primitive accumulation is the strategy the capitalist class always resorts to in times of crisis, when the command over labor has to be reasserted, since expropriating workers and expanding the labor available for exploitation are the most effective methods for re-establishing the "proper balance of power" and gaining the upper hand in the class struggle. In the era of neo-liberalism and globalization this strategy has been extremized and normalized, making primitive accumulation and the privatization of the 'commonwealth' a permanent process, now extending to every area and aspect of our existence (Caffentzis & Federici, 2014, p. 94).

When capital finds difficulties for its reproduction and accumulation, it recurs to the methods of primitive accumulation that deepen the privatization and commodification of the common. As we have seen in the Introduction of this book, this new wave of enclosures by neoliberal capitalism was theorized by Harvey as *accumulation by dispossession*, which:

> include the commodification and privatization of land and the forceful expulsion of peasant populations [...]; conversion of various forms of property rights (common, collective, state, etc.) into exclusive private property rights [...]; suppression of rights to the commons; commodification of labour power and the suppression of alternative (indigenous) forms of production and consumption; colonial, neocolonial, and imperial processes of appropriation of assets (including natural resources); monetization of exchange and taxation, particularly of land; the slave trade (which continues particularly in the sex industry); and usury, the national debt and, most devastating of all, the use of the credit system as a radical means of accumulation by dispossession. The state, with its monopoly of violence and def-

---

6 While Lenin seems to understand primitive accumulation as an historical stage of capitalism, Rosa Luxembourg reads imperialism as part of capitalism's need to incorporate non capitalist spaces through the means of primitive accumulation in order to avoid its crisis and maintain its expansion. The reflection on new enclosures that took part since the 1990s, especially since the number of *Midnight notes* on "New Enclosures", extends Luxembourg's intuition to new realms of non-capitalist social relations that capital needs to colonize. Put differently, capital always needs to produce an outside to be colonized and to enable the expansion of its process of production and accumulation.

initions of legality, plays a crucial role in both backing and promoting these processes. To this list of mechanisms we may now add a raft of techniques such as the extraction of rents from patents and intellectual property rights and the diminution or erasure of various forms of common property rights (such as state pensions, paid vacations, and access to education and health care) won through a generation or more of class struggle. (Harvey, 2005, pp. 159–169)

As we have seen in the introductory chapter, Harvey maintains that the main goal of neoliberalism was to reestablish the conditions for capital accumulation and restore the power of economic elites after thirty years of Keynesianism. In many parts of the world, this expansion of new enclosures and dispossession by neoliberal governments implied massive privatization of public enterprises and public services, a new impulse to extractivism (mining, land grabbing, etc.) at the expense of communal lands and their inhabitants, and the ever-growing weight of both public and private debt on national economies and everyday life. No wonder that neoliberal capitalism has been more successful in reestablishing the power of elites or creating new ones in an always more unequal global society than in resuming economic growth. Apart from that, the only merit Harvey recognizes in neoliberal policies is that they managed to control inflation. (Harvey, 2005)

Finally, one of the forms of reenacting primitive accumulation is the growing violence against women and their autonomy, the poor and their conditions of survival, and looting of neocolonial spaces (Federici, 2014). Indeed, a close reading of the history of capitalism suggests that economic efficiency is not necessarily the main goal of enclosures. On the contrary, they have always sought to destroy the autonomy and self-government of the commoners, transforming them into atomized and heteronomous subjects who are forced to enter capitalist relations and to produce surplus value. In this context, it is important to recall that in many parts of the world, communal property of land is not a remainder of premodern times but part of the reproduction of life in a collectivity that assumes the autonomous, self-regulated and self-determined capacity of deciding on matters that have to do with its symbolic and material production. (Gutiérrez & Salazar Lohman, 2015, p. 20) In fact, Bollier (2014) maintains that 2 billion people still rely on communal forms of management of farmlands, fisheries and water for their survival which are being destroyed by new forms of land grabbing and the promotion of private property by international agencies.

To sum up, the notion of dispossession stresses that real subsumption of labor power to capital and capitalist accumulation is a permanent reality that goes hand in hand with a violent process of commodification of practices and goods that were exterior to it. It implies both the enclosure of *material commons*—like with land grabbing, privatization of water supplies or mining—and *intellectual commons*—like with biopiracy, data mining and copyright extension. However, Harvey maintains that the difference between primitive accumulation and dispossession is that while the former opens the way to expanded reproduction and therefore can have beneficial effects for people who are being included in capitalist economy, the latter refers to the destruction of opportunities engendered by capitalism itself. In this sense, Harvey states that not every struggle against dispossession is progressive. Even though this distinction may be useful to think some contemporary experiences, it presupposes a progressive nature of true, productive capitalism based on expanded reproduction and exploitation that would be interrupted by dispossession, something that we have already put into question in the previous chapter. Therefore, Alliez and Lazzarato (2016) state that we should not separate exploitation from dispossession and class struggle from those struggles in defense of the commons to later find a dialectic bond between them, as Harvey seems to do.

In this sense, assuming the prevalence of rent over profit and the inseparability of finance from real production in present-day capitalism, Hardt and Negri refer to the *expropriation* of the common. For them, the common is formed by "the common wealth of the material world—the air, the water, the fruits of the soil, and all nature's bounty—which in classic European political texts is often claimed to be the inheritance of humanity as a whole, to be shared together" and "also and more significantly those results of social production that are necessary for social interaction and further production, such as knowledges, languages, codes, information, affects, and so forth". (2009, p. viii)

These authors share Harvey's assertion that the "main substantive achievement of neoliberalization [...] has been to redistribute, rather than to generate, wealth and income" (Harvey, 2005, p. 159). However, they maintain that critiques of neoliberalism in terms of dispossession focus too much on the expropriation of existing wealth but do not offer a proper account of the production of new wealth in contemporary capitalism. To do so, they analyze the organic composition of capital in which the key element is the productivity of living labor. For them, dispossession may explain the fate of natural commons and public enterprises that are privatized and commodified. However, the generative artificial common, where there should be no scarcity, would be the key to understand biopolitical exploitation as the main form of production and extraction of surplus value. For these authors, with the intellectualization, digitalization and affectivization of labor, wealth is produced immediately in common. If in the Fordist phase of capitalism, productive processes and social life were submitted to the rhythms of disciplinary institutions and *general intellect* was concentrated in fix capital, as Marx had already envisaged in his *Grundrisse*, in post-Fordist capitalism the hegemonic sector would be the cognitive one. In this sense, *general intellect*, which is the main source of increases in productivity and relative surplus value, is not objectified in machines anymore. Rather, it resides in the decentralized net of singularities that cooperate with ever greater autonomy from fix spaces, rhythms, and forms of organization by the corporations. Hence, the common is produced and reproduced by a multitude of affective and cognitive workers who are expropriated by a rentistic apparatus that vampirizes autonomous social cooperation and common wealth through what economists call "positive externalities", which are a mystification of the common (2009, p. 141). Examples of these externalities are the expropriation of social cooperation in the gentrification of popular neighborhoods, the use of commons-based peer-produced software by big companies that benefit in that way from unpaid labor or even biopiracy, in which multinational corporations seek to obtain property rights over seeds and plants whose nutritive or medical uses were discovered by traditional communities.

In Hardt and Negri's account, these externalities show the contradiction between capital's need of the common to create new wealth and the obstacles produced by the strategies of control it imposes on its development, reducing the productivity of a biopolitical labor that needs an open access to the common. This expropriation of the common that hinders its development occurs in two main ways: intensively, by "segmenting or draining the common bases of production" and extensively, by "privatizing the common results". (2009, p. 145) The former takes place for instance when capital imposes fetters on sharing knowledge through intellectual property rights or by defunding public education and research, which hinders the production of new knowledge, ideas, and innovation. The latter occurs when finance expropriates and privatizes "the common wealth embedded in the accumulated knowledges, codes, images, affective practices, and biopolitical relationships" created by productive networks.

In a similar vein, Rifkin (2014) maintains that the commons of knowledge, internet, energy, etc. in which cooperators build an open and decentralized architecture are much more efficient and sustainable than private or public property, leading to a society of zero marginal cost, in which an ever growing sharing economy of collaborative commons starts to replace forms of production and consumption based on competition and exclusion. The problem with Rifkin's perspective is that it seems to bet on the possibility that market capitalism will be silently replaced by collaborative commons because decentralized and autonomous digital networks are more efficient than private property and entrepreneurial management, and because the high productivity and reduction of costs is draining the bases of profit. Hence, according to this view, by its own dynamics of competition and technological change capitalism is arriving to its end.

As we can see, these perspectives focus too much on the hegemonic sector of capitalism to understand its tendencies and therefore theorize a unitary logic for heterogeneous realities. Even if Hardt and Negri recognize the need to build political institutions of the multitude to act politically, there are not many signs that the cognitariat is moving towards revolution. Hence, they implicitly seem to bet once again on the revolutionary outcome of the contradiction between the development of productive forces and social relations of production.[7]

However, we should not forget that "traditional" commons that are linked to subsistence economies with dense social ties, and which are under siege by state and private violence, are as important as digital commons, in which social ties are usually virtual and remote and in which scarcity would be artificially created by juridical rules or technical protocols.[8] In fact, the very existence of the digital economy relies in the extraction of minerals like coltan, leading to warfare in places like Democratic Republic of Congo, or to the massive waste of energy, the production of which pollutes our planet. On the other hand, the commons are not a technical solution to social problems but part of a contingent field of struggle in its aims and results. In fact, not only most commoners are not trying to overthrow capitalism or the neoliberal state but also sharing economy becomes every year a greater source of profit for private companies and of huge savings for public agencies, creating positive externalities to capital. Hence efficiency and emancipation are two goals of the commons that not always coincide (Ibañez & De Castro, 2015).

In this sense, even though Dardot and Laval agree with Hardt and Negri in criticizing the centrality of dispossession, since it overemphasizes pillage and robbery in detriment of an analysis of exploitation, they reject the idea that today's capitalism is essentially rentistic, that there is an autonomization of immaterial labor and that there is a spontaneous development of informational communism. (2019a). Indeed, the idea of an autonomous social cooperation of the multitude can be misleading, since in neoliberal capitalism there is a production and *configuration* of specific forms of social cooperation that coexists with dispossession and biopolitical exploitation. For instance, Dardot and Laval show how present-day management instrumentalizes the need to communicate,

---

7 In a critical article of 1999, which addresses the idea of the end of work, George Caffentzis shows how already in the mid 90s Rifkin and Negri fall into technological determinism in order to assert that capitalism is already dead. In that article, he also criticizes the Leninist idea, still present in Negri, that the most productive subject (in this case the intellectual workers) must be a revolutionary subject when twentieth century history has shown the opposite.

8 In this sense we must remember Lessig's idea that internet architecture is defined not only by juridical rules but by coding: Code is Law.

unite and create in common. The goal of marketing is to find an ersatz of the common adjusted to capital's needs. "The management of collective intelligence "favors a new art of collective work based on sharing, intellectual assistance, and co- creation," [...] It is all a matter of substituting "command and control" with "connect and collaborate"". (Zara, 2008, p. 229 apud Dardot & Laval, 2019a, p. 118). This exploitation of social cooperation is much more evident in the realm of marketing (and of platform capitalism) in which the community of consumers they try to build and organize is one of the most valuable assets, not only because of the financial value people's data have but also because they can reduce costs of production by using their free labor. The consumers that collaborate with their comments and evaluations or give advice in the forums organized by these firms become free and willing co-producers of commodities and participants of innovation: they become *prosumers*. Hence, firms try to build the free cooperation of consumers to produce collective knowledge that will be incorporated to the productive cycle at a very low cost. "The common is thus already a managerial category that compounds the classical exploitation of workers with the unprecedented exploitation of consumer-users". (2019a, p. 120)

Therefore, even though Dardot and Laval acknowledge the importance of Hardt and Negri's work as a philosophical account of the common, they maintain that the latter implicitly recover Proudhon's idea of a spontaneous social cooperation that is expropriated *ex post* by capital, while a coherent Marxist view would try to understand the ways in which social cooperation is effectively organized by capital. It also implies ignoring many contemporary forms of exploitation of workers and the transformations induced in social relations and subjectivity by neoliberalism.

In fact, neoliberal governmental rationality organizes modes of being, thinking, acting, desiring, and producing through a process of incitement based on strategic knowledges and discourses which are intermingled with more or less subtle forms of coercion. The new subsumption of labor under capital implies an indirect and elastic orientation of behavior (2019a). The norm of competition and maximization traverses state, society, and subjectivity, creating an entrepreneurial governance of political institutions and an entrepreneur of the self that is responsible for its own success and failure (Foucault, 2008), and to whom society does not owe anything—and who in turn owes nothing to anyone. For neoliberal rationality, everyone must partake in the competition between human capitals autonomously, without *feeling* coerced to do so by an external agency and as such must be evaluated with efficiency as the main criteria to judge every behavior. This indirect coercion is exercised by different forms of precarization of life, like indebtedness, potential or actual unemployment, low incomes, defunding of social security, etc. which oblige us to "live dangerously". That coercion is the basis which enables new forms of management that promote the idea that we not only have to give our maximum at work but also must enjoy it, (Dardot & Laval, 2013) leading to *self-exploitation* (Han, 2015), which is the ultimate utopia of neoliberal governmentality, and to the diffusion of psychic suffering and new pathologies, like depression, panic attacks, stress, attention deficit, etc.

As we can see, far from being free, intellectual labor is constantly under pressure by techniques of power that measure their performance with new forms of evaluation. Therefore, firms are not passively waiting for cognitive rent. On the contrary, they try to exploit diffuse knowledge and organize *coopetition* of workers to maximize productivity. (2019a). In that sense, contemporary management tries to achieve a more internal submission, based in the motivations of workers and adherence to the firm, what Dardot and Laval call the *subjective subsumption* of workers. They conclude:

> The techniques capital has deployed are designed to govern subjects like individual capitals who must enter into hybridized cooperative competitive relations (as is touted in contemporary management literature) in order to produce maximum economic performance. These are not neutral techniques, nor are they *post hoc* devices implemented after the theft of what is created in the pure productivity of the common. These techniques actively proceed from the underlying self- valorizing logic of capital (2019a, p. 136)

Therefore, even if the common is constantly produced in neoliberal society, it is submitted to the logic of competition and maximization, producing the subsumption of life to capital, whose goal is unlimited accumulation. Even if privatization and looting of common goods is undeniable, today's capitalism not only produces processes of enclosure and dispossession. It also introduces new relationships of dependency and submission and new disciplinary apparatuses, modifying social relationships, identities, and subjectivities. In that sense, neoliberal governmentality seeks to transform every social relation, submitting social reproduction in all its components (familiar, political, cultural, etc.) to the extended reproduction of capital through the norm of competition. (Dardot & Laval, 2019a)

In that context, Dardot and Laval maintain that the common should not only be thought as an alternative form of production in the spaces where the state and the market don't intervene, or as a principle capable of undermining capitalism from within, but as a political principle of co-obligation and reciprocity that enables the institution of self-management and self-government. In that way, the common can become an alternative to a society based on competition, expropriation and commodification.

7.3 The struggle for the common within and against the state

Bearing in mind this relationship between neoliberal capitalism and the common, it is not surprising that the commons have become a major field of struggle against dispossession but also for the construction of relationships and forms of life based on "autonomy, the re-appropriation of common goods", and "the reconstruction of a sense of justice and respect" (Gutiérrez Aguilar, 2008, pp. 35–36).

As most perspectives on the common, Gutiérrez Aguilar's advocates a form of social coexistence that differs from the modern state synthesis, which is organized trough the delegation of political representation and founded in the predominance of surplus value and competition, which in turn are based on the private property of wealth that should be common (2008, pp. 18–19). In this sense, she maintains that emancipation implies changing the social configuration by generalizing a mode of social relationship based on the use value of things and the free association of people for autonomous goals. In this view, the struggle for the common is a struggle for social, economic, and political emancipation, which implies limiting private property and political representation to their minimum expression, and promoting economic self-management, political autonomy, and self-government.

In a similar vein, Dardot and Laval maintain that the common became so important because it revokes the progressive beliefs on the state and the hope that the state can limit the disastrous effects of capitalism (2019a). Shall we conclude then, as also Hardt and Negri think, that the common is an *exclusive* alternative to capitalist market and state, liberalism and socialism? Is its relationship to the state the same as with private property and market forces?

In my view, it would be theoretically and strategically mistaken to conceive the state (but also the market) as an autonomous and immutable entity. To be sure, the modern state has emerged in a symbiotic relationship with capital. Along modernity and to this day, it has been mostly part of its war machines and an agency that enabled the commodification of the commons. It has also assumed many social functions to create positive externalities for Capital. However, I would like to suggest that the state is a field of struggle that can become a key player in the protection and promotion of the commons. For instance, because of worker's struggle and the threat of communism, in most western countries a welfare state had to be built, enabling new forms of autonomy, security, and better material conditions and rights for workers. At the same time, commons like scientific knowledge, education, health, and information usually need the support of the state to develop in complex societies and are not by chance under siege by neoliberal policies[9]. The same happens with common goods like water or sanitation, in which the state must either manage them or recognize and protect legally the autonomy of the commoners to avoid their expropriation by market forces. Also, we may ask if global problems like pollution could be solved without the intervention of public authorities at a national and transnational level. Therefore, "the social state", which was an achievement of class struggle in the previous decades, "could be understood as the form in which contemporary societies manage common goods related to matters like health, security, education or transportation". (Rendueles & Sábada, 2015, p. 44)

Therefore, rather than thinking the state as a Universal and Irreversible enemy, we should acknowledge its contingent historical and geographical configurations. In the last resort, it is a vicissitude of governmentality (Foucault, 2008) and, at the same time, a field of struggle. In that sense, the problem is not the state as such. Rather, it is the hegemony of neoliberal and conservative forces who determine its policies.

This complex relationship between the state and the common can be seen in the recent history of Latin America since it has been a great laboratory of neoliberalism and dispossession and also of political resistance and attempts to build an alternative both from below and then from above. During the '90s, when neoliberal reforms advised by the Washington Consensus and imposed by the IMF, WB and the United States in order to refinance public debt were introduced everywhere, producing a social debacle of unemployment, poverty and exclusion, different social movements emerged attempting to resist neoliberal reforms, both materially—by searching ways to survive to them—, and politically—creating new forms of collective action, protest and institutions. These movements, especially the Zapatistas in Mexico in their 1994 uprising, anticipated the general rejection to political representation that exploded in many countries by the end of the decade. After that, the political forces which wanted to rule many of these impoverished countries at a national level had to consider the demands of social movements. In the 2000s neo-left, national-popular or progressive governments in the region, some of which were the outcome of politics from below, have produced social inclusion and citizenship through the expansion of rights and access to consumption which enabled the emergence of a new middle class in some countries where it was historically very narrow. In order to do so, they recovered the participation of government in the control of strategic resour-

---

9 In fact, neoliberals maintain that those services would be much better if they were provided by private enterprises or managed with the same logic. The disastrous effects of the covid-19 pandemic in the countries with health systems that were reduced to become more efficient should serve to put those assumptions into question.

ces and in the promotion of economic growth, instituting plans against poverty, building public infrastructures, and providing social services, while recognizing in some cases the rights of autonomous, peasant or indigenous communities to manage their common resources.[10] However, despite having a critical discourse towards neoliberalism, these governments relied heavily in a subordinate position in world market as providers of raw materials in order to obtain rent and redistribute it, leading to new forms of extractivism. In most cases, it also implied the erection of strong and hierarchical leaderships that in many cases reduced the autonomy of social movements. Part of the autonomist left has experienced this process of political construction as a cooptation of social movements by a hierarchical apparatus that neglects their autonomy and accelerates capital's expropriation of the common. Accordingly, many respected intellectuals and activists that took part in the struggles against neoliberal governments, have been fiercely critical of these experiences, opposing plebeian democracy to the rule by the new professionals of the state. (Gutiérrez Aguilar, 2008, p. 38)

Even though these critiques are legitimate, we must recognize that state intervention in terms of infrastructures, services and wealth-distribution had positive effects in the daily life of millions of people. In fact, if the politics of the common are not going to be reduced to local and isolated experiences, the state becomes a strategic field of struggle in order to provide social services, protect common goods, and promote the formation of new commons, as we have seen in many "rebel cities" around Europe in the last decade (Sauvêtre, 2015). As Ostrom and Harvey after her suggested, when the management of the common resources includes a great number of stakeholders or larger systems, they may need multiple-layered and hierarchical forms of decision making. A federation of the commons both in economic and political terms might entail a process of building alliances from below to enable an alternative political rationality, based on use value, sustainability, self-management and self-government, which is totally different from the neoliberal one, based on competition, commodification, exploitation and controlled autonomy. For that purpose, a realistic politics of the common should avoid state phobia and build a strategic relationship of conflict and negotiations within the state to counter neoliberal governmentality and the ever-growing forms of violence towards populations and nature and promote a governmentality of the common. As Caffentzis and Federici recognize:

---

10 For instance, 1999 Venezuelan Constitution recognizes the right of Indigenous peoples to manage the use of their resources in their territories. 2009 Bolivian Constitution recognizes the plurinationality of the country and communal property of Indigenous communities while that of Ecuador recognizes the right to good living (*sumak kawsay*).

"One of the main challenges we face is finding ways of connecting the struggle over the public to those for the construction of the common, so that they can re-inforce each other. This is more than an ideological imperative. What we call the public is actually wealth that we have produced and we must re-appropriate" (2014, p. 102).

Therefore, the struggle for the common in complex societies can be seen not just as a suicidal way of detaching social cooperation of virtuous communities from any institutional framework. Rather, it could be understood first and fore-most as a struggle within and against capitalism and its institutions and therefore within and against the state.

8 Epilogue: Neoliberalism reloaded

This book was inspired by the observation of a process of radicalization of neo-liberal policies, especially in the period following the 2008 global financial crisis, and the rise of far-right political movements and parties, which combine an unrestricted defense of private property and competitive markets with a racist, misogynist, xenophobic and aporophobic position that takes on authoritarian and punitive overtones. For some theorists, the crisis of global financial capitalism and the subsequent bailout of the banks were signs of a terminal crisis of neoliberalism. However, we have witnessed a process of radicalization of neoliberal policies, applying austerity measures and privileging the payment of creditors over the social welfare of the populations.

If, as I have argued at the beginning of this book, in addition to being the dominant governmental rationality of our time (Dardot & Laval, 2017), neoliberalism had been a class project aimed at recovering the hegemony of capital (Harvey, 2005), "the strange non-death of neoliberalism" could be explained because —unlike what happened with the crisis of Keynesianism in the 1970s—neoliberal measures benefited the hegemonic social class, which remained the same as before: global financial capital. (Crouch, 2012)

Although this is only one of the explanatory factors that could be mentioned, the truth is that, in the face of each financial, economic, health, climate or military crisis, the plutocratic oligarchy that governs the world seems to have no replacement plan, self-convinced that there is no alternative. That is why the answer to every crisis is always: keep on the same track, but faster!

In this context, the vision of a neoliberal governmentality that sought to optimize the systems of differences and was tolerant with the proliferation of multiplicities, inspired by Michel Foucault's seminars, by the policies of the neoliberal new left or third ways, and by part of the neoliberal collective, was opposed by a view that highlighted in different ways the existence of an authoritarian or punitive neoliberalism which was also anti-democratic, belligerent, conservative and even reactionary. These characterizations were due to the fact that, far from listening to the demands of those affected by the crisis, governments continued to appeal to austericist and technocratic solutions, which do nothing more than reinforce competition at all levels, cut social spending, reduce wages, precarize labor and reimburse creditors. Of course, there was no lack of experiences that proposed an alternative to neoliberal authoritarianism, but they ended up being defeated. In Latin America, progressive governments, which in the first decade of the new century had based their redistributive and social containment policies on a subordinate insertion into the global mar-

https://doi.org/10.1515/9783110723939-010

ket through the sale of commodities and discursively recovered a horizon of emancipation and social justice, entered a stage of withdrawal that, until very recently, seemed terminal. In Europe, where the social-democratic left is the best manager of neoliberal policies, grassroots movements such as the "indignados" emerged first and then left-wing populist parties—Syriza, Podemos, *La France Insoumise*, etc.—that were defeated by more powerful forces or were integrated into the traditional political system, with little margin for alternatives that sought modifications in the economic program or in the rationality of government. The bailout of the banks that had caused the crisis in the United States gave rise to the Occupy Wall Street movement and left-wing populist leaderships such as Bernie Sanders, but also gave rise to the Tea Party, which rejected Obama's recovery plan and strengthened the alternative right, which, in the end, served as a precedent and platform for the meteoric rise of Trump. In this context, far from leading to the social transformation called for by the massive protest movements, the crisis deepened the most anti-democratic and violent features of neoliberalism, from which the new radical rightists emerged triumphant, with their appeal to an anti-establishment, anti-globalist and anti-progressive discourse.

Indeed, after a period of popular revolt that reached its climax in 2011—from the Arab Spring to the various movements in the squares in large cities around the world—social unrest and anger began to be capitalized by radical right-wing populisms that, in some cases, implied a novelty while in others were the product of more patient political constructions, as in the British, American, French or Italian case.[1] With the electoral victory of Trump, Brexit, Salvini, Bolsonaro, Johnson, Modi, the continuity of leaders such as Erdogan, Putin, Orbán, Netanyahu, etc. and with the radicalization of discourse and measures marked by hatred of immigrants, "gender ideology" and "communism", for many theorists it was no longer enough to highlight the rise of far-right forces or to observe their mainstreaming, but rather characterizations of these movements in terms of neofascism, post-fascism, neo-liberal fascism, etc. proliferated. In fact, as opposed to those who argued that there were not too many points in common between

---

1 The novelty of these far-right populist parties is often emphasized. However, as we saw, the declared strategy of a right-wing populism that led to Trump's triumph has important immediate antecedents in the paleolibertarian and paleoconservative movement of the 90s. Brexit was inspired by Thatcher's national-liberalism. The *Lega* today is the oldest party in the Italian party system. *Rassemblement National*, beyond the change of policy, originates from the Front National founded in 1972, and the list could go on. In that sense, the major novelty is not the existence of these types of parties, movements, and ideologies but how the extremes became mainstream. (Miller-Idriss, 2017)

the new right and historical fascism, there were others for whom speaking of right-wing populisms was euphemistic, while opposing it to a left-wing populism was absolutely unfeasible, because the left should address its discourse to another public and mobilize another type of passions (Fassin, 2018a; Lazzarato, 2020). What most theorists seemed to agree on was that neoliberal governmentality could no longer be analyzed as a kind of soft power, and that, although each neoliberal experience is marked by its singularity, it was also not feasible to draw such a sharp demarcation line between the experience of a global South, where neoliberalism was imposed with blood and fire, from a North where, although the transition took place without institutional ruptures and without state terrorism, repressive measures undermined the rule of law.

In this context, the debate began as to whether this authoritarian evolution of neoliberalism was an unplanned consequence unforeseeable for its original promoters or whether, on the contrary, it was inherently linked to neoliberal thought itself and to the processes of neoliberalization. In either case, the irenic vision of a neoliberal governmentality that relied on a series of environmentally designed incitements to conduct our lives as enterprises under a vaporous performance imperative began to be complemented, if not directly refuted, by analyses that emphasized the belligerent and strategic character of neoliberalism and the violent and coercive nature of its disciplinary and biopolitical apparatuses. As we saw, William Davies (2016) marked the emergence of a punitive neoliberalism that recovered that warlike and even sovereign dimension of neoliberal power dispositifs and that differed from the founding violence of Thatcher and Reagan less by the methods than by the way of constructing the enemy. Maurizio Lazzarato, who had made an update of the concept of biopolitics to think *noopolitics* (2006), then began to question the Foucauldian gaze around the functioning of neoliberal power apparatuses through a genealogy of debt (2011), and of the relationship between governmentality, wars, and capital (2016; 2021) to arrive at a sharp alternative: neoliberal fascism or revolution. Something similar can be said of Dardot and Laval. These French theorists, strongly questioned by Lazzarato himself in *Capital Hates Everyone* as promoters of the soft power thesis, in *Le choix de la guerre civile* stress the importance of strategy and politics as a continuation of civil war to understand neoliberalism, showing the anti-democratic and authoritarian character inherent to the neoliberal thought collective itself and its project of society. That is to say that the civil war continues to operate in the filigree of peace through violence and a new state of legality. (Harcourt, 2018).

For the French, one of the features of the civil wars waged by neoliberalism is that they are initiated by the oligarchy and are total: *social*, since they seek to weaken the social rights of populations; *ethnic*, since they seek to exclude foreigners from all forms of citizenship by increasingly restricting the right of asylum; *political* and *legal*, by resorting to legal means to repress and criminalize all resistance and all contestation; *cultural* and *moral*, by attacking individual rights in the name of the most conservative defense of a moral order often referred to Christian values (Dardot et al., 2021).

In this context, the new radical right only reinforces neo-liberalism. The battles between globalists and nationalists, or between open liberal democracy and populist illiberal democracy, are fights over different versions of neoliberalism. These recodifications of conflict hide the same defense of the global market order, an anti-democratic system, and a concept of freedom as the freedom to do business and consume, and affirmation of Western cultural values. (Dardot et al., 2021)

In this sense, the authors define neoliberalism as "a strategic rationality that folds to the context" (2021, p. 18). This strategic dimension, on which our book has insisted repeatedly, is made explicit in the contributions of Rougier, Hayek and others who, already in the Walter Lippmann colloquium, recognize the need for a war of ideas opposed to collectivist forms of thought. In line with what we have raised in chapter 2, Dardot et al. (2021) show that neoliberalism was conceived as an economic and political project that reacted against the forms of social regulation of the economy that universal suffrage and partisan democracy imposed on the free market in the 1920s thanks to the electoral success of social democratic parties and the recourse to economic planning by democratically elected governments. For these thinkers, the issue was not a defense of freedom as such, but the threat of politicization of the economy that democracy poses to the free market.

Indeed, Dardot et al. (2021) argue that the enterprise of re-founding liberalism is motivated by the experience of social democracy in Austria and the Weimar Republic in Germany: the emergence of a social state that they do not hesitate to designate—together with Schmitt—as the total state. At the antipodes of a policy of social risk protection, the neoliberal state seeks to build the market and protect it from the threats of regulation and control of an abusive state (2021, p. 21). To fulfill this mission, the state must be constantly on a war footing to prevent democracy from intervening in the economy. Following these premises, neoliberal governments put into practice strategies of civil war against everything that threatens "free societies", by betting on a strong state and repressing all the forces and social movements that oppose this project.

For this very reason, I have tried to show that, despite the legitimacy of the question, we are not witnessing a neoliberal fascism. As Dardot et al. (2021) point out, neoliberal violence is not a fascist type of violence exercised against a community designated as foreign but is characterized first and foremost by a violence that establishes and preserves the market order and is exercised against democracy and society. Despite their alliance with new types of nationalism, neither do they aim to restore a mythical fusional community like the fascisms of the interwar period, but to ensure that each individual and family can constitute itself in a competitive enterprise. As I have already pointed out, the question of fascism cannot be measured in terms of the psychology of a leader like Trump or Bolsonaro, and as much as there are social practices that can be characterized as "fascist", we are far from witnessing the emergence of such a political regime. If the fascists were interventionist, statist and holistic, the neoliberals are convinced that a civilization based on individual freedom and responsibility of the consumer citizen is at stake in the market order. In this framework, the competitive market functions as a categorical imperative that makes it possible to legitimize the most excessive measures, even the recourse to military dictatorship, if necessary (2021, p. 22). In line with what Davies and Lazzarato and the Foucauldian notion of a field of adversity put forward in their own way, the Frenchmen provide a definition of neoliberalism that is worth quoting in extenso:

> Neoliberalism is not only a set of theories and authors but a political project of neutralization of socialism in all its forms and of all forms of demand for equality, a project carried forward by theoreticians and essayists who are from the outset political entrepreneurs. It stems from a common political will to establish a free society founded mainly on competition, a society of private law, within the framework of laws and explicit principles, protected by sovereign states seeking to find anchors in morality, tradition or religion at the service of a strategy of complete change of society. In other words, neoliberalism must be understood as a strategic struggle against other political projects globally qualified as collectivist (Dardot et al., 2021, p. 24).

In this framework, the most brutal forms of neoliberalism do not imply a degeneration of it but refer to "an implacable dogmatic logic that does not look at the means used to weaken and crush its enemies". These enemies are always presented as enemies of freedom and civilization, which only consumer sovereignty and competition can guarantee. Hence the authors conclude that "the wars of neoliberalism are both wars for competition and against equality". (Dardot et al., 2021, p. 26).

In this sense, the concept of authoritarian neoliberalism, which I have explored following a leafy path of contemporary debate, is imprecise and insufficient. If there are authoritarian traits that are inherent to neoliberal rationality, as evidenced in its theory and praxis, it would be better to speak of *neoliberalism reloaded* to characterize our present. Indeed, the notion of authoritarian neoliberalism would imply that we consider that there was a stage of neoliberalism in which it was democratic, peaceful, and pluralist and that authoritarianism is something that obscenely distorted a pristine neoliberalism that would be marked by a heroic defense of freedom against all forms of actual or potential totalitarianism. However, it is precisely this conception of freedom that must be put into question. A freedom that for Hayek can be guaranteed by an authoritarian government—and even by genocidal dictatorships—where political rights do not exist, and which is fundamentally threatened by a democracy that tends to the unlimited and, therefore—through a demand impossible to fulfill of a mythical social justice—can become totalitarian. A freedom that, as Wendy Brown pointed out, is the freedom to lower taxes for the richest, to expand the power and rights of corporations to the detriment of workers, to try to destroy what is left of a regulatory and social state. It is the freedom that the American paleolibertarians defended four decades ago, with their phobia of the state and of the poor, Black people, Latinos, women, and sexual dissidents, that is to say, a freedom that only concerns white and male owners. It is the freedom to ignore the existence of climate change in order to continue destroying our planet or to accept only cosmetic solutions that are economically profitable, such as those proposed by free-market environmentalism. It is the freedom not to respect care measures during the covid-19 pandemic and to march against "oppressive" governments that wanted to enforce health passes. It is a negative liberty that is horrified by the power of the state, but minimizes that of capital, and which, as seen in the pandemic, conceives individuals as unrelated atoms without responsibility for each other. As Dardot et al. point out, this freedom that is "more important than life" is in reality a further attack on egalitarian logics: "the civil war against equality in the name of freedom is undoubtedly one of the main faces of current neoliberalism considered from the strategic point of view" (Dardot et al., 2021, p. 13).

In this sense, the notion of *neoliberalism reloaded* aims at thinking a genealogy where historical discontinuities can find a common thread in certain political and theoretical continuities. In this framework, we have tried to highlight not only the reactionary character of much of neoliberal thought—in many cases linked to the roots of extreme right-wing thinking—but also the violent way in which it was imposed from the 1970s onwards in different geographies.

In the Nietzschean-Foucauldian tradition, the aim of sketching genealogies is not to find an origin from which the subsequent historical evolution would develop but, on the contrary, to be able to conjure up the chimera of the origin and see how realities emerge and are invented within the framework of certain battles. In this sense, thinking about the affiliations of current neoliberalism, and even recovering some of the ideas of its founding fathers, does not imply adopting a teleological view of these processes. As Wendy Brown argues in *In the ruins of neoliberalism*, if, on the one hand, it cannot be claimed that what has been called authoritarian (Bruff, 2013) or reactionary (Fraser & Sunkara, 2019) neoliberalism are a necessary consequence of the thinking of the neoliberals of Austria, Freiburg, Virginia, Geneva or Chicago, neither can it be ignored that there are clearly antidemocratic and reactionary elements (Perrin, 2014) in the thinking of the different schools that gave rise to the neoliberal thought collective and its political heirs.

Within this framework, I have attempted to propose a genealogical view of the authoritarian evolution of neoliberalism and the rise of the new right-wing movements from South America, where the anti-democratic, violent, and predatory nature of neoliberalism is far from being a novelty. In fact, it is no coincidence that while in the 1990s certain Anglo-Saxon perspectives saw in neoliberal government rationality a kind of soft power, which came to put an end to the din of the battle to organize societies around the model of enterprise and competition, Latin American critical thought—in tune with certain updates of Marxism —understood neoliberalism as a predatory political-economic project, first imposed by violent dictatorial regimes with blood and fire along with the curse of the foreign debt and then through the Washington Consensus, which sealed a history of counterrevolutionary and neocolonial violence, which ended up irreversibly transforming the model of Industrialization by Import Substitution and a certain distributive equity between wage earners and businessmen.

On the other hand, these dictatorial regimes not only proposed to put an end to what they called the Marxist enemy—an invisible or spectral enemy, which on the one hand was foreign and on the other infiltrated the spirits of the people— but for this purpose they proposed as a central task the defense of the Western and Christian world and its moral values against the forms of life that defied them. In this sense, if today's neoliberalism goes hand in hand with the reactionary ideology of the new far right (nativist, racist, misogynist, anti-scientific, conspiratorial, fundamentalist, religious, etc.), we should not be so surprised. As I have tried to show, neoliberalism not only has strong elective affinities with various political, social, and intellectual conservatisms, but it emerged as a reaction to mass democratic politics and the threat it posed to private property. If we think of neoliberalism in terms of its strategy, its goal has always been to destroy any advance in the direction of equality, democracy, or social justice, fighting socialism, social democracy, Keynesianism, Welfarism, communism and left-wing populism.

Moreover, the new South American right-wingers cannot avoid their relationship with a recent past marked by genocidal horror, which they seek to relativize if not openly glorify, nor with the plundering produced by the policies of deindustrialization and dispossession promoted by neoliberal policies. In fact, the new far-rightists claim that liberalization and deregulation have not yet gone too far, and that we live in a socialist society, where cultural Marxism and "gender ideology"—its most abominable offshoot—predominate. This is not accidental if one considers that, since their inception, neoliberals have established an antagonistic boundary between total market liberalization in a society governed by strong property rights and competition, and everything else (Davies, 2016).

Therefore, in the absence of more precise concepts, through the notion of *neoliberalism reloaded*, I seek to think our present as marked not by a new political rationality but by a radicalization of neoliberal technologies of government. Only from this strategic point of view can we understand the authoritarian evolution of neoliberal policies and its symbiosis with extreme right-wing ideologies, which has puzzled those who saw in the neoliberal project only an economization of everything or a pluralistic and amoral libertarianism.

It is therefore no coincidence that the books that emphasize this strategic dimension of neoliberalism revise the Latin American archive (Lazzarato, 2021; Dardot et al., 2021; Harvey, 2005; Klein, 2007). The Chilean case is particularly interesting because it is not only there where neoliberalism was imposed with blood and fire as a project—paradoxically enough—of economic-social engineering, but also because this country currently shows the power of popular resistance in the face of decades of inequalities. *Will it be that where neoliberalism began, it will end?*

In any case, this book proposes that it makes no sense to look for solutions to the present situation in the neoliberal recipe book itself, but neither in the past alternatives which, besides having failed or been defeated, are today impracticable. Therefore, we have focused on the antagonism between the new neoliberal right-wing and anti-capitalist feminisms. For these rightists, the questioning of patriarchal and colonial capitalism by these feminisms is unacceptable, because by questioning the exploitation and dispossession of reproductive labor, which falls on feminized subjectivities, they shake the patriarchal and colonial order that encumbers white men. The attempt to reverse these situations and expand rights for women and LGBTQI citizens has generated enormous resentment in this social sector—among which the radical right finds its clientele—who denounce that the world is dominated by progressive forces and even by a new communism, which now operates fundamentally from the cultural and political superstructures. If there is one thing that these new rightists do well, it is to correctly identify the enemy when they oppose feminism and "gender ideology". As argued in chapter 6, if feminism fulfills the role of the new communism, it is because of its capacity to question and attempt to overcome the existing state of affairs.

However, there is no communism without a redefinition and a politics of the common(s). Therefore, we made a brief review of some debates around the common and the commons in neoliberal capitalism. The common appears, from different points of view, as an alternative rationality to the neoliberal one, and, therefore, capable of serving as a principle for a society based on self-government and self-management. However, although the common is an alternative to both the private and the public spheres, it cannot ignore the existence and relevance, in many cases, of both forms of ownership and management of resources. Therefore, a policy of the commons, in its search for a radically egalitarian society, cannot be implemented in frontal opposition to the public and the private, but must be able to articulate with them and imbue them with a collective and radically democratic logic. In short, there are commons that can only be preserved or act efficiently with the help of the public sector and where the important thing is not so much to whom an asset belongs but how it is managed and to whom it benefits. Far from falling back into phobia towards the state, which is a field of struggles between alternative political forces and rationalities, the commons must be able to transcend the state-market opposition and be able to establish a type of social bond in which care for the planet and the beings that inhabit it is the priority. This implies a collective responsibility towards others. If for the neoliberals this would imply a loss of freedom, for the commoners there can be no freedom without responsibility, solidarity, and co-activity. Because it is clear that in order to be able to respond to the challenges represented by global phenomena such as a pandemic or climate change—perhaps the danger that should make our shared condition of vulnerability most evident—we cannot follow the same path of privatization and commodification, which seek to transfer the costs of pollution to others, appealing to individual salvation. On the contrary, we need a system of production and distribution and a collective organization alternative to neoliberal capitalism that is sustainable in social, ecological, and economic terms. We have been calling this alternative, together with others, the alternative of the common.

Bibliography

Acha, B. (2021). *Analizar el auge de la ultraderecha.* Barcelona: Gedisa (ebook).

Agamben, G. (1998). *Sovereign power and bare life. Meridian: Vol. 1.* Stanford, CA: Stanford University Press.

Agamben, G. (2005). *State of exception.* Chicago: University of Chicago Press.

Agamben, G. (2011a). *The kingdom and the glory: For a theological genealogy of economy and government. Meridian, crossing aesthetics: II, 2.* Stanford, CA: Stanford University Press.

Agamben, G. (2011b). Introductory Note on the Concept of Democracy. In G. Agamben, A. Badiou, D. Bensaïd, W. Brown, J-L. Nancy, J. Rancière, K. Ross & S. Žižek. (eds.), *Democracy in what state?*, pp. 1–5. New York: Columbia University Press.

Alabao, N. (2019). ¿Por qué el neofascismo es antifeminista? In A. Guamán, A. Aragoneses & S. Mar (eds.), *Neofascismo; La Bestia Neoliberal*, pp. 205–218. Madrid: Siglo XXI.

Alcaraz, F., Beck, I., Elman, J., Hernández, P., Rodríguez, P. & Vallejos, S. (2021). Entre el Estado como enemigo y "la ideología de género", la juventud antiprogresista. *elDiarioAR*, June 16, 2021. https://www.eldiarioar.com/la-reaccion-conservadora/ene migo-ideologia-genero-juventud_132_8030547.html (accessed April 18, 2022)

Alliez, É. & Lazzarato, M. (2016). *Wars and Capital.* South Pasadena, CA: Semiotext(e).

Antón-Mellón, J. & Hernández-Carr, A. (2016). El crecimiento electoral de la derecha radical populista en Europa: parámetros ideológicos y motivaciones sociales. *Política y Sociedad* 53(1), 17–28. https://doi.org/10.5209/rev_POSO.2016.v53.n1.48456 (accessed August 8, 2022)

Applebaum, A. (2020). *Twilight of democracy: the seductive lure of authoritarianism.* New York: Doubleday (ebook).

Aragoneses, A. (2019). La construcción del enemigo como base del (neo)fascismo. In A. Guamán, A. Aragoneses & S. Mar (eds.), *Neofascismo; La Bestia Neoliberal*, pp. 121–136. Madrid: Siglo XXI.

Arendt, H. (1973). *The origins of totalitarianism.* New York: Harcourt Brace Jovanovich.

Audier, S. (2012). *Néo-libéralisme(s): Une archéologie intellectuelle. Mondes vécus.* Paris: Bernard Grasset.

Audier, S. (2016). "Néolibéralisme" et démocratie dans les années 1930: Louis Rougier et Louis Marlio. *Revue de philosophie économique* 17, 57–101. https://www.cairn.info/ revue-de-philosophie-economique-2016-1-page-57.htm?ref=doi (accessed April 19, 2022)

Badiou, A. (2019). *Trump.* Cambridge UK, Medford MA: Polity.

Barry, A., Osborne, T. & Rose, N. S. (eds.). (1996). *Foucault and political reason: Liberalism, neo-liberalism, and rationalities of government.* Chicago: University of Chicago Press.

Bassets, M. (2016). Con Trump tenemos una especie de cuasifascismo populista, no un fascismo plenamente desarrollado: Entrevista con el historiador Robert O. Paxton, autor de 'La anatomía del fascismo'. *El país*, June 6, 2016. https://elpais.com/internacional/ 2016/06/05/estados_unidos/1465162717_340531.html (accessed April 18, 2022)

Beck, U. (1992). *Risk society: Towards a new modernity. Theory, culture & society.* London, Newbury Park, CA: SAGE Publications.

Bensaïd, D. (2011). Permanent Scandal. In G. Agamben, A. Badiou, D. Bensaïd, W. Brown, J.-L. Nancy, J. Rancière, K. Ross & S. Žižek. (eds.), *Democracy in what state?*, pp. 16–43. New York: Columbia University Press.

https://doi.org/10.1515/9783110723939-011

Berardi, F. (2009). *The soul at work: From alienation to autonomy.* Los Angeles, CA: Semiotext(e).

Berardi, F. (2010). *Precarious Rhapsody: Semiocapitalism and the pathologies of post-alpha generation.* London: Minor Compositions.

Berlin, I. (2002). *Liberty: Incorporating four essays on liberty.* Oxford: Oxford University Press.

Betz, H-G. (2021). Forty years of radical right-wing populism: an assessment. In Pereyra Doval, G. & Souroujon, G. (eds.), *Global resurgence of the right: Conceptual and regional perspectives,* pp. 7–40. Abingdon Oxon, New York, NY: Routledge.

Bhattacharyya, G. (2018). *Rethinking racial capitalism: Questions of reproduction and survival. Cultural studies and Marxism.* Lanham: Rowman & Littlefield Publishers.

Biebricher, T. (2020). Neoliberalism and Authoritarianism. *Global Perspectives* 1(1), 11872. https://doi.org/10.1525/001c.11872 (accessed April 18, 2022)

Boiral O. (2003). Pouvoirs opaques de la Trilatérale. *Le Monde diplomatique,* november 2003. https://www.monde-diplomatique.fr/2003/11/BOIRAL/10677 (accessed April 18, 2022)

Bollier, D. (2014). *Think like a commoner: a short introduction to the life of the commons.* New Society.

Borón, A. (2019). Bolsonaro y el fascismo, *Página 12,* January 2, 2019. https://www.pagina12.com.ar/165570-bolsonaro-y-el-fascismo (accessed April 18, 2022)

Brandes, S. (2019). The Market's People: Milton Friedman and the Making of Neoliberal Populism. In W. Callison & Z. Manfredi (eds.), *Mutant Neoliberalism,* pp. 61–88. Fordham University Press.

Brown, W. (2015). *Undoing the demos: Neoliberalism's stealth revolution.* New York: Zone Books.

Brown, W. (2018). Where the fires are. Wendy Brown interview with Jo Littler. *Soundings* 68, Spring 2018. https://www.eurozine.com/where-the-fires-are/ (accessed, April 18, 2022)

Brown, W. (2019). *In the ruins of neoliberalism. The rise of antidemocratic politics in the West.* New York: Columbia University Press.

Bruff, I. (2014). The Rise of Authoritarian Neoliberalism. *Rethinking Marxism* 26(1), 113–129. DOI: 10.1080/08935696.2013.843250 (accessed April 18, 2022)

Bruff, I. & Tansel, C. B. (2019). Authoritarian neoliberalism: trajectories of knowledge production and praxis. *Globalizations.* 16(3), 233–244. DOI: 10.1080/14747731.2018.1502497 (accessed April 18, 2022)

Bruff, I. & Tansel, C. (eds.). (2020). *Authoritarian Neoliberalism: Philosophies, Practices, Contestations.* London: Routledge.

Buchanan, P. (1998). *The Great Betrayal: How American Sovereignty and Social Justice are Being Sacrificed to the Gods of the Global Economy.* Little, Brown and Company.

Buffett, W. (2011a). Buffett: There has been class warfare for 20 yrs and my class has won. Interview with W. Buffett, by Alison Kosik for CNN on September 30, 2011. https://cnnpressroom.blogs.cnn.com/2011/09/30/buffett-there-has-been-class-warfare-for-20-yrs-and-my-class-has-won/ (accessed April 18, 2022)

Buffett, W. (2011b). Stop Coddling the Super-Rich. *New York Times,* August 14, 2011. https://www.nytimes.com/2011/08/15/opinion/stop-coddling-the-super-rich.html (accessed April 18, 2022)

Bullrich, E. (2016a). Speech in the framework of the panel "La Construcción del Capital Humano para el Futuro" at the Investment and Business Forum, Kirchner Cultural Center,

September 2016. https://www.youtube.com/watch?v=1dvO-jorNow&ab_channel=Francis coJos%C3%A9Bessone (accessed April 18, 2022)

Bullrich, E. (2016b). Speech delivered at the inauguration of the Veterinary School Hospital of the National University of Río Negro in Choele Choel, Río Negro, Argentina. September 16, 2016. https://www.clarin.com/politica/ministro-bullrich-campana-desierto-desato_0_rycAGitn.html (accessed April 18, 2022)

Caffentzis, G. & Federici, S. (2014). Commons against and beyond capitalism. *Community Development Journal* 49(51), 92–105.

Camus, R. (2002). *Le grand remplacement*. Published by the Author.

Camus, J.-Y. & Lebourg, N. (2017). *Far-right politics in Europe*. Cambridge, MA: Harvard University Press.

Caré, S. (2016). La dérive des continents néolibéraux: essai de typologie dynamique. *Revue de philosophie économique* 17(1), 21, 21–55. https://doi.org/10.3917/rpec.171.0021 (accessed August 8, 2022)

Caré, S. & Châton, G. (2016). Néoliberalisme(s) et démocratie(s). *Revue de philosophie économique* 17(1), 3, 3–20. https://doi.org/10.3917/rpec.171.0003 (accessed August 8, 2022)

Castro Santos, M. & Tavares Teixeira, U. (2013). The essential role of democracy in the Bush Doctrine: the invasions of Iraq and Afghanistan. *Revista Brasileira de Política Internacional* 56(2), 131–156.

Castro, E. (2011). *Lecturas foucaulteanas. Una historia conceptual de la biopolítica*. La Plata: Unipe.

Casullo, M. E. (2019). *¿Por qué funciona el populismo?* Buenos Aires: Siglo XXI.

Catanzaro, G., Stegmayer, M. & Rolón Machado, P. J. (2019). The New Neoliberal Turn in Argentina. *Critical Times* 2(1), 133–158. https://doi.org/10.1215/26410478-7615035 (accessed April 18, 2022)

Cavallero, L. & Gago, V. (2021). *A feminist reading of debt*. London: Pluto Press.

Chomsky, N. & Foucault, M. (2006). *The Chomsky-Foucault debate: On human nature*. New York: New Press. Distributed by W.W. Norton.

Cooper, M. (2017). *Family values: Between neoliberalism and the new social conservatism*. New York: Zone Books.

Cooper, M. (2021). The Alt-Right: Neoliberalism, Libertarianism and the Fascist Temptation. *Theory, Culture & Society* 38(6), 29–50. https://doi.org/10.1177/0263276421999446 (accessed August 8, 2022)

Coriat, B. (2015). Qu'est ce qu'un commun? Quelles perspectives le mouvement des communs ouvre-t-il à l'alternative sociale? *Les Possibles* 5(winter 2015), 18–24.

Cornelissen, L. (2020). Neoliberalism and the racialized critique of democracy. *Constellations* 27(3), 348–360. DOI: 10.1111/1467–8675.12518 (accessed April 18, 2022)

Crouch, C. (2012). *The strange non-death of neoliberalism*. Cambridge: Polity.

Crozier, M., Huntington, S. & Watanuki, J. (1975). *The Crisis of Democracy*. New York: New York University Press.

Dardot, P. & Laval, C. (2013). *The new way of the world: on neoliberal society*. London, New York: Verso.

Dardot, P. & Laval, C. (2019a). *Common: On revolution in the twenty-first century*. London, New York: Bloomsbury Academic.

Dardot, P. & Laval, C. (2019b). *Never ending nightmare: The neoliberal assault on democracy.* London, New York: Verso.

Dardot, P., Sauvêtre, P., Guéguen, H., Laval, C. (2021). *Le Choix de la Guerre Civile: Une Autre Histoire du Néolibéralisme.* Québec: Lux editeur.

Davidson, N., Saull, R. (2017). Neoliberalism and the Far-Right: A Contradictory Embrace. *Critical Sociology* 43(4–5), 707–724. DOI: 10.1177/0896920516671180 (accessed August 8, 2022)

Davidson, N. (2017). Crisis Neoliberalism and Regimes of Permanent Exception. *Critical Sociology* 43(4–5), 615–634. https://doi.org/10.1177/0896920516655386 (accessed August 8, 2022)

Davidson, N. (2018). Neoliberalism as a Class-Based Project. Un D. Cahill, M. Cooper, M. Konings & D. Primrose (eds.), The SAGE Handbook of Neoliberalism, pp. 55–69. Los Angeles, London, New Delhi: SAGE.

Davies, W. (2016). The New Neoliberalism. *New left review* 101, Nov–Oct 2016, 121–134.

De Angelis, M. (2001). Marx and primitive accumulation: The continuous character of capital's 'enclosures', *The commoner* n.2, September 2001.

De Büren, P. (2020). *Contraofensiva neoliberal: La Escuela Austríaca de Economía en el centro estratégico de la disputa.* Buenos Aires: Instituto de Investigaciones Gino Germani – UBA.

Deleuze, G. (1992). Postscript on the Societies of Control, *October*, 59, 3–7. http://links.jstor. org/sici?sici=0162-2870%28199224%2959%3C3%3APOTSOC%3E2.0.CO%3B2-T (accessed April 18, 2022)

Demirović, A. (2018). El populismo autoritario como estrategia neoliberal de gestión de la crisis. *Constelaciones. Revista de teoría crítica* 10, 116–134.

Duménil, G. & Lévy, D. (2004). *Capital resurgent: Roots of the neoliberal revolution.* Cambridge: Harvard University Press.

Duménil, G. & Lévy, D. (2013). *The crisis of neoliberalism.* Cambridge, MA & London, England: Harvard University Press.

Dvoskin, N. (2019). El anarcoliberalismo como terraplanismo económico. *Cuadernos de Economía Crítica* 5(10), 159–168.

Elman, J. (2018). La derecha sub-30. ¿Quién le teme a Agustín Laje? *Revista Anfibia.* http://re vistaanfibia.com/cronica/quien-le-teme-a-agustin-laje-2/ (accessed August 8, 2022)

Elyachar, J. (2019). Neoliberalism, Rationality, and the Savage Slot. In W. Callison & Z. Manfredi (eds.), *Mutant Neoliberalism*, pp. 177–195. Fordham University Press.

Esposito, R. (2008). *Bíos: Biopolitics and philosophy.* Minneapolis: University of Minnesota Press.

Expósito, J. (2021). *Feminismos revolucionarios. Hacia una teoría materialista del capitalismo patriarco-colonial.* Vicente López: Red Editorial.

Fabry, A. (2019). *The political economy of Hungary: From state capitalism to authoritarian neoliberalism.* Cham, Switzerland: Palgrave Macmillan.

Fagioli, A. (2020). *Octubre chileno: rebeldía y multitud.* Vicente López: Red editorial.

Falquet, J. (2017). *Pax Neoliberalia.* Buenos Aires: Madreselva.

Fassin, D. (2018). *The will to punish.* New York: Oxford University Press.

Fassin, É. (2018a). *Populism left and right.* Chicago, IL: Prickly Paradigm Press.

Fassin, É. (2018b). Le moment néofasciste du néolibéralisme. *Mediapart*, June 29, 2018. https://blogs.mediapart.fr/eric-fassin/blog/290618/le-moment-neofasciste-du-neo liberalisme (accessed August 8, 2022)

Federici, S. (2014). *Caliban and the witch*. 2nd revised ed. New York: Autonomedia.

Federici, S. (2020). *Revolution at point zero: Housework, reproduction, and feminist struggle*. 2nd ed. Oakland: PM Press.

Federici, S. (2021). *Patriarchy of the wage: Notes on Marx, gender, and feminism*. Spectre. Oakland CA: PM Press.

Feher, M. (2019). Disposing of the Discredited: A European Project. In W. Callison & Z. Manfredi (eds.), *Mutant Neoliberalism*, pp. 146–176. Fordham University Press.

Ferrarese, M. R. (2014). Governance: A Soft Revolution with hard Political and Legal Effects. *Soft Power. Revista euro-americana de teoría e historia de la política* 1(1), 34–56. http:// www.softpowerjournal.com/web/wp-content/uploads/2014/09/articolo-3-governance.pdf (accessed August 8, 2022)

Foucault, M. (1982). The Subject and Power. *Critical Inquiry* 8(4), 777–795. http://www.jstor. org/stable/1343197 (accessed April 19, 2022)

Foucault, M. (1998). *The will to knowledge. The history of sexuality: Vol. 1*. Harmondsworth: Penguin Books.

Foucault, M. (2003a). *Psychiatric power: Lectures at the Collège de France, 1973–1974*. New York: Picador.

Foucault, M. (2003b). *Society must be defended: Lectures at the Collège de France, 1975–76*. New York: Picador.

Foucault, M. (2007). *Security, territory, population: Lectures at the Collège de France, 1977–78*. Basingstoke, New York: Palgrave Macmillan; République Française.

Foucault, M. (2008). *The birth of biopolitics: Lectures at the Collège de France, 1978–79*. Basingstoke England, New York: Palgrave Macmillan.

Foucault, M. (2010). *The government of self and others*. Houndmills Basingstoke Hampshire, New York: Palgrave Macmillan; St Martin's Press.

Francis, S. (1994). Message from MARs: The Social Politics of the New Right. In *Beautiful Losers: Essays on the Failure of American Conservatism*, pp. 60–78. University of Missouri Press.

Fraser, N. (2016). Contradictions of Capital and Care. *New Left Review* 100, Jul–Aug 2016.

Fraser, N. (2017). From Progressive Neoliberalism to Trump—and Beyond, *American Affairs* 1(4). https://americanaffairsjournal.org/2017/11/progressive-neoliberalism-trump-beyond/ (accessed August 8, 2022)

Fraser, N. & Sunkara, B. (2019). *The old is dying and the new cannot be born. From progressive neoliberalism to Trump and beyond*. London, New York: Verso.

Friedman, D. (1997). *Hidden order: the economics of everyday life*. New York: Harper Business.

Friedman, M. (1988). Discussion of Capitalism and Freedom with Milton Friedman. In M. Walker (ed.), *Freedom, Democracy and Economic Welfare: Proceedings of an International Symposium*, pp. 121–125. Vancouver, British Columbia: Fraser Institute.

Friedrich, S. (2016). *Lexikon der Leistungsgesellschaft. Wie der Neoliberalismus unseren Alltag prägt*. Berlin: Matthes & Seitz.

Fukuyama, F. (1989). The End of History? *The National Interest* 16, 3–18. http://www.jstor. org/stable/24027184 (accessed April 19, 2022)

Gago, V. (2020). *Feminist international: How to change everything.* London, New York: Verso.

Gago V. & Mezzadra. S. (2017). A Critique of the Extractive Operations of Capital: Toward an Expanded Concept of Extractivism. *Rethinking Marxism* 29(4), 574–591. DOI: 10.1080/08935696.2017.1417087 (accessed April 19, 2022)

Galindo, M. (2019). Bolivia: La noche de los cristales rotos. *La vaca,* 11/11/2019. https://www.lavaca.org/notas/bolivia-la-noche-de-los-cristales-rotos-por-maria-galindo/ (accessed April 19, 2022)

Gallino, L. (2008). Biopolitihe del lavoro. In L. Demichelis & G. Leghissa (eds.), *Biopolitiche del lavoro.* Milno-Udine: Mimesis.

García Olascoaga, O. (2018). Presencia del neofascismo en las democracias europeas contemporáneas. *Revista Española de Investigaciones Sociológicas* 162, 3–20.

Giroux, H. (2018). Neoliberal Fascism and the Echoes of History. *truthdig,* August 2, 2018. https://www.truthdig.com/articles/neoliberal-fascism-and-the-echoes-of-history/ (accessed April 19, 2022)

Graeber, D. (2011). *Debt. The first 5000 years.* Melville House.

Graeber, D. (2012). Of Flying Cars and the Declining Rate of Profit. *The Baffler* 19. https://thebaffler.com/salvos/of-flying-cars-and-the-declining-rate-of-profit (accessed April 19, 2022)

Gramsci, A. (1971). *Selections from the prison notebooks of Antonio Gramsci.* New York: International Publishers.

Gulliver-Needham, E. (2018). Adam Smith to Richard Spencer: Why Libertarians turn to the Alt-Right. *Medium,* February 22, 2018. https://medium.com/@elliotgulliverneedham/why-libertarians-are-embracing-fascism-5a9747a44db9 (accessed April 19, 2022)

Gutiérrez Aguilar, R. (2001). Forma comunal y forma liberal de la política: de la soberanía social a la irresponsabilidad civil. In Á. García, R. Gutiérrez, R. Prada & L. Tapia (eds.), *Pluriverso: Teoría política boliviana,* pp. 55–73. La Paz: Muela del Diablo/Comuna.

Gutiérrez Aguilar, R. (2008). *Los ritmos del Pachakuti. Movilización y levantamiento indígena-popular en Bolivia.* Buenos Aires: Tinta limón.

Hall, S. (1985). Authoritarian populism: A reply to Jessop et al. *New Left Review,* 1(151), May–June, 115–124.

Hall, S. (ed.). (1990). *The politics of Thatcherism.* London: Lawrence and Wishart.

Hamann, T. H. (2009). Neoliberalism, Governmentality, and Ethics. *Foucault Studies,* 37–59. https://doi.org/10.22439/fs.v0i0.2471 (accessed August 8, 2022).

Han, B.-C. (2015). *The burnout society.* Stanford University Press.

Harcourt, B. (2018). *The counterrevolution: How our government went to war against its own citizens.* New York: Basic Books.

Hardin, G. (1968). The tragedy of the commons. *Science* 162(3859), 1243–1248. http://www.jstor.org/stable/1724745 (accessed April 19, 2022)

Hardin, G. (1974). Lifeboat Ethics: the Case Against Helping the Poor. *Psychology Today,* September 1974. Published in *The Garrett Hardin Society.* https://www.garretthardinsociety.org/articles/art_lifeboat_ethics_case_against_helping_poor.html (accessed August 8, 2022)

Hardt, M. & Negri, A. (2000). *Empire.* Cambridge, MA: Harvard University Press.

Hardt, M. & Negri, A. (2004). *Multitude: War and democracy in the age of Empire.* New York: The Penguin Press.

Hardt, M. & Negri, A. (2009). *Commonwealth.* Cambridge: Harvard University Press.

Harrison, G. (2019). Authoritarian neoliberalism and capitalist transformation in Africa: all pain, no gain. *Globalizations* 16(3), 274 – 288. https://doi.org/10.1080/14747731.2018.1502491 (accessed April 21, 2022)

Harvey, D. (2003). *The new imperialism.* Oxford University Press.

Harvey, D. (2005). *A Brief History of Neoliberalism.* Oxford University Press.

Harvey, D. (2011). The Future of the Commons. *Radical History Review* 109, 101 – 107. DOI: 10.1215/01636545 – 2010 – 017 (accessed August 8, 2022)

Hayek, F. (1981). En el momento actual nuestra principal tarea es limitar el poder del gobierno. Interview by R. Sallas. *El mercurio,* April 12, 1981, 8 – 9.

Hayek, F. (2003). *The road to serfdom.* London: Routledge.

Hayek, F. (2011). *The Constitution of Liberty: The Definitive Edition: Vol. 17.* University of Chicago Press.

Hayek, F. (2013). *Law, legislation and liberty: A new statement of the liberal principles of justice and political economy.* Abingdon: Routledge.

Hess, C. & Ostrom, E. (2008). *Understanding Knowledge as a Commons. From Theory to Practice.* Massachusetts: MIT Press.

Hoevel, C. (2014). Las contradicciones culturales del neoliberalismo. *Economía y Política* 1(2), 39 – 72. DOI: 10.15691/07194714.2014.006 (accessed August 8, 2022)

Hoppe, H.-H. (2001). *Democracy—the god that failed: The economics and politics of monarchy, democracy and natural order.* New Brunswick, NJ: Transaction Publishers.

Ibáñez, R. & De Castro, C. (2015). Los comunes en perspectiva: eficiencia versus emancipación. *Economistas sin fronteras* 16, 2015, 8 – 12.

Jessop, B. (2019). Authoritarian Neoliberalism: Periodization and Critique. *South Atlantic Quarterly* 118(2), 343 – 361. DOI: 10.1215/00382876 – 7381182 (accessed August 8, 2022)

Judis, J. B. (2016). *The populist explosion: How the great recession transformed American and European politics.* New York: Columbia Global Reports.

Kant, I. (2016). *Perpetual Peace. A Philosophical Essay.* Gutenberg Project.

Karsten, F. & Beckman, K. (2012). *Beyond democracy: Why democracy does not lead to solidarity, prosperity and liberty but to social conflict, runaway spending and a tyrannical government.* Createspace.

Klein N. (2007). *The shock doctrine: The rise of disaster capitalism.* New York: Picador.

Klein, N. (2020). *On Fire: The (Burning) Case for a Green New Deal.* Simon & Schuster.

Laclau, E. (2005). *On populist reason.* London, New York: Verso.

Laclau, E. (2007). *Emancipation(s).* London: Verso.

Lazzarato, M. (2006). The Concepts of Life and the Living in the Societies of Control. In M. Fuglsang & B. Sorensen (eds.), *Deleuze and the Social,* pp. 171 – 190. Edinburgh University Press.

Lazzarato, M. (2012). *The making of the indebted man: An essay on the neoliberal condition.* Los Angeles, CA, Cambridge, MA & London, England: Semiotext(e); MIT Press.

Lazzarato, M. (2015). *Governing by debt.* South Pasadena, CA & Cambridge, MA: Semiotext(e); MIT Press.

Lazzarato, M. (2021). *Capital hates everyone: Fascism or revolution.* South Pasadena, CA: Semiotext(e).

Leghissa, G. (2008). Il modello dell'impresa e le radici della governamentalità biopolitica. In G. Leghissa & L. Demichelis (eds.), *Biopolitiche del lavoro,* pp. 73 – 90. Milano-Udine: Mimesis.

López Hernández, I. (2020). Los claroscuros de la crisis permanente y el desfile de los monstruos. A modo de introducción. In *Familia, raza y nación en tiempos de posfascismo*. Madrid: Traficantes de Sueños.

Lorey, I. (2015). *State of insecurity: Government of the precarious. Futures*. London, New York: Verso.

Main, T. J. (2018). *The rise of the alt-right*. Brookings Institution Press.

Mansuy, D. (2016). Jaime Guzmán: une synthèse libérale-conservatrice. *Revue de philosophie économique* 17(1), 209 – 229. https://doi.org/10.3917/rpec.171.0209 (accessed August 8, 2022)

Marcuse, H. (1991). *One-dimensional man: Studies in the ideology of advanced industrial society*. Boston: Beacon Press.

Márquez, N. & Laje, A. (2019). *The black book of the New Left: Gender ideology or cultural subversion* (ebook).

Marx, K. (1906). *Capital: A Critique of Political Economy*. New York: Random House.

Marx, K. & Engels, F. (1998). *The German ideology: Including Theses on Feuerbach and introduction to The critique of political economy. Great books in philosophy*. Amherst N.Y.: Prometheus Books.

Marzocca, O. (2011). *Il Governo dell'Ethos. La produzione politica dell'agire economico*. Milán: Mimesis.

Mattei, U. (2010). *Beni comuni. Un manifesto*. Bari: Laterza.

Mbembe, A. (2017). *Critique of Black reason*. Durham: Duke University Press.

Mbembe, A. (2019). *Necropolitics*. Durham: Duke University Press.

Mcmurtry, J. (1999). *The Cancer Stage of Capitalism*. Sterling, VA: Pluto Press.

Mezzadra, S. (2008). Attualità della preistoria. Per una rilettura del capitolo 24 del primo libro del Capitale, "La cosiddetta accumulazione originaria". *La condizione postcoloniale. Storia e politica nel presente globale*. Verona: ombre corte.

Mezzadri, A. (2019). On the value of social reproduction. Informal labour, the majority world and the need for inclusive theories and politics. *Radical Philosophy* 204, Spring 2019, 33 – 41. https://www.radicalphilosophy.com/article/on-the-value-of-social-reproduction (accessed August 8, 2022)

Micocci, A. & Di Mario, F. (2018). *The fascist nature of neoliberalism*. London: Routledge.

Midnight notes collective & friends. (2009). Promissory Notes: From Crisis to Commons. http://www.midnightnotes.org/Promissory%20Notes.pdf (accessed April 19, 2022)

Midnight notes collective. (1990). *Midnight Notes* 10 "The New Enclosures" (1990). http://www.midnightnotes.org/newenclos.html (accessed April 19, 2022)

Miller-Idriss, C. (2017). *The extreme gone mainstream: Commercialization and far right youth culture in Germany*. Princeton: Princeton University Press.

Mirowski, P. (2013). *Never let a serious crisis go to waste: How neoliberalism survived the financial meltdown*. London: Verso Books.

Mirowski, P. & Plehwe, D. (2009). *The road from Mont Pèlerin: The making of the neoliberal thought collective*. Harvard University Press

Mises, L. v. (1951). *Socialism. An Economic and Sociological Analysis*. New Haven: Yale University Press.

Mises, L. v. (1985). *Liberalism in the classical tradition*. 3rd ed. San Francisco, CA: Cobden Press.

Mises, L. v. (1998). *Human Action. A Treatise on Economics*. Auburn, AL: Mises Institute.

Mouffe, C. (2019). *For a left populism.* London: Verso.

Mudde, C. (2018). *The far right in America.* London, New York: Routledge Taylor & Francis Group.

Mudde, C. (2019). *The far right today.* Cambridge UK, Medford MA: Polity.

Mudde, C. & Rovira Kaltwasser, C. (2017). *Populism: A very short introduction.* New York: Oxford University Press.

Murillo, S. (2011). Estado, sociedad civil y gubernamentalidad neoliberal, *Entramados y perspectivas. Revista de la carrera de sociología* 1(1), Jan–Jun 2011, 91–108.

Nicoli, M. & L. Paltrinieri. (2014). Il management di sé e degli altri. *aut – aut* 362, 49–74.

Nietzsche, F. W. (1997). *Twilight of the idols, or, How to philosophize with the hammer.* Indianapolis: Hackett Pub.

Orsi, F. (2015). Reconquérir la propriété: un enjeu déterminant pour l'avenir des communs. *Les Possibles* 5(winter 2015). https://france.attac.org/nos-publications/les-possibles/nu mero-5-hiver-2015/dossier-les-biens-communs/article/reconquerir-la-propriete (accessed April 19, 2022)

Ortega y Gasset, J. (1993). *The revolt of the masses.* New York: W.W. Norton.

Ostrom, E. (1990). *Governing the Commons. The evolution of institutions for collective action.* Cambridge University Press.

Palti, E. (2009). Acerca del desencuentro entre democracia y liberalismo. Una aproximación histórico-conceptual al debate político en la Argentina del s. XIX. *La biblioteca* 8, 58–69.

Paltrinieri, L. (2013). Anarchéologie du management. In D. Lorenzini, A. Revel & A. Sforzini (eds.), *Michel Foucault: éthique et vérité (1980–1984),* pp. 217–237. Paris: Vrin.

Patnaik, P. (2021). Why Neoliberalism Needs Neofascists. *Boston Review,* July 19, 2021. https://bostonreview.net/class-inequality-politics/prabhat-patnaik-why-neoliberalism-needs-neofascists (accessed April 19, 2022)

Paxton, R. (2005). *The Anatomy of Fascism.* New York: Vintage Books.

Paxton, R. (2021). I've Hesitated to Call Donald Trump a Fascist. Until Now. *Newsweek,* January 11, 2021. https://www.newsweek.com/robert-paxton-trump-fascist-1560652 (accessed April 19, 2022)

Peck, J., Brenner, N. & Theodore, N. (2018). Actually Existing Neoliberalism. In D. Cahill, M. Cooper, M. Konings & D. Primrose (eds.), *The SAGE Handbook of Neoliberalism,* pp. 3–16. Los Angeles, London, New Delhi: SAGE.

Perrin, J. (2014). *Libéral-reac: Les racines réactionaires du néolibéralisme.* Paris: Francois Bourin.

Pézet, É. (2004). Discipliner et gouverner: influence de deux thèmes foucaldiens en sciences de gestion. *Finance Contrôle Stratégie* 7(3), 169–189.

Piketty, T. (2014). *Capital in the twenty-first century.* Cambridge, MA & London: Harvard University Press.

Blanco, J. P. (2018). Isaiah Berlin, Friedrich Hayek y Milton Friedman pasean por villa miseria. Los límites de la concepción liberal de la libertad. *Tabula Rasa* (29), 183–201. https://doi.org/10.25058/20112742.n29.09 (accessed April 19, 2022)

Preciado, P. B. (2013). *Testo junkie: Sex, drugs, and biopolitics in the pharmacopornographic era.* New York: The Feminist Press at the City University of New York.

Ramas San Miguel, C. (2019). Social-identitarios y neoliberales autoritarios: dos corrientes en la nueva internacional reaccionaria. In A. Guamán, A. Aragoneses & S. Mar (eds.), *Neofascismo: La Bestia Neoliberal*, pp. 73–88. Madrid: Siglo XXI.

Ramírez Gallegos, F. (2019). La pendiente neoliberal: ¿neo-fascismo, postfascismo, autoritarismo libertario? In A. Guamán, A. Aragoneses & S. Mar (eds.), *Neofascismo: La Bestia Neoliberal*, pp. 19–38. Madrid: Siglo XXI.

Reinhoudt, J. & Audier, S. (2018). *The Walter Lippmann Colloquium: The birth of neo-liberalism*. Cham, Switzerland: Palgrave Macmillan.

Rendueles, C. & Sábada, I. (2015). Los bienes comunes en un entorno de fragilidad social: El caso del crowdfunding. *Economistas sin fronteras* 16, 42–47.

Reuters (2020). Brasil debe dejar de ser "un país de maricones", dice Bolsonaro sobre miedo al coronavirus, November 10, 2020. https://www.reuters.com/article/politica-bolsonaro-idESKBN27Q39V (accessed April 19, 2022)

Riley, D. (2019). What is Trump? *New Left Review* 114, 5–31.

Rockwell, L. (1990). The Case for Paleolibertarianism. *Liberty Magazine* 3(3), 34–38.

Rodrigues, J. (2018). Embedding Neoliberalism: The Theoretical Practices of Hayek and Friedman. In D. Cahill, M. Cooper, M. Konings & D. Primrose (eds.), *The SAGE Handbook of Neoliberalism*, pp. 129–142. Los Angeles, London, New Delhi: SAGE.

Rodríguez, P. (2015). Espetáculo do Dividual: Tecnologias do eu e vigilância distribuída nas redes sociais. *Revista Eco-Pós* 18(2), 57–68. https://doi.org/10.29146/eco-pos.v18i2. 2680 (accessed, April 19, 2022)

Röpke, W. (1950). Barriers to Immigration. In G. Hoover (ed.), *Twentieth Century Economic Thought*, pp. 605–645. New York: Philosophical Library.

Röpke, W. (1950). *The social crisis of our time*. Toronto: The University of Chicago Press.

Röpke, W. (1964). South Africa: An Attempt at a Positive Appraisal. *Schweizer Monatshefte* 44(2), May 1964, 8.

Röpke, W. & Commun, P. (2009). *Au-delà de l'offre et de la demande. Bibliothèque classique de la liberté: Vol. 16*. Paris: les Belles lettres.

Rose, C. (1986). The Comedy of the Commons: Custom, Commerce, and Inherently Public Property. *University of Chicago Law Review* 53(3), Article 1, 711–781. https://chicagounbound.uchicago.edu/uclrev/vol53/iss3/1 (accessed April 19, 2022)

Rose, N. (2003). Neurochemical selves. *Society* 41, 46–59. https://doi.org/10.1007/BF02688204 (accessed April 22, 2022)

Ross, K. (2011). Democracy for Sale. In G. Agamben, A. Badiou, D. Bensaïd, W. Brown, J.-L. Nancy, J. Rancière, K. Ross & S. Žižek (eds.), *Democracy in what state?*, pp. 82–99. New York: Columbia University Press.

Rothbard, M. (1994b). Race! That Murray Book. *Rothbard Rockwell Report* V(12), 1–10.

Rothbard, M. (1992). Right-Wing Populism: A Strategy for the Paleo Movement. *Rothbard-Rockwell Report*, 5–14.

Rothbard, M. (2000). *The Irrepressible Rothbard: The Rothbard-Rockwell Report, essays of Murray N. Rothbard*. Burlingame: Center for Libertarian Studies.

Rothbard, Murray. (1995). 1996! The Morning line. *Rothbard-Rockwell-Report*, 1–12. http://www.rothbard.it/articles/the-morning-line.pdf (accessed April 19, 2022)

Ruidrejo, A. (2015). Jesuitismo y biopolítica en las misiones del Paraguay. *Sociología Histórica* (5), 237–256. https://revistas.um.es/sh/article/view/232461 (accessed April 19, 2022)

Rüstow, A. (1932). Freie Wirtschaft – Starker Staat. *Schriften des Vereins für Socialpolitik* 187, 62–69.

Ryan, M. D. (2019). Interrogating 'authoritarian neoliberalism': The problem of periodization. *Competition & Change* 23(2), 116–137. https://doi.org/10.1177/1024529418797867 (accessed August 8, 2022)

Sacchi, E. (2020). Elementos para una genealogía de la crueldad neoliberal: gubernamentalidad, post-fordismo, acumulación originaria y colonialidad. *Dorsal. Revista de Estudios Foucaultianos* 8, 11–33.

Salzinger, L. (2019). Sexing Homo OEconomicus: Finding Masculinity at Work. In W. Callison & Z. Manfredi (eds.), *Mutant Neoliberalism*, pp. 196–214. Fordham University Press.

Sauvêtre, P. (2019). National-néolibéralisme: de quoi le populisme est le nom. http://sens-public.org/articles/1470/ (accessed April 19, 2022)

Sauvêtre, P. (2015). Quelle politique du commun? Les cas de l'Italie et de l'Espagne. *SociologieS*, October 19, 2016. http://journals.openedition.org/sociologies/5674 (accessed April 19, 2022)

Schmitt, C. (1996). *The Concept of the Political, Translated and with an Introduction by George Schwab*. Chicago & London: University of Chicago Press.

Segato, R. (2016). *La guerra contra las mujeres*. Madrid: Traficantes de sueños.

Shiva, V. (2002). The Enclosure and Recovery of the Biological and Intellectual Commons. In D. Marothia (ed.), *Institutionalizing Common Pool Resources*, pp. 675–684. New Delhi: Concept Publishing Company.

Singh Chaudhary, A. & Klion, D. (2021). Neofascism After Trump: Interview. Jan 22, 2021. https://jewishcurrents.org/neofascism-after-trump/ (accessed April 19, 2022)

Slobodian, Q. (2018). *Globalists: The end of empire and the birth of neoliberalism*. Cambridge, MA: Harvard University Press.

Slobodian Q. & Plehwe, D. (2019). Neoliberals against Europe. In W. Callison & Z. Manfredi (eds.), *Mutant Neoliberalism*, pp. 89–111. Fordham University Press.

Solchany, J. (2016). Le problème plus que la solution: la démocratie dans la vision du monde néolibérale. *Revue de philosophie économique 17*, 135–169. https://doi.org/10.3917/rpec.171.0135 (accessed August 8, 2022)

Stallman, R. (2002). *Free Software, Free Society: Selected Essays of Richard M. Stallman*. Boston: GNU Press.

Stanley, J. (2018). *How fascism works: The politics of us and them*. New York: Random House.

Stefanoni, P. (2021). *¿La rebeldía se volvió de derecha? Cómo el antiprogresismo y la anticorrección política están construyendo un nuevo sentido común (y por qué la izquierda debería tomarlos en serio)*. Buenos Aires: Siglo XXI.

Summers, R. T. (2017). The Rise of the Alt-Right Movement. *Media and Communication Studies Summer Fellows* 11, 1–47. https://digitalcommons.ursinus.edu/media_com_sum/11 (accessed April 19, 2022)

Svampa, M. (2019). *Neo-extractivism in Latin America: Socio-environmental conflicts, the territorial turn, and new political narratives*. Cambridge University Press.

Sztulwark, D. (2019). *La ofensiva sensible. Neoliberalismo, populismo y el reverso de lo político*. Buenos Aires: Caja Negra.

Tansel, C. B. (2017). *States of discipline. Authoritarian neoliberalism and the contested reproduction of capitalist order*. London: Rowman & Littlefield.

Thatcher, M. (1988). Speech to the College of Europe ("The Bruges Speech"), Sep 20, 1988. https://www.margaretthatcher.org/document/107332 (accessed April 19, 2022)

Tocqueville, A. (2012). *Democracy in America*. Indianapolis: Liberty Fund.

Traverso, E. & Meyran, R. (2019). *The new faces of fascism: Populism and the far right*. London, Brooklyn, NY: Verso.

Valencia, S. (2018). *Gore capitalism*. South Pasadena, CA & Cambridge, MA: Semiotext(e); MIT Press.

Vercelli, A. & Thomas, H. (2008). Repensando los bienes comunes: análisis socio-técnico sobre la construcción y regulación de los bienes comunes. *Scientiæ Studia*, São Paulo, 6(3), 427–442.

Villacañas, J. L. (2020). *Neoliberalismo como teología política: Habermas, Foucault, Dardot, Laval y la historia del capitalismo contemporáneo*. Barcelona: NED.

Wacquant, L. (2009). *Punishing the Poor*. Duke University Press.

Weber, I. (2018). China and Neoliberalism: Moving Beyond the China is/is not Neoliberal Dichotomy. In D. Cahill, M. Cooper, M. Konings & D. Primrose (eds.), *The SAGE Handbook of Neoliberalism*, pp. 219–233. Los Angeles, London, New Delhi: SAGE.

Zacharenko, E. (2019). Combustible neoliberal para el movimiento antifeminista. *Nueva Sociedad*, Nov 2019. https://nuso.org/articulo/combustible-neoliberal-para-el-movimiento-antifeminista/imprimir/ (accessed April 19, 2022)

Zara, O. (2008). *Le management de l'intelligence collective. Vers une nouvelle gouvernance*. 2nd updated and extended ed. Paris: M21 Editions.

Whyte, J. (2019). *The morals of the market: Human rights and the rise of neoliberalism*. London: Verso.

Index

Concepts

https://doi.org/10.1515/9783110723939-012

Names, places, institutions

9 783111 619880